Japan: Beyond the End

'David Williams has written a provocative and important book about the challenge that Japan's modern public policy presents for Western and particularly Anglo-American thought about the state and its role in economic growth and social planning. . . . an intelligent and incisive discussion that will help to clarify issues of immense contemporary importance to readers in many countries.'

Professor Marius B. Jansen, *Princeton University*

Japan: Beyond the End of History assesses Japan's significance, in fact and in theory, for the Western traditions of political philosophy and practice from Adam Smith and Hegel to the French deconstructionists and today's 'end of history' theorists. The issues covered range from the industrial policy of the founders of the Meiji state to the painful recession and political upheaval of the early 1990s.

Francis Fukuyama has famously argued that, with the collapse of Soviet communism, the only viable system for the future is liberal-democratic capitalism in the Anglo-American mould. This would suggest that East Asian mercantilism, state-led and often authoritarian, is doomed. This book considers an alternative theory: that Japanese-style nationalist development offers a far greater challenge to Western theory and values than the fallen systems of Eastern Europe ever represented.

David Williams has taught Japanese government and political philosophy at Oxford University and is now an editorial writer for *The Japan Times*. He regularly comments on Japanese affairs for the *Los Angeles Times*.

The Nissan Institute /Routledge Japanese Studies Series

Other titles in the series:
The Myth of Japanese Uniqueness, *Peter Dale*
The Emperor's Adviser: Saionji Kinmochi and Pre-war Japanese Politics, *Lesley Connors*
Understanding Japanese Society, *Joy Hendry*
A History of Japanese Economic Thought, *Tessa Morris-Suzuki*
The Establishment of the Japanese Constitutional System, *Junji Banno, translated by J.A.A. Stockwin*
Industrial Relations in Japan: the Peripheral Workforce, *Norma Chalmers*
Banking Policy in Japan: American Efforts at Reform During the Occupation, *William M. Tsutsui*
Education Reform in Japan, *Leonard Schoppa*
How the Japanese Learn to Work, *Ronald P. Dore and Mari Sako*
Japanese Economic Development: Theory and Practice, *Penelope Franks*
Japan and Protection: The Growth of Protectionist Sentiment and the Japanese Response, *Syed Javed Maswood*
Japan's Nuclear Development, *Michael Donnelly*
The Soil, by Nagatsuka Takashi: a Portrait of Rural Life in Meiji Japan, *translated and with an introduction by Ann Waswo*
Biotechnology in Japan, *Malcolm Brock*
Britain's Educational Reform: a Comparison with Japan, *Mike Howarth*
Language and the Modern State: the Reform of Written Japanese, *Nanette Twine*
Industrial Harmony in Modern Japan: the Invention of a Tradition, *W. Dean Kinzley*
Japanese Science Fiction: a View of a Changing Society, *Robert Matthew*
The Japanese Numbers Game: the Use and Understanding of Numbers in Modern Japan, *Thomas Crump*
Ideology and Practice in Modern Japan, *Robert Goodman and Kirsten Refsing*
Technology and Industrial Development in Pre-War Japan, *Yukiko Fukasaku*
Japan's First Parliaments 1890–1910, *R.H.P. Mason, Andrew Fraser, and Philip Mitchell*
Militarization in Contemporary Japan, *Glenn D. Hook*
Emperor Hirohito and Showa Japan, *Stephen S. Large*

Japan: Beyond the End of History

David Williams

London and New York

First published 1994
by Routledge
11 New Fetter Lane, London EC4P 4EE

Simultaneously published in the USA and Canada
by Routledge
29 West 35th Street, New York, NY 10001

© 1994 D. Williams

Typeset in Times by Megaron, Cardiff, Wales
Printed and bound in Great Britain by T. J. Press (Padstow) Ltd, Padstow,
Cornwall

Printed on acid free paper

British Library Cataloguing in Publication Data

A catalogue record for this book is available from the British Library

Library of Congress Cataloging in Publication Data has been applied for.

ISBN 0-415-05243-2 ISBN 0-415-09662-6 (pbk)

To Professor Ōtsuka Hisao and Professor S.E. Finer,
two scholars who encouraged me to be one

In the East, anything is possible!

Pierre Loti, *Aziyadé*

Contents

In place of a foreword   xi
Acknowledgements   xix
Chronological note and conventions   xxii

Introduction

1 Policymaking in an economic superpower   3
2 Understanding the new Japan: Some ideological pointers   10

PART I THE POLITICS

Policymakers and the Japanese political system

3 Why the centre holds   19
4 Gentlemen and players in the policy contest   36

The Japanese state at work

5 Four policy lessons from the 1980s   51
6 The Ministry of Finance and the Japanese miracle   65
7 Japanese industrial policy: The great debate   75
8 Politics and policies since the bubble   92

PART II THE PHILOSOPHY

The foundations of the Japanese approach

9 A Japanese lesson: Language and nationalism   105
10 Japan, Germany and the alternative tradition in modern
      public policy   117
11 Making history: Japan's grand narrative and the policymaker   133

Theories and controversies

12 The revolutionary 1980s and the rise of Japanese public
       policy studies   145
13 Yellow Athena: The Japanese model and 'The End of History' 157
14 Japanese public policy as foreign policy: A post-war
       revolution?   171
15 Unblinking politics: McCarthyism, grand theory and wild
       empiricism   180

Coda

16 The receding roar: Last thoughts on the Japanese miracle   203

       Notes and references   206
       List of works cited   221
       Index   229

In place of a foreword

One learns to play jazz to become an adult. This is because jazz, at its essence, is about adult experience. What is true of jazz is also true of politics. Public policy is an adult affair, just as mastering political science is an adult pleasure. The young genius of modern politics, whether an American founding father or a creator of the Meiji state or Pitt the Younger, must bring a sovereign maturity to his task. But this also suggests why the youthful encounter with the world of politics may be so pleasurable: it savours of things to come.

This introduction to the politics of Japanese public policy has been written for the intelligent adult who wants to know how contemporary Japan has changed the way we understand the relationship between politics and the economy. It has been designed with three types of thoughtful reader in mind.

First, and most broadly, it is for anyone with a lively and serious interest in public affairs. For any adult, that is, who has given some thought to how the world works, and who can, as a consequence, both understand and take issue with a vigorous piece of journalism or political analysis such as that found in *The Economist* or *Foreign Affairs* or the 'Opinion' section of the *Los Angeles Times*.

The second type of reader that this book has been written for is the university student of Japanese politics. My hope is that it may serve as an introduction for students on an advanced course – someone reading the Japanese government paper in the Honour School of Philosophy, Politics and Economics ('Modern Greats') at Oxford or an upper division political science elective on Japanese politics such as is taught at Princeton, to cite two examples of which I have personal experience – who seek either to put their thoughts or impressions about Japan in perspective or to learn enough about that Oriental polity to make some useful comparisons with public policy practice in other advanced industrial democracies.

The third kind of reader is the teacher. The substance of this book deals with the facts and arguments about Japan as they are addressed in the writings of the best newspaper commentators and reporters, but the text is informed by a decade of academic research on the government of Japan. Indeed, many of the issues raised in this text cannot be addressed without reference to works by professional students of Japan, political scientists or historians, economists or sociologists. It is unfortunate that some of the best introductory texts on Japanese government concentrate almost exclusively on party politics and also that so much of what is most incisive in academic writing on Japanese public policy is contained in weighty monographs or in scarce copies of scholarly articles. It is my hope that this text may serve to bridge this gap in the literature between the reader and the specialist. Perhaps it may even find a place on the reading lists of the growing number of comparative politics courses now being taught in Europe, North America and Australia.

At a crucial phase in his development as a writer, V.S. Naipaul observed that 'no novel offered itself to me'. If great novelists complain of 'creative gaps', then social scientists suffer the reverse fate: the intellectual problem that clings to their lives like the mists and fogs that hug the hills and valleys of the Somerset coast. I have brooded on the Japaneseness of Japanese government for more than two decades. It has been the unyielding intellectual concern of the eighteen years that I have spent in Japan as a student, translator, journalist and scholar. This book has been a long time in coming.

It owes its beginnings to the lectures delivered by Professor Ōtsuka Hisao on national economics or *kokumin keizai* at International Christian University (ICU) in Tokyo during the early 1970s.[1] It was then, in the still aftermath of a bitter student uprising, that the first stirrings of the project that became *Japan: Beyond the End of History* were set in motion.

Most important was my initial encounter, via Ōtsuka's writings, with the German Historical School, following on Friedrich List's *The National System of Political Economy*. This was crucial because List was the nineteenth century's finest thinker about the foundations of what we now call 'industrial policy', a set of ideas and practices that have been decisive to the economic rise of modern Germany and Japan.[2] A further five years spent doing work for the Industrial Research Department (*Sangyō-chōsa-bu*) of the Industrial Bank of Japan (IBJ) in Tokyo during the late 1970s refined my understanding. Of particular importance were the long hours of discussion of the Japanese economic 'miracle' with the late Morishima Tōzō, deputy president of IBJ between 1975 and 1977. Another five years spent studying British public policy at

Oxford, where I took my doctorate, under Professor S.E. Finer, forced me to rethink the foundations of the German and Japanese approach. This was followed by a further seven years as a journalist in Tokyo, during a period, from the 1985 Plaza Accord to the 1992 American presidential election, when the structure of the Japanese economy became a focus of world concern. Finally, a year of teaching Japanese government at Oxford in 1990–1 brought home to me the rewards and difficulties of trying to put into satisfying order the central political lessons of Japan's post-war rise to economic ascendancy.

Two volumes are the result of this long process of germination. The first is this introduction. The second is a very different kind of work in which I shall attempt to come to grips with the formidable theoretical issues that must be addressed if the mind of Europe is to grasp the true significance of the Japanese experience of government.

A NOTE ON THE TITLE OF THIS BOOK

At the close of 1992, *The Economist* (26 December 1992) took a backward glance at recent global developments and concluded that, 'The collapse of communism brought universal agreement that there was no serious alternative to free-market capitalism as the way to organise economic life.' This 'universal agreement' defined for many what they believed Francis Fukuyama meant when he asked, in a famous 1989 essay, whether history had ended. The wide debate sparked by Fukuyama's question and the even wider consensus about the virtues of market capitalism struck students of post-war Japan and East Asia as implausible. Indeed, the revisionist critics of American foreign policy towards Japan had concentrated much of their fire on the assumption that Japanese-style economics conformed to Anglo-American practice and, perhaps just as important, free-market economic ideals.

Such revisionist doubts were fuelled by a growing body of evidence and theory – Chalmers Johnson's *MITI and the Japanese Miracle*, Ronald Dore's *Flexible Rigidities* and Robert Wade's *Governing the Market* – that demonstrated the proposition that East Asian economic policy and practice broke radically with the free-market positivism that underpins all the main schools of Anglo-American economic thought: Keynesianism, monetarism and rational expectations or new classical economics. Revisionists also showed that such unorthodoxy was, for most Japanese, Korean and Taiwanese businessmen, politicians, bureaucrats and consumers, the stuff of manifest common sense.

For such revisionists, therefore, the Western obsession with Soviet economic policy was a dangerous illusion because the collapse of

European communism suggested the birth of a consensus about a *false* theory of how the world worked. But good Hegelians, such as Fukuyama, bring an important corollary to their musings on the end of history. Not for them the passive conclusion of *The Economist* that communism's demise produced a significant intellectual accord. Rather, Hegelians see ideas, including economic liberalism, as acting on the world. For the Hegelian, capitalism undermined the Soviet Union, which was crushed by the closing of history's door.

In the wake of the puncturing of Japan's speculative bubble during the early 1990s, an influential group of Japanese commentators and economists began to insist that their country should abandon its nationalist approach to business and growth, and surrender to the new consensus about how to organize economic life. In Hegelian terms, the same door that closed down Lenin's state may now be shutting on Japan. This book offers the view that history will not end until Japan, and much of East Asia with her, is made to conform to this new consensus. Until this happens, the world will stand beyond the end of history regardless of what has happened in Eastern Europe.

In 1993, one-party rule collapsed in Japan and the coalition government of Hosokawa Morihiro was born. Post-war economic success made this 'liberal hour' affordable. The LDP's fall was otherwise unthinkable. But the agony of Japan's socialists and the corruption that broke LDP unity confounds the hopes of the post-war constitutionalists who sought to make politicians 'the ultimate arbiters of political power' (Curtis). The rooted irresponsibility and poverty of vision of party politicians, no less than the sorry legacy of peasant politics (*hyakushō seiji*), have compromised democratic virtue.

Is Japan's miracle-working regime therefore doomed? Best-sellers such as *Seihin no Shisō* (The idea of holy poverty), by Nakano Koji, and *Risō no Kuni* (Rebuilding a nation), by Ohmae Kenichi, suggest a new climate of opinion. Bureaucratic controls are being eased. Some critics even blame the bureaucracy for Japan's troubles.

The old regime still dominates the landscape. Ozowa Ichirō, a symbol, for many, of LDP corruption, played kingmaker for the Hosokawa coalition. The success of the breakaway Shinseitō and Sakigake parties depended on old LDP voter loyalty. The eclipse of the policy tribes (*zoku*) and the inexperience of the new coalition strengthened the hands of the bureaucracy. The Hosokawa government's commissioning of a fresh Maekawa Report reflects the tested logic of structural change and mercantilist ambition. Japanese nationalsim has outlasted Soveit communism. The Soviet Union was no Japan.

A NOTE ON THE STRUCTURE OF THE BOOK

I have divided this book into two parts, 'The Politics' and 'The Philosophy' of the Japanese approach to public policy. As most books and journalism in English about Japanese government contain little or nothing that resembles philosophy, while manuals of social scientific methodology offer no factual analysis of Japanese politics, the basic structure of *Japan: Beyond the End of History* may be seen to offer a fresh departure in how we think about the Japanese political system.

The first plan of the book put the philosophy first, and the politics after. But this approach was strongly criticized by two people for whom I have considerable intellectual regard, one an Oxford don and the other a well-published computer expert with a classical education. Both insisted that the sensibility of the Anglo-American reader demanded that the factual description of Japanese policymaking should precede any analysis of the thinking that underwrote such a description. Having eaten the cake, they suggested, it might then be sensible to discuss recipes.

An author working in the tradition of Continental Europe feels the need to specify his first principles, to reveal his ideological stance and to clarify his cultural orientation early in his exposition. The modern British schoolman who believes that common sense mitigates the problems of first principles, ideology and cultural difference will want to proceed immediately with setting out the facts of the case. One result is that the Continental mode tempts the writer to impose a good deal of himself on his reader before he unveils his portrait of Japan, while British practice insists that the author present his 'Japan' to the reader without preamble, but in a way that forces the reader to tease out the philosophical, ideological and cultural biases which inevitably colour the 'Japan' presented.

The persuasiveness of the British approach rests in its respect for the illusion of textual narration, which in turn reflects our attitudes towards writing itself. But this effective illusion is conjured at the price of making the formidable exercise of describing Japan's political culture in the English language, an inherently unlikely business, seem easy and uncontentious.

Here I have yielded to Anglo-American wisdom. My commitment to clarity about first principles and my doubts about the contrived character of political scientific exposition has therefore been kept to the margins, especially in the first half of the book. Politics before philosophy; facts before ideas: I have surrendered to this formula with some hesitation. My reasons as a journalist for being hesitant are made more explicit in Chapter 2 and indeed form an important theme in the second part of this book, titled 'The Philosophy'.

Why has this portentous word been used? Part of the reason is cast of mind. Another is the recent turn in philosophical writing on both sides of the English Channel towards the problems of politics, culture and ethnocentricity. Richard Rorty's classic study *Philosophy and the Mirror of Nature* helped to confirm this new trend in philosophical thought that may yet prove to be as important politically as the earlier 'linguistic turn' proved scientifically fruitful.[3] The issue is, despite its overt philosophic character, anything but academic.

The traditional British approach to the political and social sciences must be seen for what it is: anti-cultural in bias, universal in ambition. In criticizing this approach, Charles Taylor, the Canadian political philosopher and student of Hegel, has drawn a cardinal distinction between two theories of modernity, which he calls 'cultural' and 'acultural'. He evokes

> the picture of the plurality of cultures, each of which has a language and a set of practices which defines specific understandings of personhood, social relations, states of mind/soul, goods and bads, virtues and vices, and the like. *These languages are often mutually untranslatable.*[4]

The opposing tradition seeks to understand history as an unfolding of a universal paradigm of modernization. It sees modernity as a set of transformations that have shaped the modern West, but also as a process that has been decisively influenced by modern Western thought.

The Modernization School which dominated American research about Japan from the late 1950s to the early 1970s was much criticized for suggesting that history was moving in a single direction, which had been pioneered by the modern West and which Japan was condemned to follow. But Francis Fukuyama, anticipating Western jubilation at the collapse of European communism and the demise of the Soviet Union, has resurrected this challenge, in his controversial essay *The End of History?*, as the European Revolution of 1989–91 unfolded, and the implication for the student of Japan of this new Hegelian universalism is treated in Chapters 13 and 15. Indeed, the question of whether history, in the sense Hegel defined it at the conclusion of *Phenomenology of Spirit* (1807), can end without transforming Japan propels much of the argument of this book.

Professor Taylor not only attacks such Hegelian universalism, he also contests the *methods* used by social scientists in understanding Japan and other non-Western cultures. The Western practitioners of economic positivism and certain forms of empiricism, in journalism and political science, insist that their methods are acultural and therefore transcend the limits of any particular culture.

But there is a price to be paid for the universalist impulse in these Western methods, and Taylor believes that the cost is too great:

> [A] purely acultural theory distorts and impoverishes our understanding of ourselves, both through misclassification . . . and through too narrow a focus. But its effects on our understanding of other cultures is even more devastating. The belief that modernity comes from one single universally applicable operation imposes a falsely uniform pattern on the multiple encounters of non-Western cultures with the exigencies of science, technology and industrialization . . . . As long as we leave our own notions of identity unexamined, we will fail to see how theirs [other cultures'] differ and how this difference crucially conditions the way in which they integrate the universal features of "modernity".[5]

There is no political culture to which this philosophic dissent from the claims of universal Western science may be more profitably applied than modern Japan. Our failure to make explicit, even to ourselves, our first principles and guiding ideologies, carries with it considerable risks. These risks have an intellectual and methodological edge:

> In short, exclusive reliance on an acultural theory unfits us for what is perhaps the most important task of social sciences in our day: understanding the full gamut of alternative modernities that are in the making in different parts of the world. It locks us into an ethnocentric prison, condemned to project our own forms onto everyone else, and blissfully unaware of what we are doing.[6]

As an exercise in analysis, *Japan: Beyond the End of History* is above all committed to freeing the reader from such ethnocentric prisons, to combating Western projectionism, and to adding, however slightly, to our awareness of what we are doing when we contemplate the facts and theories of Japanese public policymaking.

D.W.
Somerset, England

Acknowledgements

To write a book is to be in debt to others. I would like to take this opportunity to thank Professor J.A.A. Stockwin of the Nissan Institute of Japanese Studies, Oxford, and Mr Peter Sowden of Routledge, for commissioning this book, and Professor Stephen Wilks of Exeter University for first encouraging me to write a book about Japanese public policy.

The Tokyo press corps has served as a superb forum in which to learn and test ideas. Special thanks are due to Mr Suzuki Junichirō, president of *The Japan Times* between 1985 and 1993 and to Mr Mataebara Yūtaka, the newspaper's chief editorial writer since 1985. My job as editorial writer at *The Japan Times* has given me a privileged position from which to follow and comment on events as they have unfolded during the past seven years in Asia's new giant. I wish to express my appreciation to Mr Nick Valery, who now covers Japan for *The Economist*. It was during Mr Valery's former incarnation as editor of the Barclays de Zoete Wedd investment magazine *Japan* that he provided me with repeated opportunities to hammer out my views on the US–Japan trade relationship. Few readers are as demanding as those practised sceptics who invest in the Tokyo stock exchange.

I offer my grateful thanks to Mr Marvin Seid, editorial writer for the *Los Angeles Times*, the late Mr Art Seidenbaum, veteran editor of the 'Opinion' section for the paper, and Mr Frank del Olmo, now deputy editor of the editorial pages. It is because of them that I have had the privilege of writing about Japan for one of America's largest and most sophisticated readerships on Asia affairs.

I would also like to express my gratitude to Mr Kamio Akio and the staff of the monthly *Tokyo Business Today*, between the years 1987 and 1989, when Mr Nakaoka Nozomu was editor and I served as the magazine's principal writer. Tōyō Keizai, which publishes *Tokyo Business Today*, is one of Japan's premier organs of reporting on the international and national economy. Working on *TBT* gave me the opportunity to cover major stories, such as the Bush administration's Structural Impediments Initiative (SII), with veteran reporters of the rare calibre of Mr Nakaoka and Mr Yamagata Yuichirō. It was the sort of experience that every foreign journalist working in Japan should have.

To Professor Helmut Wagner of the Free University Berlin, my intellectual mentor for over a decade now, I owe much. Also in Germany, I would like to thank Professor Peter Pantzer of Bonn University as well as Professor Erich Pauer and Dr Ulrike Schaede of Marburg University who published an early version of Chapter 12 in the Occasional Paper Series of his Centre for Japanese Studies.

Senior scholars in the United States who have helped me at various stages of the work include Professors Marius Jansen, Sheldon Garon and Kent Calder, all of Princeton, Professors Ronald Dore and Richard Samuels of Massachusetts Institute of Technology, Professors Ezra Vogel and Susan Pharr, both of Harvard, and Professor Robert Hardgrave of the University of Texas at Austin, and finally in California, Mr Frank Gibney, President of the Pacific Basin Institute in Santa Barbara and Professor Chalmers Johnson of the University of California at San Diego. I would also like to extend a word of thanks for editorial advice to Mr David Holzgang and Ms Shirley Grant of The Cheshire Group in Santa Rosa, California.

The academics and intellectuals in Japan who have taken time to discuss various aspects of the book have been too numerous to mention, but I do wish to acknowledge the help of Professor Shirai Atsushi of Keiō University. Mr James Gibney of the US Embassy in Tokyo and Mr Kenneth Jones of Teikyō University were generous with their advice and criticism.

In Australia, my thanks go to Professor Sydney Crawcour of the Australian National University (who gave an excellent series of seminars on Japanese economic development at St Antony's College, Oxford, during Trinity Term 1990) and to Dr Rikki Kersten of the University of Sydney.

In England, I would like to express my gratitude to the Warden, Sir Ralf Dahrendorf, and the Fellows of St Antony's College, Oxford, for their hospitality during the 1990–1 academic year, as well as to the director, Professor J.A.A. Stockwin, Mrs Dorothy Storie, and the teachers, Dr Ann Waswo and Dr Jenny Corbett, and the staff of the Nissan Institute of Japanese Studies, Oxford, for their help and comradeship during my stay there.

I must also thank Professor Ian Neary of Essex University who kindly included a slightly altered version of Chapter 13 under the title 'Yellow Athena: The Japanese Model and the East European Revolution' in his *War, Revolution and Japan* (Japan Library, 1993).

At Routledge, this text benefited from the editorial labours of Mr Gordon Smith and Mr James Whiting. Finally, I must thank Mr Robin Reilly, who generously read the final draft of the work with unstinting attention. Any remaining errors or infelicities are my own.

Chronological note

Modern Japanese imperial era names

Meiji (1868–1912)
Taishō (1912–1926)
Shōwa (1926–1989)
Heisei (1989–present)

CONVENTIONS

Throughout this book, Japanese names are given in their proper order, with the surname first and the personal name second. With names of Westerners of Japanese descent, Western order is preserved.

Introduction

1 Policymaking in an economic superpower

INTRODUCTION

Japan matters. It has changed the way the modern world understands itself, and Japanese public policy has been one of the key vehicles in promoting this change. The principal goal of this book is to show in what ways this claim will or will not stand. The testing of so large an assertion demands caution as well as clarity. Only then we will be able to assess properly the pressure that Japanese policy success and failure exerts on Western ideas about how the world works.

How essential is individualism to democracy? Can bureaucracies be effective? Is the frequent handover of power from one political party to another necessarily a good thing? Do industrial policies work? What is the relationship between the state and the market; and is it more subtle and complex than the contemporary heirs of Adam Smith assume? Can the state contribute significantly to economic growth? Is economic individualism the only valid approach to understanding social and political behaviour? Should producers be favoured over consumers in setting economic priorities? What exactly is an 'export'? The rise of Japan and its impact on the modern world has forced Westerners to answer these questions in very different ways from those that we might have chosen even two or three decades ago. Such questions form the subtext of this book.

The central conclusion of this text is that some knowledge of Japan is indispensable to a sound grasp of the contemporary world. Japanese public policy is seen to stand at the heart of this understanding. One perception in particular governs the whole of the analysis presented here: Japan is a nationalist polity that is becoming a more liberal one. If the modern Japanese experience of government invites us to be clearer about the meaning of two ideas – liberalism and nationalism – then Japan's influence on the contemporary world would merit our applause.

THE ARGUMENT

A new age

We have reached the crowning heights of Japan's rise as an economic power. Her status as a commercial, manufacturing and financial juggernaut is no longer a matter of debate or qualification. Japan's name is now almost certain to be added to that very select list of nations – Venice, Holland, England, Germany and the United States – which have successively stood at the cutting edge of economic change during the past 500 years.

This is a singular achievement. Against enormous odds and the weight of history, Japan has transcended her obvious weaknesses (her dependence on imported raw materials, for example) to play the predominant role in a historic transformation: the shift of the centre of economic vitality and initiative from the Atlantic to the Pacific. More than the decolonization of the Third World or the great European civil war of 1914–1945, this marks the end of the long era of Western domination of world history.

All this can be argued with confidence; yet it appears to be equally true that the consequences of Japan's emergence to the front ranks of economic influence and power have been only poorly grasped outside East Asia. This remains true in Europe, but it is also to a surprising degree the case in the United States, as well as in the Commonwealth powers of the Pacific: Canada, Australia, and New Zealand.

The effort to understand East Asia's most important economy has nonetheless been prodigious. The rise of Japan to its present status as the world's pre-eminent industrial and financial power has fuelled enormous academic and journalistic interest in this distant nation. Such attention reflects an astute realism. Public and private sector policies made in Tokyo now decisively influence the management of Third World debt, the financing of America's massive federal deficit, and even the level of industrial unemployment in Wales. So crucial is the role of the Japanese government in the making of such choices that we have an unprecedented need to know how Japan's public authorities reach their decisions, and what set of ideas and goals informs this process.

But the challenge of equipping both policymakers and public opinion in the West with a sound but generalized understanding of the consequences of the growth of Japanese productive power has been magnified by the extraordinary pace of change during the past decade. It is only since the mid-1980s that the Japanese have arrived on the international financial and trade fronts with irresistible force. Future historians may come to judge the years 1985–6 as the turning point in the coming of the so-called 'Pacific century', a suggestive if imprecise designation.

In 1985 Japan replaced the United States as the world's largest creditor nation. At almost the same time, Tokyo overtook New York as the richest stock market. In 1986, Japan became the globe's most generous dispenser of foreign aid. During the same year Japan's defence spending leapfrogged that of both Britain and France, thus making its military budget the third largest in the world. With the ending of the Cold War and the demise of the Soviet Union, Japan may well be the world's second largest defence spender. Futurologists now debate whether Japan's gross national product (GNP) will surpass that of the United States in 2010 or 2025. The weight of such changes, long in the making, have been felt only since the mid-1980s.

During the economic and policy revolution of the 1980s, Japan started to change in significant and unprecedented ways. The impact of this metamorphosis has made it more important than ever that we understand the 'new Japan'. This transformation has been both statistical and qualitative, and it throws into doubt many of the key assumptions made about Japan by Western scholars and journalists writing before 1985.

This change has not been confined to the international arena. Quite the contrary, it has begun to affect many branches of domestic Japanese social policy. The altered status of women in the Japanese workforce, the new power of consumers, a flood of legal and illegal workers from the Third World, the erosion of Japan's work ethic among younger workers, a leisure and travel revolution, an extraordinary property boom and bust, have all helped to overturn existing interpretations of Japan's social make-up. As a consequence, the country's leaders are recasting the agenda of Japanese public policy in the social field, already under considerable pressure because of the rapidly ageing composition of Japan's population. The forces driving change in the new Japan are therefore to be found in both public and private life, in the work-place and the home, in the traded and non-traded sectors, in global expansion and domestic constraints.

But for the Western student of Japan – whether a policymaker or opinion leader, an academic or journalist, a student or serious reader – the overriding focus of interest in the new Japan is her power. *Pace* the perennial Japanese anxiety about national weakness or the ongoing debate over whether Japanese power has peaked, the fact of relative Japanese economic dominance will continue to cast a shadow of enormous importance over international affairs. Japanese power is here to stay. It is this new fact of global life which the Western world must learn to live with, and, better still, to understand.

Home truths

This understanding must be rooted in a sophisticated appreciation of Japanese public policy. The force of this claim may be demonstrated by reference to the developments that have transformed global society during the twentieth century. Amid the turbulent tides and eddies of the past nine decades, which changes have mattered most?

Sir Isaiah Berlin, the Oxford political philosopher, has broached the question in an elegant essay titled 'The Pursuit of the Ideal'.[1] He identifies the growth of the natural sciences and technology (the object of broadest consensus among writers on this question) together with the 'ideological storms' unleashed by the Russian Revolution of 1917 as 'two factors that, above all others, have shaped human history in this century'.[2]

Peter F. Drucker, the doyen of American business thinkers, also has addressed this issue in *The New Realities*, where he sets out his list of the forces – what he calls 'the main realities' of our time – at work in bringing one century to a close as it sets another in motion.[3] Drucker cites:

1 the retreat of the Western belief in the Enlightenment doctrine of 'salvation by society' and the revolutionary or interest politics it inspired;
2 the collapse of Russian imperialism;
3 the decline of armaments as effective instruments of international policy.

About the importance of the rise of science and technology, there is little debate. The impact of Soviet or Russian imperialism would indeed appear to mark the final chapter in the retreat of European imperialism. The demise of aggressive and unenlightened ideologies is more controversial. The new apparent impotence of any geo-politics grounded in military strength alone will be tested by practitioners of traditional *realpolitik* for some time to come. The perceived limits of state power, particularly in English-speaking countries, is, by contrast, one of the ruling dogmas of the age. To this list, it might be wise to add consumer-driven economics and the unprecedented growth in the size of national economies (the cult of GNP expansion) that has transformed the world since the ending of the Second World War.

The Japanese experience of government in our century puts all these changes in a unique and powerful light, which has its source in the ambitions, successes and failures of Japanese public policy. Take Berlin's two factors: the scientific-technology revolution and the ideological earthquake that have resulted from the great Russian Revolution of 1917, and its turbulent aftermath. The Japanese drive to dominate the markets in consumer-friendly technologies has encouraged the rest of the world to suspect the facile equation of the scientific with the technological. It is the Japanese example that has highlighted the apparent paradox that a nation may have strong foundations in basic science (including a bevy of Nobel Prize-winning scientists) and still fall victim to an ever-deepening dependence on imports of technology, as may be seen in the case of Britain.

At the same time, growing Japanese supremacy in high-tech markets also casts doubt on the classic Western divide between disinterested basic research, often left to the university, and profitable product development, the work of the venture-capitalist. The Japanese experience presses home the implausible conclusion that a country may boast a Bell Laboratory and a Silicon Valley enterprise culture and the market muscle of an IBM, yet still be unable to hold its own in world high-tech markets.

It is such policy conundrums that put into fresh and unflattering perspective General Charles de Gaulle's snobbish dismissal in 1962 of Japanese Prime Minister Ikeda Hayato, author of his country's dash for growth in the 1960s, as a pathetic 'transistor salesman'. There are some curious contradictions of Western public policy common sense at work in these conundrums. Nothing in conventional Western public policy practice prepared us to understand the impact of a single agency of government – the Ministry of International Trade and Industry (MITI) – on so many areas of Japanese national life. Take, for example, MITI's role in the battle over the import of American transistor technology in the 1950s; or the way it broke IBM's hold on the Japanese electronics industry in the 1960s; or its effort to force the development of fifth-generation technology during the 1980s; or its contribution, by outsmarting the US trade negotiators, to the rout of American semiconductor manufacturers. Despite Western disclaimers to the contrary, there is clearly more involved in electronic industry success than *laissez-faire*. Public policy counts here, too.

Berlin's other point, about Russia, is a complex one. In our times,

> great ideological storms have altered the lives of virtually all mankind
> . . . totalitarian tyrannies of both right and left and the explosions of
> nationalism, racism, and, in places, of religious bigotry, which,
> interestingly enough, not one among the most perceptive social
> thinkers of the nineteenth century had ever predicted.[4]

Japan has been no exception to the explosive impact of ultra-nationalist ideologies or to the tortured politics of national expansionism. But Japan has been more than a victim. The Japanese example confounds the modern perception that nationalism is always irrational. The contemporary heir of the adult politics initiated by the Enlightenment will readily dismiss the blood-feuds that tear at the Balkans and the patchwork ethnicities of the defunct Soviet Union as a reactionary surrender to nineteenth-century nationalist madness in a world preparing for the advent of a high-tech utopia. But the Japanese example, and much East Asian experience with it, permits the formulation of the contrary doctrine of 'thinking nationalism', of the effective mobilization of national energies in the cause of economic and technical advance. Indeed, the conclusion might be that societies unable to promote analogous national projects are doomed to run second in the competition to make the world's future. In the task of 'dreaming forward', Asian nationalists stand at the forefront.

The key word in Berlin's formulation is 'ideological'. Nations are ancient; nationalisms are new. Nationalism, more often than not, is a new creed that would wrap itself in the native dress of what it is not: cultural antiquity. Japanese nationalism is best understood not as a cultural or religious phenomenon (though it borrows selectively from Japanese tradition) but as an ideology, a modern intellectual construct as artificial as it has proven effective. The struggle to transform an apolitical peasantry into a modern nationalist-minded population capable of sustaining state goals has stood at the heart of the Japanese programme of nation-building.

The Japanese schoolhouse since Meiji, the careful creation of the Japanese Ministry of Education, has been the epicentre of this change. In *Japan's Modern Myths: Ideology in the Late Meiji Period*, Carol Gluck observes that,

> The schools, along with the army, clearly constituted the most pervasive tutelary apparatus of the state. The ideological message purveyed to elementary schoolchildren was probably the most codified in content and single-minded in goal of any to which late Meiji Japanese were exposed. [5]

Families and the mass media have come to reinforce the Japanese sense of nationalist identity because parents and opinion leaders have passed through the same school room. In this sense, the most singular achievement of Japanese public policy over the past twelve decades may have been the creation of the modern Japanese 'nation' itself.

The abrupt ending of the superpower rivalry between the United States and the Soviet Union, and the resulting massive cuts in the military budgets of most major and middling powers stands behind Drucker's insistence that, 'After three hundred or more years in which armaments were "productive" and worked as instruments of policy, they have become "counterproductive".'[6]

The result may be a radical shift in perspective, even in world view. We may be leaving an age which produced thousands of volumes on the battles, weapons and leaders of the military conflicts of the past century, but hardly any studies of the factors of production and of economic power, its creation, mobilization and management, that sustained such conflicts, indeed made them possible. The suggestion would be that economics as a discipline and a way of looking at the world has become the new focus of concern in foreign policy analysis, and thus has ended the old, and all too exclusive, stress on diplomacy, military tactics and geo-politics. Post-war Japan, particularly in its effective and total substitution of economic competition for military expansion, exemplifies in an unrivalled way the forces that would sweep away the Cold War world order. As no other polity, Japan has forced the world to rewrite the diplomacy guidebooks and manuals of strategic thinking that formed the intellectual underpinnings of the post-war global order. Since 1945, Japan has lacked both nuclear weapons and the freedom to act in an autonomous way in the military sphere. Even the constitutional status of its army has remained uncertain. Nevertheless, Japan has emerged as an economic superpower.

Reflecting on the pivotal issues of:

1 the relationship between technology and science, and how both influence economic competitiveness;
2 the progressive potential of modern nationalism;
3 the new primacy of the economic in international affairs,

it would appear that Japanese public policy has indeed been one of the key vehicles in changing the way the world understands itself.

The importance of Japanese public policy is not confined to these large questions. On the contrary, in the struggle to protect the global environment, in the contentious business of trade imbalances, in the financing of aid programmes to the Third World, in the regulation of capital flows, and in the generation of direct investment across international boundaries, Japan is a prominent player that other governments and interest groups seek to influence. And more often than not, the target of such effort is Japanese public policy.

Japan does indeed matter. To appreciate the force of this conclusion, the past evolution and present character of her public policy, especially in the financial and industrial sphere, must be examined.

2 Understanding the new Japan

Some ideological pointers

Nations are the products of their experience. In this way nations resemble individuals. Thus, while it is a fact that individual human beings, certainly as biological organisms, share a great deal, it is also true that an individual's experience of life gives a different – one is tempted to say a unique – cast to a person's values and way of living. So it is with nations.

Such differences in national experience matter. They have, for example, coloured the long and sometimes acrimonious debate over the future of the European Community (EC). Mrs Thatcher, always alert to the intellectual failures of others, challenged her Continental European colleagues at EC summits for departing from what she saw as 'common sense'. Such wrangles touched on the most rooted assumptions of a nation's experience. The British Prime Minister insisted that common sense teaches us that a baby must be able to crawl before it can walk. In the name of this 'step-by-step' approach, she objected to the ambitions of her German and French colleagues to set goals to be achieved five or ten years hence without having the institutional means to reach those goals already in place. Without tested tools in hand, what was the point of some grandiose plan?

In part, this was an argument about national philosophies. Such philosophies both reflect and influence every aspect of national life. In writing about multiculturalism and the reform of British education, Clifford Longley, the columnist of *The Times* (London), has observed that,

> If [British] Muslims look at the present status of denominational schools in Britain, they will find no clear statement of public policy. The system has emerged in the traditional British way, as a series of solutions to practical problems, rather than as the application of first principles.[1]

Longley's observation is consistent with a crucial feature of the Thatcherite critique of the Continental European penchant for setting goals and then inventing the means to reach them. The practical man, in British parlance, is just as uncomfortable with the unnecessary rigidities of first principles as with the untested dreaminess of distant goals.

Yet establishing objectives, however distant, and then creating the tools to achieve them is one of the central features of the Japanese approach to life. Japan has been called a 'goal-orientated society' or 'goal-achieving culture' and this fundamental orientation (determine the goal, then set about achieving it) influences all aspects of Japanese social practice. It defines the Japanese philosophy of social action, and it casts a long shadow over the activities of the individual, the family, the firm and the state. In fact, Japanese public policy, old and new, cannot be understood without reference to this philosophy.

Thus there appears to be a curious parallel between the British critique (call it 'empiricism') of European long-range thinking and American discontent with the practices, forms and ideology of Japanese public policy. This rooted similarity between the Continental European and Japanese approaches will be examined in Chapter 10. But there is a recent bone of contention between the USA and Japan that illustrates the point at issue: the rancorous negotiations over the structure of the Japanese economy known as the Structural Impediments Initiative or SII.

These talks became the lynchpin of the Bush administration's trade policy towards Japan from 1989. Despite a window-dressing of reciprocity, the negotiations were not in fact about how the USA and Japan could structurally change their economies, but rather about how the Japanese could alter theirs to ease the mammoth current account trade deficit between the two countries. The Japanese surplus offended Washington because, after years of effort by the Reagan administration to erode Japan's advantage in trade, America's deficit still averaged around $40 billion during Bush's first three years in office.

The key word here is 'structure'. The economic structure of a country is one of the most complex of all social phenomena. It constitutes the main economic framework of a nation, reflecting the impact of millions of consumer preferences, growth in population, advances in technical innovation, and the long-term influence of government policies, mainly in the macroeconomic sphere. An economic structure mirrors what a nation is. Such structures are very resistant to change, especially in the short term. In this sense, quick 'structural change' as an object of public policy is, for the economist, a contradiction in terms.

Given the nature of economic structures and the fact that they are so difficult to alter, the Bush administration strategy was improbable. Indeed, the word 'impediments' in 'Structural Impediments Initiative' suggests that the economists on the Bush negotiating team were aware of the unorthodoxy of their approach. It was much more plausible to talk about changing mere 'impediments' than economic 'structures'. The problem was that the Bush administration economists were in a quandary. They believed, with most economists, that the US–Japan trade imbalance was the result of macroeconomic factors, such as Japan's post-war propensity towards high rates of savings, and macroeconomic factors reflect structural conditions. Because they regarded structural change as impossible in the short term, they attempted to finesse the problem with half-measures (targeting impediments), and hoped for the best.

This approach was vulnerable to criticism for being poorly thought out. The policies proposed were never going to redress the trade imbalance in either the short or the long term. But what kept the Bush strategy from verging on the ridiculous was one crucial factor: the Japanese believe in structural change. Indeed their policymakers are past masters of structural change. Japan would never have become an economic superpower in so short a time without a national commitment by policymakers, politicians, business leaders and union members to meet the challenges demanded by successful structural change.

Such structural change is all about setting ambitious objectives, and then, as required, inventing the means to achieve them. The Bush administration would never dream of attempting such structural change in the United States. It would violate the values, the habits, the 'common sense' of the whole nation. But the modern Japanese economy had been built with such structural policies, and therefore it could just as adroitly undo the impact of them. In short, American economists thought that the existing structures of the Japanese economy were artificial because unnatural, and unnatural because they violated the tenets of free-market economics. Changing Japan would, in other words, make Japan 'normal'. That is, like America and Britain.

This point about a 'return to normalcy' illuminates an important lesson for the student of Japanese public policy because it forms a conspicuous thread throughout most writing, in English, about the new Japan. The theory that the social and economic changes that began in the late 1980s will 'disincorporate Japan', will 'liberalize' Japan, will 'open up' Japan, all turn on the perception, and the hope, that the unleashing, of market forces in particular, will make Japan economically normal at last. The implicit message is that the old Japan, the Japan before 1985, can now safely be forgotten.

This book rejects that assumption. On the contrary, it seeks to raise and to answer the question: How much of the old Japan is still alive in the new Japan? This book is built on a non-conformist belief: that the greatest source of error and misconception in contemporary Western writing about Japan, in the media or in academe, derives directly from a failure to grasp the nature of the Japanese political and business system before 1985. As Giuseppi Verdi remarked in a famous 1871 letter: 'Let us return to the past; it will be a step forward.'

PART I   THE POLITICS

Policymakers and the
Japanese political system

3 Why the centre holds

A NATIONALIST SOLUTION

From the standpoint of the policymaker, particularly the nationalist addressing the state's core concerns, the supreme fact of Japanese political life has been the existence of more than one centre of authority, legitimacy and policymaking initiative. This condition has prevailed throughout the country's long experience of government, from the sixth century of the Christian era to the present. As a political system, Japan has been polycentric. This polycentrism has taken two forms.

First, for a variety of practical political reasons, but also as a result of a set of mental habits many Japanese would describe as 'cultural', those who have enjoyed ultimate power have on numerous occasions sought to exercise their authority from 'behind the throne'. This persistent duality between the nominal holder of power and the true wielder of power has been the classic political 'discovery' of foreign travellers to Japan for centuries.

The earliest example of this arch feature of Japanese statecraft is probably the Fujiwara family's usurpation of imperial prerogatives throughout most of the Heian period (794–1185). Imperial powers lost to the Fujiwara were subsequently seized by the Kamakura shoguns and the Hōjō regents of medieval times, the warlords of the Warring States period (1482–1558), the Tokugawa shoguns of the long Edo peace (1600–1867), and the Meiji oligarchs, who ruled on behalf of the nominally absolute emperor, the formal apex of the 1890 Meiji Constitution. Since the Pacific War (1941–5), there is much evidence to suggest that the bureaucracy has often dominated, though the postwar constitution has officially assigned that function to the Japanese parliament or Diet. There is the conspicuous example of ex-Prime Minister Tanaka Kakuei who dominated ruling party politics from disgraced retirement. Recent proponents of the theory that the most senior leaders of the so-called policy 'tribes' (*zoku*) set state priorities in the name of these much larger interest groups subscribe, certainly by implication, to the same 'shadow' or 'dummy general' ('*kagemusha*') theory of Japanese political power.

This is one of the conceits of Japanese political sensibility. Take, for example, the 1980 film by Kurosawa Akira, *Kagemusha* (shadow warrior), which is a meditation on the medieval exploitation of the idea. Arthur Stockwin crystallizes the point in his observation on the 1890 Meiji Constitution: 'According to that document, sovereignty resided in the emperor, but the emperor did not rule personally, and it was not at all clear who *was* supposed to.'[1]

Nor did the replacement of the Meiji Constitution by the 1947 MacArthur Constitution cure such obscuring tendencies. This is how *The Economist*, in a 1992 article, attempted to discover who takes decisions on setting interest rates on behalf of the Bank of Japan:

> In appearance, the Bank of Japan is less free [compared to America's Federal Reserve Board]. It operates under the Bank of Japan Law of 1942, which placed it firmly under government control and gave the minister of finance the right to overrule BOJ policy.
> A 1949 amendment, however, set up a Policy Board as the top decision-making body. . . . The board sets the discount rate. But open-market operations are decided by an Executive Committee, equivalent to the FOMC [the Federal Open Market Committee in America]. This consists of the governor, the deputy governor and seven BOJ executive directors, appointed by the minister of finance. Thus, on the face of the law, it is unclear who really holds the monetary reins. Supposedly, the Policy Board takes the decisions. But the finance minister can overrule it. The relationship between the bank and the ministry is therefore uneasy.[2]

These examples demonstrate not Montesquieu's 'separation of powers', but a divide between power and legitimacy. The Japanese Diet, as the representative body of a constitutionally sovereign people, is the legitimating organ (just as the emperor was in the Meiji Constitution) of the Japanese state. Whatever the claims of the Japanese Diet also to be a working parliament, legitimation is its prime constitutional function.

No defence of parliamentary power can credibly insist that the higher Japanese bureaucracy is composed of pliant 'yes, minister' civil servants. Since the war, the bureaucracy has normally dominated the legislative process, and in this narrow sense can be said to have ruled while the Diet reigned. Similarly, Tanaka Kakuei brought his formidable political skills and patronage to bear on the legislative procedures of the Diet, in the pursuit of very different goals, but was rarely constrained by them.

The Diet, as opposed to the political parties, has been above the often sordid struggle for party advantage, and this has preserved its prerogatives despite the evident imperfections of Japanese democracy.

Behind Western probing to discover the true nexus of power a misconception is sometimes at work. The Japanese do not share, to anything like the same degree, Western exasperation with institutional ambiguity. Their attitude towards power bears greater affinity with the key notions of French deconstructionist theory. Thus, just as the deconstructionist of a poetic text holds that meaning is a momentary weakness in the play of semantic markers, so the exposure of the true circuits of power and policymaking within a political system is a temporary failure of sheltering ambiguities, instructive but unlikely to persist.

But even French theory falls short of the Japanese reality, because an institution such as the Bank of Japan is a not a semantic marker but a powerful organ of government. Despite the ambiguities, or perhaps because of them, the BOJ succeeds in a way untrue of the Federal Reserve Board. It is the success of Japanese monetary policy that demonstrates that, *pace* Roland Barthes, Japanese government is more than 'an empire of signs'. It works. Hence the suspicion that the Meiji Constitution did not fail because it was ambiguous, but because Japanese policymakers, habituated to such ambiguities, could not manipulate them with sufficient skill. Western insistence on organizational clarity and constitutional lucidity may be entirely beside the point when applied to Japan. The anti-liberal character of the Meiji Constitution is of course another matter.

The distinction drawn in the Japanese language between *tatemae* (principle) and *honne* (motive) is relevant here. *Tatemae* is often rendered, in a rough and ready way, as 'surface' and *honne* as 'reality'. This will sometimes do, but not here. The distinction between Diet and bureaucracy or emperor and shogun, viewed as an example of *tatemae* and *honne*, is closer to the English contrast between 'form' and 'content', that is, between the legitimizing, and therefore indispensable, form and the substance of power. In talking about the location of Japanese political power, the proper rendering of *honne* might be 'the always obscured *locus* of true power' and *tatemae* as 'the indispensable legitimacy of certain necessarily conspicuous political forms'. The notion of *honne* is well developed in Japan not because the Japanese have a penchant for mistaking appearance for reality, but because they recognize political 'forms' (*tatemae*) as being anything but superficial.

The second form that Japanese political polycentrism takes is even more important. The power of the Japanese polity, even when conspicuously concentrated, has been divided between more than one centre. Though it often subtly blends with *kagemusha* polycentrism, this division of power has been a notable feature of Japanese politics in modern times. All generalizations are vulnerable, and this is no exception. Thus it is not being claimed that Japan is unique in this respect nor that the meticulous historian could not find much that would make this generalization fray at the edges, but it is to insist that the polycentric quality of the Japanese political system – ancient, medieval and modern – is one of the most remarkable features of Japanese governance.

This emphasis on the polycentric character of the Japanese political system should not encourage the shallow conclusion that there is no such thing as the Japanese state. Modern Japan is not only a state, it is a unitary state: a political system that admits few of the federalist or decentralizing or devolving impulses that have so influenced the nature of the American, British, German or Canadian polities. The Japanese state admits no constitutional dilutions of its authority. By the standards of Canada's powerful provinces or America's fifty states, Japanese prefectures, the largest constitutional units of local government, have until recently tended to be mere shadows that more closely resemble French *départements* at their most feeble. As a capital, modern Tokyo is the twentieth-century answer to nineteenth-century Paris. It rules.

Japan has no equivalent of the devolutionary demands pressing on unitary Britain or its well-developed traditions of independent local government. Rather, most political actors in Japan acknowledge that central government, particularly the bureaucracy, remains the prime agent of innovation and reform within the system. There are no exact analogies to the Japanese state among English-speaking democracies, but the unchallengeable power of central administrative initiative within the Japanese system may be usefully compared with the strong centralizing thrust of the British state under Thatcherism at its most dynamic or with the role of the US Department of Justice, particularly under Eisenhower, Kennedy and Johnson, in overturning the reactionary legal structures of racial discrimination in the old Confederacy.

But Japanese centralism is not an occasional feature of the political system; quite the contrary, it has been true of the higher state bureaucracy for the entirety of Japan's modern experience as a nation. On balance, the Western student in search of a model of constitutional and policy practice will discover that, on this count, modern Japan more closely resembles Britain under Thatcher or France under de Gaulle, both unitary states, than any post-war federal system. Imperial and

Weimar Germany also offer arresting analogies to the modern Japanese experiment in centralized rule.

Yet given the fundamental orientation of Japanese statecraft, including its pronounced weakness for dispersing power or for obscuring the actual *loci* of power, why is Japan not a federal state? The regime before the Meiji Restoration has been described, to the irritation of historians of medieval France, as a bureaucratic feudal regime. The emperor in Kyoto was nominally responsible for the affairs of the country, the shogun in Edo (Tokyo) actually in charge as the emperor's vicar, but with a substantial amount of wealth and power retained in a string of semi-autonomous domains outside the immediate jurisdiction of the shogunate government (*bakafu*).[3]

Given such an experience, why did Japan not adopt a federal structure after 1868? Why did not one of the more cohesive of those semi-autonomous domains, Satsuma or Chōshū, emerge as the Japanese equivalent of California, which is rich, powerful and a long way from Washington?

The answer is complex. The Japanese view is that the country's survival as an independent polity was endangered by the late-nineteenth-century thrust of Western imperialism (American, Russian, British and French) into the Far East, and that only a centralizing nationalist solution provided an adequate defence against the threat of Western colonialization or commercial domination.

National vulnerability gave the statist campaign among a significant section of the samurai elite a persuasive urgency, and encouraged a break with traditional Japanese assumptions about how power was to be organized and for what purposes. Thus the most important of the Meiji nationalist reformers moved rapidly and decisively from the view that Japan was endangered as a nation to the conviction that only a unitary state could ease the foreign threat; from the conviction that the emperor had to be revered and the Western barbarians expelled (*sonnō-jōi*) to the assumption that the only final cure for national vulnerability was to achieve economic and miltary superiority over those nations that threatened Japan ('ō-*bei ni oikose*' or 'overtake Europe and America'); and, finally, from the view that traditional polycentrism was untameable, to one that embraced the German imperial model. This followed a brief flirtation with the French system, until the Franco-Prussian War (1870–1) demonstrated the superiority of Bismarck's approach. The British and American models were never serious contenders.

The nationalist spur was crucial. It encouraged the belief that the Japanese, as a race, were inherently superior to the peoples of the West, and this quality would manifest itself in a competitive struggle. The Meiji reformers were also convinced that this inherent superiority would become apparent only if the state, and therefore society at large, could be reorganized along effective lines. Just the same, the attractiveness of a unitary polity housing a nationalist state suggests a historic reorientation of mind, in many ways out of step with both Japanese historical practice and the impoverished realities that defined Japan at the end of the Edo era.

Reflecting on Japan's long modernization drive, it is clear that the nationalist programme was responsible for winning many of the key battles to reform Japanese consciousness and to foster state power on a scale consistent with the ambitions of the late Edo and Meiji periods. Nevertheless, polycentrism continues to define the Japanese experience of government.

This would not have surprised the Meiji modernizers. They were the products of the polycentric Japanese tradition. The modernizing experiments carried out by Satsuma when Ōkubo Toshimichi served the *han* government were only possible because the *han* was relatively free from interference from Edo. Such leaders knew the political realities of their country. Experience told them that the most powerful commercial families were not going to be brought to heel. The peasantry was profoundly unpolitical in any modern sense. The Japanese elites had long displayed a pronounced weakness for cabals and group in-fighting. Even the future loyalties of the samurai class were uncertain. The Meiji oligarchs were furthermore divided among themselves. All this meant that modernization was going to be very difficult to accomplish.

These constraints shaped the Meiji compromise between the fact of polycentrism and the need for an effective modernizing state. Just as James Madison, aware of the constitutional dangers of factions, tried to fashion a political system that could finesse them, the Meiji modernizers designed a state powerful enough to overcome Japan's obvious weaknesses.[4]

Nationalist attempts to combat polycentrism are responsible for many of the anti-liberal features of modern Japanese government. Only a strong state had any chance of overcoming the fractured nature of Japanese politics. Liberalism was a virtue that nationalists believed Japan could not afford. The propagandizing schoolroom, the episodes of police repression, and the tireless pursuit of elite consensus are all part of this effort. The Meiji pioneers suspected that a federalist solution would make their task infinitely more difficult because federalism would encourage the deeply rooted polycentric tendencies of the regime that they had inherited from the Tokugawas. Only a unitary state would do.

In this contest between national weakness and reforming vision rests the answer to the conundrum: Why is the Japanese state at once strong and weak? The Meiji state and its Shōwa successor are manifestly strong states with certain domestic powers and prerogatives unavailable to more liberal Western states, especially since 1945. The divided character of the Japanese political system is such that the state has to be strong in the public-policy sphere to get anything done. The fact that the state is frequently thwarted by other political forces merely underscores the kind of resistance that central bureaucrats must contend with. In such a political context, it should be obvious why state officials work so hard at networking and nurturing elite consenses.

It is the first business of the state to bridge the chasms that divide national and private interests. Many examples of bureaucratic paralysis, of policy immobilism, are the direct consequence of the fractures in carefully constructed consensus at the highest level. The campaigns of successive American administrations to restructure Japan have failed because all the main Japanese elite groupings are aware that such reforms would invite dangerous tampering with the main fault line in Japanese politics: the gap between corporate and state or bureaucratic interest. This is the feature of Japanese political geology that the great American diplomatic efforts of the 1980s and 1990s – the Plaza Accord, the Maekawa Reports, the semiconductor market-share battle, the Structural Impediments Initiative (SII) and President Bush's ill-starred effort to win the 1992 'Tokyo primary' – have stumbled over.

If US policymakers had done their homework, they would have known that Japanese policymakers and nationalist opinion leaders have repeatedly struggled to compensate for the polycentric and sometimes destabilizing proclivities of other political actors, whether interest-group-corrupted politicians, romantic idealists with a weakness for political violence or grasping businessmen keen to line their own pockets at national expense. Centralized solutions, in the eyes of such nationalists, were indispensable. Nevertheless, all the key elite actors recognized that, if national goals were to be achieved, such objectives had to be consistent with the character of the polity as it already existed. The chief lesson of the modern Japanese experience of government is that aberrant tendencies were overcome only with difficulty, and without eliminating the polycentric character of Japanese government.

This may beg another important question: In what sense did the Japanese nation exist in 1868? The Japanese may have been conscious of themselves as a cultural, linguistic, religious, even racial collectivity, but were they a nation in the modern sense? In what sense were the Meiji ruling elite 'nation-builders'?

Meiji nationalism was an invented ideology that had its roots in the growth of patriotic consciousness during the eighteenth century. But the Meiji elite sought new methods to channel and shape this national consciousness. This meant taking a largely apolitical peasant population and turning them into nationalist-minded soldiers, savings-minded housewives and patriotic schoolchildren, all willing in spirit to make sacrifices for the nation. Before 1945, this involved anchoring national loyalties in the person of the emperor, the concept of the nation-state being too abstract and unreal for such purposes. After 1945, the idea of being a Japanese acquired a persuasive unchallenged quality long sought by nationalist policymakers. For better or worse, Japan has opted for a nationalist solution to her problems. The resulting vessel of statecraft has proved to be one of the most formidable in modern history.

THE LONG REVOLUTION

The impact of the Japanese political system on the outside world has been one of the great themes of twentieth-century history, from the Russo-Japanese War (1904–5), through the First World War, the imperialist assault on China, the Second World War, to Japan's new status as an economic superpower since the early 1980s. The domestic story has been as remarkable. This nationalist dynamic has been a response to the turbulence of twentieth-century global politics. But it has also given modern Japan its goal-driven coherence, even if the process has sometimes shaken the foundations of the Japanese polity.

The leading players of late Edo society included the imperial court at Kyoto, the *bakufu* with its capital at Edo, the principal *daimyō* (including the descendants of Tokugawa Ieyasu's most important opponents at the decisive battle of Sekigahara in 1600) and the wealthiest of the country's commercial class. The Meiji Restoration set in motion a redistribution of power between these contending centres. The Tokugawa shogunate was the main loser. The elite who overthrew the *bakufu* were drawn mainly from the middle and lower ranks of the larger and more remote semi-autonomous domains or *han*. In bringing down the shogunate, the rebels had sought to have the emperor revoke the legitimating powers he had conferred on the Tokugawas. The rebels moved the imperial court to Edo, where they took over the main branches of shogunal administration and transformed them into a nascent imperial bureaucracy. The merchant class did not play a significant role in this *coup d'état,* but neither were their powers and riches touched by the conflict in any way that prevented them from exercising a prominent role in the new state.

By the time of the Russo-Japanese War (1904–5; Meiji 37–38), the emperor had been made the head of the state – absolute in law, nominal in practice – by the Meiji Constitution of 1890. Real power was divided. First, there were the elder statesmen (*genrō*), the founding fathers of the Meiji state. Second, there was the higher bureaucracy, reformed and modernized into a civil service on the imperial German model. The power of the samurai class had been broken and the class dissolved, partly replaced by a new aristocracy. Samurai valour and virtues flowed into the most powerful and ultimately destructive of Meiji legacies: the imperial armed forces. The elite bourgeois business class steadily grew in wealth and influence, and close ties between the emerging zaibatsu and the leaders of the Meiji state strengthened the power of both. Finally, there were the party politicians who struggled for control of the Japanese Diet, Asia's oldest parliament, which was created by the Meiji Constitution and reflected the impact of Western models. From the start, the legislative system was penetrated from above by the *genrō*, the bureaucracy and the military, and corrupted by interest politics from below. All subsequent parliamentary reformers in Japan have had to struggle against these and similar problems.

From 1918 to the late 1920s, Japan experienced a liberal era that was eventually overwhelmed by the forces unleashed in the Great Depression. The gradual passing of the *genrō* and the military's uncertain popularity brought party politicians into greater prominence. The zaibatsu strengthened their hold on the Japanese economy. Frequently hampered by the authorities, the mass media and the Japanese intelligentsia acquired new influence. The weak economic performance of the liberal period gave way to a deep depression in Japan's still large farming sector. Japanese military involvement on the Asian continent further chilled the liberal climate at home. Discontent fuelled a new, violent radicalism of left and right. In the name of the emperor, cabinet ministers, some with zaibatsu connections, were cut down by right-wing extremists, plunging Japan into an era of 'government by assassination'.

Party politics was in decline. Increasingly, policy initiative passed back into the hands of committed anti-liberal nationalists, reform bureaucrats and patriotic generals. Liberal economic orthodoxy was abandoned and Keynesian expansionism, funded by war-related expenditure, produced an era of unprecedented growth. Between the Japanese invasion of China proper and the attack on the Pacific possessions of the USA and Britain, party politics was rendered impotent, while economic organizations committed to nationalist policies were strengthened (because the old zaibatsu were too independent). The powers of bureaucracy were enhanced, while the military, particularly the army, attempted to mobilize the nation for world war.

Power was redistributed in 1945, but not as much as is sometimes assumed. The main losers of the war were the militarists. In post-war Japan, the higher bureaucracy of the police has exercised more influence on policy than the country's constitutionally hobbled armed forces. The claim of the imperial house to be the uncontested focus of national unity was badly compromised. The zaibatsu were partially dismantled by the US Occupation. The more oppressive arms of the higher bureaucracy, particularly the Home Ministry (*Naimushō*), were broken up and the powers of the police circumscribed. The principal beneficiaries of the post-1945 changes were the economic bureaucracy – particularly the Ministry of Finance (MOF) and the Ministry of International Trade and Industry (MITI), reconstituted in 1949 – and civilian politicians and their parties.

By 1955, conservative politicians, the higher economic bureaucracy and the business elite of the country's principal industrial groupings (*keiretsu*) had coalesced into a powerful establishment capable of seeing off the left-wing opposition as well as the country's large but politically ineffective labour unions, while managing Japan's new strategic alliance with the United States. The struggle between the conservative Liberal Democratic Party, which has ruled uninterrupted since the party's formation in 1955, and the left-wing opposition parties has dominated the headlines since 1955, but the most important political battles were fought between the main players of Japan's tripartite establishment: the bureaucracy, the largest established firms and the LDP.

A series of corruption scandals continues to confirm the popular perception of ruling party politics as venal and self-seeking. Nevertheless, the LDP has been adept at pork-barrel patronage and at responding to sudden shifts in voter concern, the classic 1970s examples being pollution reforms and demands for welfare entitlements. The most significant factor in the changing mosaic of elite power since the 1980s has been the expansion of corporate Japan. The 1989 Recruit scandal was precipitated by a *nouveau riche* firm in an expanding industry trying to buy its way into the elite golden circle dominated by heavy industry and banking. The globalization of the Japanese economy has eroded some of the privileges of the public sector but not as much as foreign commentators have tended to assume. Even the drive to liberalize the Japanese economy has of necessity been orchestrated by the post-war establishment.

CENTRE VERSUS PERIPHERY

The post-war tripartite alliance of the Japanese bureaucracy, the ruling Liberal Democratic Party and the best-established of large businesses embodies the 'centre' of Japanese politics, the pivot of the state and society. This is the orthodox view, and it is correct for almost the entire post-war period. Outside this golden circle stands a variety of interests and groupings: the political opposition, the major trades unions, citizen protest groups, much of the progressive intelligentsia and a large number of firms in new industries (some services, for example) that are regarded as *arriviste*. These are public actors on the periphery of political life.

Two broad distinctions underpin the institutional divide between 'centre' and 'periphery'. There is the contest between the ruling elite and Japan's counter-elite, the latter consisting of anti-conservative political forces, particularly of the left, and the new sectors of the economy whose representatives remain second-class citizens in Japan's corridors of power. Second, the divide between 'centre' and 'periphery' is the latest manifestation of the old separation between the elite and the peasant mass. The century-old drive to transform the non-elite population into nationalists has been successful on several levels, but Japan is still unambiguously ruled from above, despite democratic elections. Public attitudes mirror this fact after more than a generation of liberal dispensation under the 1947 constitution. But there is more to this division between elite and non-elite than one-sided manipulation. At root, a great number of Japanese do not wish to identify with the nation's elite because they are profoundly ambivalent in their attitudes towards the corruption endemic to power politics. Many Japanese outside the golden circle nurse doubts about the price that Japan has paid for its post-war success.

Behind this ambivalence stands a complex strand of Japanese tradition. Tetsuo Najita describes it as 'the elemental axis' of Japanese political history. One strand is 'bureaucratism' (*kanryōshugi*) in which 'effective, measurable, bureaucratic performance is viewed as central to the realization of national well-being', while the other opposing strand 'denies the primacy of bureaucratic norms. It affirms an old and deeply felt value placed on the purity of human spirit (*ningensei*; *kokoro*), or the idealistic capacity in men to create and serve without regard to the self.'[5]

This contrary impulse within the Japanese polity has not prevented public acquiescence in orchestrated drives from above to enhance Japan's wealth and power by the fostering of industrial strength. Nor does it contribute to any widespread denial of the bureaucracy's role in defining these goals nor to its indispensable role in their achievement.

But bureaucratism, it is widely felt, 'is not an ideology that concerns itself with the spiritual and intellectual, or nutritive need of the nation as a whole, but is primarily an affair among elites to satisfy their own interests'.[6]

Thus many Japanese vote for the ruling Liberal Democratic Party, even more concede the pivotal leadership role of the bureaucracy, and perhaps still more take pride in the competitive feats of Japan's corporate elite. But there remains 'a conspicuous lack of emotional loyalty' towards this leadership and its elite privileges.[7]

Why might this be so? First, there is the unapproachable character of the higher central bureaucracy. As the Master observes in the Confucian Analects, 'A gentleman who lacks gravity does not inspire awe'.[8] Japanese bureaucrats are the spiritual heirs not only to the samurai-administrators who ran Tokugawa Japan, but also to the Confucian tradition of the mandarin gentleman. The Japanese bureaucracy has always cultivated an effective *gravitas*. The traditional awe in which senior officials, or even junior ones sent to the provinces, are still held in Japan mirrors the psychology at work. This condition, as much as any other, explains why the revelation that nearly twenty senior politicians had taken bribes from the Recruit company counted for less than the fact that a single senior bureaucrat from the Labour Ministry had done so. Japan's senior administrators are expected to observe a higher code, and almost invariably do. Thus, in Najita's summary:

> Bureaucratic service in Japan is not simply a prestigious career or an avenue to accrue vast sums of personal wealth; it is a 'mission' (*shimei*) to enhance the well-being of the nation through the systematic creation of industrial wealth.[9]

This sense of mission extends to membership of Japan's outstanding firms. It even softens the consistently dismissive attitudes of the public towards party politicians, many of whom see their careers less as exalted missions of state than as thinly disguised paths to wealth. Robert Kennedy's celebration of politics as 'an honourable profession' has little resonance in Japan. Nevertheless, Japan's democratic constitution secures the place of these all too often venal and self-seeking men (women are few) within the charmed circle of the Japanese political centre.

The centre is also protected by the values of the periphery. Various material reasons are offered to explain why, for example, Japan's socialist party has never captured a majority in the powerful lower house of the Japanese Diet. There is no doubt that poor organization and inadequate campaign coffers have contributed to the dismal electoral record of the opposition, but there is also an unmistakable psychology at work in these successive defeats, which might be called the 'nobility of failure'. It is better not to win than to stain one's hands with the dirty realities of power. Successful Japanese politicians have too obviously broken with the selfless ideals of Japanese civic virtue.

But who in Japanese political life have best kept faith with the self-denying moral imperatives of the 'human spirit' (*kokoro*), purity, humanity (*ningensei*) and cultural idealism that form the alternative axis of Japanese political sensibility? Even a select list will include many surprises for the casual reader of Western reporting on modern Japan. Only four examples will be touched on here: student radicals, the *yakuza*, kamikaze pilots and the emperor himself.

The Japanese peasantry may have burned down many of the schoolrooms of the early Meiji state, but Japan is a culture which reveres learning and young students. In a poor society, they were the privileged few, nascent men of talent, in whose hands the fate of society would eventually rest. Until very recently, students of secondary and university education in Japan formed a conscious elite which sought to influence national politics. By Confucian tradition, Japanese students were young in a peculiarly idealistic way. In a word, Japanese students were 'pure' (*junsui*): their motives were above suspicion. To such students, the conscience of their society, fell the idealistic burden of righting wrongs and fighting injustice by public protest and demonstration, always urged on by the intelligentsia. This made students a force in society across the face of Confucian East Asia.

The same psychological dynamic was in full flood in Tiananmen Square in 1989 and it has defined the whole thrust of protest politics in South Korea since independence. This traditional attitude towards student protests, from both the left and the right, defined Japanese street politics. It was certainly at work during the 1960 student demonstrations against the US–Japan Security Pact and in the early stages of the student uprising against the pact's renewal in 1970. Confronted by student sincerity, the average subject or citizen, morally offended by their rulers, has tended to applaud. Only under the most extreme provocation have the police or army dared to move against these protestors. In East Asia, student power has been a genuine force.

The perception of purity also influences the Japanese public reaction to the *yakuza* or gangster. Often linked with traditional crafts and skills – carpentry and timber cutting, for example – the *yakuza* in his idealized guise embodied an appealing dimension of Japanese tradition, of loyalty until death and a profound sense of obligation to his betters. The hierarchies that govern *yakuza* life are warm, violent and feudal. For many Japanese, *yakuza* are romantic outlaws, an appealing conceit in a society of conformists and the marginalized, closer to the image of Robin Hood than Al Capone. That some *sōkaiya – yakuza* groups which extort money by interrupting shareholders meetings – are renowned for disclosing shady dealings in the boardrooms of Japan's business elite confirms this view. Besides, massive cross-holdings between giant firms ensure that meetings of their shareholders are tame affairs. So not every Japanese is displeased that the privileged are subject to public discomfiture on occasion. But, consistent with the rooted Japanese preference for purity over power, it is instructive that the recent commercialization of the Japanese mafia, dramatically exposed once again in the security companies scandal centred on Nomura and the Tokyo Sagawa Kyūbin affair during the early 1990s, has further contributed to the sharp decline in the *yakuza's* moral prestige. Some dirty hands are dirtier than others.

Asked which decade of modern Japanese history saw the greatest contemporary flowering of national idealism, many older Japanese would, with some embarrassment, name the country's war years between 1937 and 1945. The reasons are straightforward. A time of war in any country is one of conspicuous self-sacrifice and collective struggle. Few wartime actions so embodied the idealistic spirit of the Japanese nation as the kamikaze, men who knowingly threw their lives away in the defence of the nation. This is a romanticized image, but there is no question that the outbreak of war with America and Britain forced Japanese society to put aside some of its more damaging quarrels and to unite behind the emperor, the supreme symbol of national purity. The soothing effect of unity, but also the nobility of failure (the pilots would not return even if their sacrifice brought victory) gave the Shinto rituals that pilots engaged in before flying off to attack the American carrier fleet a particular poignancy. Few Japanese, even those who disapprove, can fail to be moved by such selfless heroism. In cultural idealism, the honoured dead are pure; only the guilty survive.

The imperial institution stood at the apex of this cult. The emperor's role in Japanese society was more important and complex than Allied wartime propaganda or peacetime reporting have suggested. It is almost impossible to reconcile the image of the emperor from the Pacific struggle – that of Oriental generalissimo astride a grey charger – with the imperial role in Japanese history as lynchpin of radical anti-establishment protest. Granted the Tokugawa *bakufu* was overthrown in his name – that is what the term 'Meiji Restoration' means – but the emperor's name was evoked to justify attacks against the officials of the declining *bakufu* as well as the anarchist impulse behind the assault on the Meiji constitutional state and the campaign for a Showa Restoration during the 1920s and early 1930s. This is Najita's explanation:

> As the ultimate source of *de jure* power, [the imperial institution] sanctioned the industrial revolution, but as a symbol of Japan's continuous cultural history it stood also for the principle of pure and selfless commitment to the national community. Above all, as god-king the emperor stood for a cultural ideal that confirmed a capacity in ordinary men to transform themselves into something extra-ordinary, to fully realize the dynamic and creative potential embedded in the self. The identification with this ideal sometimes led to decisive action against the present, justifying such action with the imagery and rhetoric of imperial justice for all of society. [10]

Japanese cultural idealism, as conceived under imperial dispensation, retained something of its pre-war radical, and therefore subversive, potential in the post-war era. This potential was demonstrated with some drama during the last four months of the life of Emperor Hirohito (Japanese usage now favours the term 'Emperor Shōwa'), his passing on 6 January 1989, and his burial seven weeks later on 24 February. This brief period gave form to one of the more solemn chapters in the political and psychological, some would say spiritual, life of Japan in this century. For the Japanese people, especially for the young, educated since the demise of the cult of imperial divinity, this media crisis offered something of an education in national sentiment. For many, over this short but moving period, the lesson was as profound as our hurried age allows. It was certainly a reminder that the periphery of Japanese life, in terms of amoral power and administrative authority, retains its ability to worry secular Japan, especially its mass media.

This imperial drama, deep in the liberal phase of the national experience, posed surprising risks for the post-1945 constitutional order.[11] However much the imperial institution had been adapted to post-war circumstances, the late emperor retained his nimbus of divinity for millions of older Japanese. Every prime minister of the Emperor Shōwa's long reign was born not only before the emperor's renunciation of divinity in 1946, but before he ascended the throne in 1926. For nationalists and their critics, the emperor remained the unique embodiment of the ancient regime: its myths, its purities and its aura of unviolated Japaneseness. It was not necessary for the emperor to say or do anything to evoke these sentiments, only to be.

For most, perhaps every, thinking Japanese, the imperial institution has throughout the long post-war period stood at a sensitive fault line in the national psyche. For this reason, it may be argued that during the nervous five months between onset of the late emperor's final illness and his burial, Japan's post-war settlement, including its democratic constitution, was more vulnerable to challenge, however modest, than at any time since the massive street protests of 1960. The underlying cause of this crisis of nationalist sentiment was almost certainly Japan's fractured experience of modernization.

Nationalism and industrialism have rooted deeply in the modern Japanese psyche. This is not true of either democracy or liberal values. There has been considerable progress over the past four decades, but neither set of progressive ideals has yet acquired an authentic native feel. The post-war reforms that Western liberals find so hopeful were the consequence of defeat and foreign occupation. Japan's present constitution, with its commitment to parliamentary democracy, is a foreign product wholly at odds with the assumptions of traditional Japanese governmental practice or theory. But for the shogunate of General MacArthur, the present constitution would not exist. Although for many Japanese it represents some guarantee of political stability and a check on executive arrogance, for others it retains the odour of a colonial imposition.

Post-war de-colonization in the Third World has often involved the substitution of native rule for good government. The Japanese experience reverses this choice. After a period of nativist constitutionalism, the Japanese have been the unwilling beneficiaries of a constitutional arrangement far more conducive to good government than its Meiji predecessor. They have retained the 'Potsdam system' because it works, not because it is their own. But the Meiji Constitution has had a formidable afterlife. Whatever its flaws, the 1889 document reflected Japan's modern political culture in a way unmatched by its 1947 successor. The state-shinto cult of the Meiji modernizers, contrived and opportunist though it may have been, had impact. However secularized, however much the product of post-war democratic education, the dilute Meiji inheritance still allows Japanese intuitively to appreciate the French Revolutionary image of *la Patrie* as the sole object of legitimate worship.

The emperor stood at the heart of the Meiji Constitution, his premodern 'charismatic image' shining through this constitutional arrangement. Japan's defeat in 1945 doomed the emperor's constitutional status while undermining his charismatic stature. At the insistence of the occupying powers, the Shōwa Emperor renounced his divinity, and the post-war constitution reflects this change. But the frustrated campaign to restore real power to the emperor (the so-called 'Shōwa restoration') fanned the sparks of national discomfort, especially among conservatives, with the Potsdam system. For forty years after 1945, the imperial question, with all of its ambiguities, quietly ticked just below the floorboards of the post-war settlement because the status of the late Emperor Hirohito remained the focus of nationalist as well as ultra-nationalist discontent.

Japan endured the tremors of late 1988 and early 1989 – the national cult of restraint, the overt muffling of dissent (the mayor of Nagasaki was later shot for his criticism of the emperor's war role), the massive but nerved-racked reporting of the story, the rocket attacks on the imperial funeral cortege, even vague rumours that the Shōwa emperor's successor might be assassinated for his liberal stance – much as it weathered the crisis of 1960 over the US–Japan security pact, the student uprising of 1968–9 and the psychic upset provoked by Mishima's suicide in 1970, without suffering any permanent scars. But the apparent invisibility of such spasms should not encourage empirical obtuseness. There is ample reminder in the tensions that surrounded the death of the Shōwa Emperor why Itō Hirobumi, the key architect of the Meiji Constitution, was so keen to make the emperor the focus of the modern Japanese state. What better way was there to neutralize the subversive character of the imperial throne.

The imperial climax of 1988–9 points to a larger lesson. During its modernization drive, Japan's elite has had to endure revolt, assassination and mute but palpable public disaffection because of the conscious choice of the Meiji modernizers and their successors to pursue a secular, materialist and anti-idealistic course. It has been the singular achievement of this elite to prevent the conflicting axes of national belief from grinding the political centre to dust. Failure has threatened more than once.

Japanese and Western liberals tend to frown on the troublesome side of such cultural idealism. After all, the forces and values that animate resistance to establishment powers are so often aliberal, even anti-liberal, because so very Japanese. But any sceptism towards the idealist impulse in the Japanese character, any sense of the need to lean even slightly in the opposite direction, towards materialistic practicality and *realpolitik*, offers a unique opportunity for the outsider to acquire a native feel for the reasons why, in modern Japan, the centre has held.

4 Gentlemen and players in the policy contest

PARTY PRETENSIONS

It is in the interest of almost everyone involved in the making of public policy in Japan to exaggerate the influence of the Liberal Democratic Party (LDP), the conservative coalition that has formed every government since the party was launched in 1955. This iron rule of Japanese politics remains in force even as the liberalization of the Japanese economy reveals more facts about the extraordinary impact of ruling party politicians on the country's everyday affairs. Their influence extends even to the management of Japan's thousands of unofficial business cartels.

In late 1991, Japan's enfeebled Fair Trade Commission brought a suit against eight manufacturers of the cling film used by supermarkets to wrap food. It was the first suit brought against a cartel in more than a decade, and it sparked a brief but intense period of media probing into how cartels work in Japan. As they are the most formidable non-tariff barrier against penetration of the Japanese market by foreign firms, the question is of more than academic interest.

The rigid discipline that cartels impose on business competition was repeatedly confirmed in reports on business practices. One of the more revealing concerned price-fixing in the ambulance distribution and sales system. A local city office had put out an order for new ambulances to competitive tender as the law requires. One daring member of the local cartel decided to seek commercial advantage by breaking ranks with his comrades and underselling the competition. His bid was the lowest and the city office in question accepted it. But word got out about this market-force machination, and not one motor manufacturer would sell him the ambulances he required. Unable to fulfill his obligations to the city, the cartel rebel was officially censured by the public authorities for breach of contract. In desperation, he began to try to mend fences with cartel members, but his efforts were rejected. Finally, he received a call telling him what the conditions were for his acceptance back into the cartel. Both he and the reporters covering the story (the telephone calls in question were recorded and broadcast on national television) were in no doubt that the intermediary was a senior politician in the LDP, probably the (honorary) president of the local ambulance wholesalers association, which was in turn an important contributor to that politician's re-election coffers.

This ambulance story was a media scoop precisely because it brought to light one of those rare occasions when the enforcement of a cartel broke down. Normally such price-fixing is a smooth operation. Its very effectiveness encourages the incestuous relationship between business-men and politicians that all experts agree is ubiquitous in Japan but rarely exposed.

The late 1980s battle of US trade negotiators to win market access for American producers of oranges and beef pivoted on winning over some of the grandees of the LDP who held key positions in the affected Japanese producer associations in rural Japan, home to the traditional backbone of LDP strength in the Diet. Adam Smith's warning that every businessman would achieve a monopoly if he could is no more than a plaintive cry in Japan, so endemic is the country's cartel constitution (*dangō taishitsu*), both as predisposition and fact.

Despite the pervasive influence of senior ruling party politicians (the politician is more important than the party), the rule about exaggerating the role of the LDP will stand. Party politicians overstate their weight in national affairs because it ameliorates their corrupt and often comic image to do so, but it is precisely this image that encourages the mass media to pay excessive attention to their petty feuds and larger failings. Party politicians make for better copy than discreet civil servants. Businessmen overstate the importance of politicians because, by doing so, they distract attention from their own equally pervasive impact on policymaking and the political process. Bureaucrats stress the function of politicians because policy is easier to design and enforce when the real *locus* of state power is obscured. Idealists pathetically invest their hopes in the political parties, across the ideological spectrum, because the parties are supposed to reflect the workings of genuine democracy. Japanese political parties are important, but vested interests have artificially magnified their influence in often corrupt ways. Finally, Western political scientists, especially those working in English-speaking democracies, contribute to the inflated reputation of Japanese political parties because they appear to be the most familiar feature of the Japanese political landscape.

G-men

Bureaucrats are unlikely heroes. In a world dominated by huge bureaucratic structures – civil, military and corporate – the modern 'organization man' rarely struts or preens his feathers. Perhaps this is because bureaucratism appears to corrode romantic heroism; it neither charms, astounds nor enthrals. Yet the civil servant, singly or *en masse*, has left his mark on the vision of modern times fabricated by the media. The invention of the 'intellectual *montage*' by Eisenstein, and its effective exploitation by contemporary film directors, has fostered a respect for organizational strength. Thus the hero of *The Day of the Jackal* (the film rather than the novel) is the French security services, mobilized, in scene after scene, to protect Charles de Gaulle, the embodiment of the French state. In *The Caine Mutiny* (again the film rather than the play), the story's protagonist may be Captain Queeg, but the hero is the US Navy. The films *Fail Safe* and *Seven Days in May* make a similar point about the American armed forces, viewing them less as a fighting force than as a disciplined bureaucracy patriotically serving the nation. What are the FBI G-man (short for 'government man') and Le Carré's George Smiley but bureaucrats with guns? Such examples lend plausibility to the unlikely notion that civil servants, too, can be heroes. What is striking about Japan, and modern Prussia, is that economic bureaucrats are regarded there as achievers of great deeds, as heroes.

Such heroism encourages the view that Japan's experience of government challenges one of the iron rules of all political analysis: the precept that bureaucracy is always a negative phenomenon. This negativity transcends political and cultural divides. The commentator may be ancient or modern, Asian or European, but his suspicious tone will hardly vary. The historicist who insists that different eras are closed books to one another need only recall the persistently jaundiced light that is cast almost everywhere on bureaucracies. Is this negative consensus the result of incisive clarity or intellectual sloth, or it is it an unedifying surrender to cant, prejudice or even fear?

The contrast between modern East Asian reflection on bureaucracy and the treatment of bureaucracy by Western writers, especially in English-speaking countries, may provide an answer. In countries heir to the Confucian tradition of elite state service, bureaucracy is often feared and criticized but rarely belittled or dismissed as ineffective. On the contrary, bureaucrats who work at the heart of East Asian states and polities are the beneficiaries of considerable prestige. Bureaucracy may be criticized as unresponsive and heavy-handed but rarely as unnatural or unnecessary.

The lessons of this Oriental response to the fact of bureaucracy, to its enduring power and presence in East Asian statecraft, have not been entirely neglected in recent Western writing on Pacific Rim politics. Hofheinz and Calder assess the differences in bureaucratic philosophies in these terms:

> In sharp contrast with the freewheeling Americans, who have distrusted government from the beginning of their historical experience, the Eastasian peoples have embraced government and bureaucracy as a high art. The ancient Chinese conception of public service as a moral responsibility, the traditional stress on ritual as the cement of society, the strict ordering of officialdom by rank and by extensive written rules – all these ancient characteristics lie at the heart of the current Eastasian economic rebirth. . . . Even in relatively individualistic Korea, state officials adopt easily the same elitism found in Japan and Taiwan, where a post in government is considered a mark of superiority.[1]

This is the stuff of an intellectual revolution, especially in the English-speaking world. Alas, the few studies produced during the brief era of positive assessments of Japan's bureaucracy, during and after the second oil shock, failed to spark the overthrow of the conventional Western view of bureaucracy as necessarily ineffective. Indeed, the staying power of this anti-bureaucratic prejudice is amply demonstrated in modern writing on the Western civil service. Among work by journalists, Peter Hennessy's *Whitehall* remains an outstanding example of the pro-bureaucratic revisionist view.[2] Such revisionists are still a tiny minority. This venerable but also vulnerable tradition of anti-bureaucratism requires sceptical scrutiny if writers and readers schooled in this mode are to make sense of the pro-bureaucratic tradition of East Asia, especially of modern Japan. But this demands an acceptance of the possiblity that human beings, working together within state structures, can achieve sound administration, perhaps even something as remarkable as a national economic miracle.

Ignore the perceived muddle in the universal discourse on bureaucracy and it will be impossible to grasp, for example, the core issues at stake in the policy debate generated by a decade of negotiations between Washington and Tokyo over how to ease the bilateral trade imbalance between America and Japan. Fail to understand the importance and potential of effective bureaucracy, and one will misconstrue the insights contained in the Maekawa Reports (1986–7), or the bureaucratic dynamic at work in the Structural Impediments Initiative (SII), or the significance of the Japanese discussion over liberalization and internationalization. Such failure will even conspire against understanding the bureaucratic critique that Namiki Nobuyoshi has recently aired in his best-selling tract, *Tsūsanshō no Shūen* [The End of MITI] or, in a similar vein, *Ōkura Kanryō no Shihai no Shūen* [The End of MOF Domination] by Yamaguchi Jirō.[3]

'No, minister'

History encourages the conviction that the Japanese bureaucracy will, despite short-term setbacks, remain the crucial bedrock of the nation. Recent suggestions of a decline in bureaucratic morale and an erosion of the bureaucracy's *raison d'être* with the liberalization of the Japanese economy points to the opposite view, that the long era of bureaucratic supremacy may be coming to a close. Certainly, evidence of bureaucratic retreat has been seized upon with glee by many foreign observers who have been keen to welcome recent changes because they cannot understand or accept the notion of an efficient bureaucratic polity.

The issue is not just bureaucratic power. The unsettling sparkle of 'Yes, Minister', the British comedy about the struggle between politicians and higher civil servants to dominate Whitehall policymaking, was the result of the disturbing suggestion that cunning bureaucrats might, in an unconstitutional way, run the show. But it is one thing to suspect that the deference owed by civil servants to elected politicians, encapsulated in the phrase 'Yes, Minister', is a sham, and quite another to argue that a system, such as the Japanese, which legitimates the powers of bureaucrats to say loudly and frequently 'No, Minister!', is both proper and more effective. But this is exactly the position argued in some of the more incisive pages of recent Western political science on Japan.

What is the view of the Japanese themselves? Recalling with nostalgia the high era of outstanding Japanese civil servants at MITI, such as Sahashi Shigeru ('Mister MITI'), one corporate leader has observed that, 'In the old days, MITI looked after us and fought off foreign interests; now they take flight at the first sighting of opposition'.[4] This businessman's complaint was partly in response to his perception of MITI's failure during the 1986 Tōshiba affair, when it was discovered that Tōshiba Machine, a member of the Tōshiba corporate group, had sold sensitive submarine technology to the Soviets. The incident provoked ferocious criticism in the USA and a ban on Tōshiba sales there. MITI led the damage-control exercise on the Japanese side.

In a similar vein, the stinging criticism of the Japanese bureaucracy contained in Uchibashi Katsuhito's '*kaisetsu*', at the end of Sakata

Makoto's *Nihon Kanryō Hakusho* (White Paper on the Japanese Bureaucracy), begins with a rhetorical attack on the Japanese bureaucratic consensus:

> It is often remarked that the Japanese bureaucrats are good at their jobs (*yūshū*). One continues to hear their praises sung, that things will be all right if one lets them get on with the task at hand, and that their contribution has, at many points, been decisive to Japan's rise to the status of a great economic power. This country's business elite believes this to be the case, and they have repeatedly said so in public.[5]

Whatever the force of contemporary criticism of the Japanese bureaucracy, even its severest critics, such as Uchibashi, must concede the existence of a broad unifying orthodoxy that has underwritten and continues to underwrite the bureaucracy's prestige in post-war Japan. Not to acknowledge this fact of Japanese political life, before engaging in a vigorous critique of bureaucratic perogatives and failings, would deny such a work any plausibility. This culture of positive bureaucratic appraisal extends to industrial policy, the *bête noire* of conservative business commentators and dyed-in-the-wool liberal free-marketeers. Yet, here again, industrial policy is the object of broad support in Japan, especially among the elite of the business community (see Chapter 7).

Despite their much-advertised commitment to tough and clear-sighted empiricism, it is not Western journalists but Western scholars who have done most to bring the true character of the Japanese polity to light. Tetsuo Najita's incisive gloss on the Japanese bureaucratic tradition has already been cited. T.J. Pempel, a critic of the 'straw men' that sometimes deface Western writing about Japan, weighed the pros and cons of the debate over the Japanese state and bureaucracy and concluded that, 'Instead of government by autonomous agency, Japan has had government by central design'.[6]

In his study of public policy, *The State and Labour in Modern Japan*, Sheldon Garon has insisted on putting bureaucrats at the centre of Taishō Japan's reform effort:

> How the parties and bureaucracy confronted the complex problems of domestic division and social inequities tells us much more about the life and death of Taishō democracy than either the several accounts of the rise and fall of the parties per se or the attempts to measure the Japanese commitment to democracy as an abstract notion.[7]

Then there is the provocative conclusion that Chalmers Johnson draws in *MITI and the Japanese Miracle*. He forcefully rejects the 'anything but politics' bias in explanations of Japan's post-war economic success. The issue most deserving of scholarly scrutiny is the complex process of structural economic change viewed as an outcome of policy influence and bureaucratic will, in conjunction with Japanese industry and banking. Johnson insists that the 'shift of industrial structure [between c. 1955 and c. 1965] was the operative mechanism of the economic miracle'.[8] He insists that there is a prima-facie case for arguing that MITI's role in this structural shift was significant. It is precisely this argument that makes his contention that 'the LDP has reigned but the bureaucracy has ruled' so fruitful. Johnson's effective case for bureaucratic polity as overseer of a developmental state has made *MITI and the Japanese Miracle* the most consequential text generated by Western political science about Japan since the war. In a way unmatched by the journalism of the period, much of it fine in its perceptions and discriminations, scholarship has reasserted its claim to stand at the heart of our understanding of how Japan really works. The legacy to political science has been a series of excellent monographs, written in vigorous agreement or dissent.

It may nonetheless be true that it is easier to write favourably about bureaucracy when one does not have to live under such a regime as Japan's. Or one may reverse the conceit and insist that greater liberty is the just compensation for any society which does not benefit from effective bureaucracy. The question is, however, whether in a system of free-trade, regulatory states, such as the United States and Britain, can withstand competition from developmental states such as Japan, South Korea and Taiwan. A decade of research and, more important, real-world experience has not delivered a reassuring answer. Whether bureaucrats should exercise authority independent of elected politicians, a virtue often admired in the central banker, may be one of the key issues of the age.

MONEY-CHANGERS IN THE TEMPLE

The most serious flaw in post-war reporting and scholarly writing on Japanese government has been the exaggerated attention paid to party politics. The public policy studies revolution of the 1980s has done much to correct this mistaken picture. But one of the most provocative studies of the 1980s was a revolt against this new trend in political analysis: Kent Calder's *Crisis and Compensation: Public Policy and Political Stability in Japan, 1949–1986*.[9] This monumental study is either the last hurrah of the defenders of the primacy of Japanese party politicians or one of the most serious pieces of counter-revisionism in the field of Japanese political science. It sets forth an intellectual argument on the scale that only the giant monograph permits. Calder confines his study to the years between 1949 and 1986. His thesis pivots on the assumption that party politicians have 'compensated' the perceived victims of political and economic 'crises'. This has determined his choice of period. Yet it is essential to see that it starts four years into the post-war revival of political parties. To suggest a similar role for Japanese political parties between 1929 and 1944, for example, would be unconvincing.

The year 1986, Calder's end-point, is also significant for any advocate of crisis-compensation dynamic. First, 1986 witnessed the beginnings of forceful recovery in Japan's manufacturing sector (see Chapter 5) that owed little to LDP pork-barrel politics but reflected a triumph of long-term corporate and bureaucratic, or national goals. Second, the mid-1980s also saw the first hints of a significant abandonment of agricultural protectionism (in beef, oranges and rice), a crucial form of pork-barrel compensation, by the LDP. As Japan's 'farm problem' provided the original context for the development of the 'crisis-compensation' dynamic, 1986 was a watershed. The world trade of the late 1980s and 1990s has been as stressful as any post-Occupation crisis that Calder describes, but this new 'crisis' has provoked not compensation but a more resolute attitude towards the inefficient and unproductive.

Calder's subtitle reads: 'Public Policy and Political Stability in Japan'. The key difference between mainstream Western scholarship on Japan before and after 1980 is the shift in focus from electoral politics to public policy. On this point, Calder's use of the term 'public policy' represents a bow to the new political scientific orthodoxy and confirms the impact of the 1980s public policy revolution in Japan studies. This revolution should also help to redefine the way we understand the sensitive issue of Japanese 'political stability'. This constitutes the soft underbelly of Japanese public policy. As a broad set of policy tools, values and targets, the Japanese miracle has made compensation possible: the growing international traded sector has generated the financial surplus which has allowed the inefficient non-traded to survive. This is why the system can afford to compensate 'crises'.

The Meiji state was brought down not only by war but by a crisis on the Japanese farm. But, however coddled during the post-war period, farming and other inefficient sectors were never the stuff of a Japanese miracle. The main vehicle of that success has been the international traded sector, cheer-led by the ruling party and sustained by the central bureaucracy, particularly MITI and MOF. The main goal of traded-sector industrial policy was growth and market-share domination; the chief concern of the non-traded-sector public policy was political stability. Calder addresses one vital dimension of the problem by focusing on the stability question, but to make his thesis more tart, he has of necessity neglected industrial policies designed to foster economic growth and international comparative advantage. The larger issue must be how the two-stroke dynamic – traded and non-traded sectors – of post-war public policy was managed.

In Calder's main title, 'Crisis and Compensation', the term 'crisis' refers to three distinct periods of post-war Japanese history:

1 the turbulence that led to the 1955 system *(gōju-go-nen taisei)*, the major realignment of political party forces on both sides of the ideological divide;
2 the crisis of confidence before and after the 1960 struggle over the US-Japan mutual security pact;
3 the dislocations resulting from the first Nixon shock and the great oil shock of 1973–4.

These are what Calder labels as 'crises' for Japan's ruling LDP, and he argues that these moments of lost nerve produced significant changes in Japanese public policy programmes. There is little question that Japanese opinion leaders perceived these periods as particularly stressful. The need to foster a stable conservative majority in the Diet in the mid-1950s, to prepare Japan for a significant weakening of protectionist barriers in the early 1960s, and to guide the Japanese economy through the rigours of the first oil shock (1973–4) all focused bureaucratic minds on the problem at hand.

But the importance of such crises must not be overstated. In the heady world of Japanese tabloid journalism, every day is a crisis. The headline crisis is exactly what it claims to be: the most eye-catching story of a single day; 365 days translated into 365 crises. The old war horses of the LDP delight in these *tatemae* crises, this surface noise of what is in reality a remarkably stable political system. The Japanese love of a good old-fashioned emergency has to be factored into ('discounted' in the language of stock market analysis) a broader picture that also recognizes the formidable strengths of Japanese economic and bureaucratic fundamentals as well as the caution of the Japanese electorate. More important, these varied crises have never resulted in compensation, in Calder's sense, for the elite that govern Japan: the bureaucracy, big business and the LDP. One has only to recall the tough-minded enforcement of higher energy costs by the bureaucracy at the short-term expense of Japanese industry in the wake of the 1973 oil crisis, which was a genuine if temporary crisis for the Japanese economy.

There is no question that floods of money, passing through the hands of ruling party politicians, is a way of 'buying off' (the term 'compensation' is imprecise) non-elite discontent that might interfere with the great national goals of rapid growth and market-share expansion. LDP politicians are notoriously venal and self-seeking, but their corruption has not been allowed to derail the Japanese miracle. Japan's rise to economic superpower status remains the pre-eminent concern for the student of post-war Japanese government, not the paid-off peasant-minded electorates of rural Japan. It is this success story that makes Japan one of the important polities of the twentieth century.

The issue of compensatory policies nevertheless needed to be tackled. The fiscal politics involved have been prodigious. Calder rightly observes that the typhoons in contemporary Japan are not what they used to be:

> In 1983 Shimane Prefecture was hit by a typhoon and subsequent flooding that killed 103 people. Within hours, hundreds of Self-Defense Force servicemen and scores of medics, together with three cabinet ministers, were descending on the Shimane capital of Matsue, population 130,000 . . . . In time, national-government compensation for typhoon damage mounted to over ¥20 billion (roughly $93 million). This equalled the entire Shimane prefectural budget for three weeks and represented more than $117,000 (sic) for every man, woman, and child in the entire prefecture.[10]

This typhoon was a genuine 'crisis' for the residents of Shimane. A poor public policy response to this natural disaster *might* have caused some electoral difficulty for the prefecture's formidable representation in the Japanese Diet, which includes Takeshita Noboru, Japan's senior party faction boss and prime minister from 1987 to 1989, when he was brought down in the Recruit bribery scandal. But this was not a national crisis, although it reflects the small-beer politics at work in the crisis-compensation cycle.

Commenting on the ability of Shimane, a pork-barrel fiefdom at its worst, to attract funding from central government, Calder remarks that, 'Reinforcing the power of Shimane in the policy process was its strong leverage in the conservative political world'.[11] This proposition may be recast. Shimane has little influence on Japanese politics or public policy. Certainly it exerts none on elite-guided national goal achievement outside the party politics of a few LDP faction bosses. The rural prefecture is being 'bribed' to return politicians to the Diet, and these politicians have exploited their party position to acquire wealth and power. They have often exercised important influence on public policy, but Shimane itself, as a community or as a political factor, has no influence on the main thrust of Japanese public policy, particularly in the all-important traded sector. Its suggested place of prominence is, in any case, the result of a constitutional fluke and rural over-representation in the Diet.

Shimane's electoral influence is the consequence of changes in the Japanese political system made by MacArthur: land reform and the constitutional strengthening of political parties. No thinking member of the Japanese elite in 1945 would willingly have conceded such influence to any rural community. What prevented the rolling back of Occupation reforms after 1952 was memories of the disastrous rural crisis (this was not a *tatemae* storm in a teacup) during the 1930s, a convulsion that contributed powerfully to the rise of the militarists. What the post-war experience of Japan demonstrates unambiguously is that MacArthur's democratic ambitions, no doubt inspired by New Deal liberalism, have led to astonishing pork-barrel excesses.

> Shimane in 1984 was only thirty-sixth among Japan's forty-seven prefectures in terms of per capita income, with an average ¥1,700,000 per person. But it was number one in terms of new public works construction contracts, bringing an additional ¥248,920 per person, or nearly 15 per cent of prefectural income, from the national government that year. Despite its poverty and relative isolation, Shimane had more museums and art galleries per capita than all but one other prefecture and more town auditoriums than all but five. It also ranked thirteenth among Japan's prefectures in the number of public libraries per person. Yet in national tax payments Shimane ranked forty-third per capita, even lower than its ranking in individual income.[12]

This venal largesse, described by Calder, is not the result of a 'crisis and compensation' dynamic because Shimane voters, the post-war landlord class excepted, have never suffered from any real crisis. Rather, this Japanese answer to the American 'spoils system' is the direct consequence of three factors: naïve Occupation reforms; the panic response of conservative politicians to these reforms; and the cunning of the Shimane electorate who have learned how to milk the system with the help of politicians regularly returned to the Diet. The same analysis may be applied to the Niigata fiefdom of the late Tanaka Kakuei and dozens of other rural constituencies.

But the key point must be that there was a system to milk. Such peasant cunning, unconstrained by elite leadership, might have subverted the policy process and helped to keep Japan poor forever. It has been only the tireless and effective pursuit of state goals at the national level that has generated the wealth so liberally showered on otherwise feeble rural constituencies in Shimane and Niigata. They, and others like them, have benefited, by historical accident, from powerful politicians pursuing venal prefectural 'interests' at the expense of national goals at the centres of elite policymaking in Tokyo. However fantastic the sums involved in this redistributive politics, it is clear that, on balance, the flow of talent, expertise, manpower and capital in post-war Japan has overwhelmingly favoured the centre, Tokyo, over the periphery, however broadly defined.

Despite the drag of pork-barrel politics, Japan has achieved unrivalled economic success. Japan, as a nation, has managed its accounts carefully enough to fund the greatest economic investment campaign in human history and still have money to spare. This surplus has been used partly to buy off the inefficient and grasping at the margins of Japan's GNP machine. This fact of Japanese political life forces the conclusion that any 'crisis and compensation' cycle was only a smaller part of the grander design called the Japanese miracle. It could not have been paid for otherwise. This miracle, not the crisis and compensation cycle, defines the central dynamic of post-war Japanese policymaking and politics.

The masters of Japan's unedifying system of 'money politics' (*kinsen-seiji*), with its elections costing billions of dollars to buy votes or influence voters, have made Japanese party politicians into the money-changers of the Japanese temple of state. In contrast, the elite economic bureaucrats and the best business leaders have been the system's saviours.[13] It is they who have harnessed the vast capacity of the Japanese people to work, study and save their way to national greatness. In this triumph, it should be amply clear who were the gentlemen (in both the Confucian and English senses) and who were the players. Politicians have often influenced policy, but bureaucrats have made the policies that have counted. And every Japanese politician knows it.

What other conclusion should be drawn from the sorry record of corruption that came to light after Japan's 1980s bubble burst? The Ministry of Finance eased its controls over financial markets during the 1980s in response to a secular economic trend towards 24-hour trading, the dangers of a general stock market collapse in 1987, and under pressure from Japanese firms. But these same firms exploited their new freedoms to push structural corruption to new depths. To blame the bureaucracy for the way Nomura and other securities houses abused the new freedoms to line pockets, in alliance with the *keizai yakuza* (economic gangsters), is not persuasive. Better to have the bureaucracy run Japan than to permit a political system to flourish where a major Japanese bank, apparently with *yakuza* links, has been credited with 'creating' the first Takeshita cabinet.

The shaming revelations of the Sagawa Kyūbin and other scandals raise crucial doubts about the virtues of the so-called policy tribes or *zoku*. The corrupt machinations of *zoku* leaders such Kanamaru Shin or Takeshita Noboru, again in league with gangster interests, should be the main object of public ire and critical scrutiny, not the crime-fighters at the Tokyo District Public Prosecutors Office (*Tokyo Chihō Kensatsu-chō*), which in any case was hobbled by feeble legislation, internal divisions, and pressure from LDP faction bosses. It may indeed be the case that political ministers exert new powers over their ministries, but the expertise that underwrites such power has not always served the public interest. The licensing powers of the Japanese Ministry of Transport were no doubt abused in the Sagawa Kyūbin affair, but there are already some signs of ministry efforts to reform its procedures.

But the MOT's vulnerability to outside influence should be laid at the feet of corrupting politicians and their *zoku* alliances. Such failures raise questions, not about the ability of *zoku* bosses to interfere with bureaucratic decision-making, but about the contribution of LDP leadership, since Tanaka Kakuei's rise, to sustaining Japan's miracle and its climb to superpower status. The corrupt frenzy of some of Japan's greatest companies, once the administrative leash was eased during the late 1980s, highlights the importance of the economic bureaucracy in keeping Japan responsibly managed and its economic miracle on course. In altering circumstances, from the post-war reconstruction to the liberalizing present, the bureaucracy has indeed made the policies that have best served Japan's interests. It may or may not have 'ruled' but whatever its flaws or weaknesses, the central bureaucracy has governed, and often well.

The Japanese state at work

5   Four policy lessons from the 1980s

Japan emerged as a world power during the 1980s. That crucial decade witnessed many other changes of great importance, one of the most consequential being the growth of global financial markets. This was the decade of the 'big bang', privatization and liberalization. Those ten years made the ugly-sounding terms 'internationalization' and 'global-ization' into something approaching household words. But if the growth of Japanese power during the 1980s is ignored or somehow side-stepped, then the true lessons to be learned from that remarkable period will not be mastered.

The Japanese husbanding of their power through the course of the decade is frequently described in the Western media as either wicked or stupid. Those who subscribed to the 'Japan as an evil empire' theory were sometimes rather inadequately termed 'revisionists'. The principal tenet of vulgar revisionists was that Japan is involved in a conspiracy to take over the world. Those who hold that the Japanese are merely being foolish tended to cling to free-market theory as if it were a wiser, older sister who could do their thinking for them. The view taken here is that the Japanese are neither fiends nor fools. Rather than perverse or irrational, Japan's economic policies and trade diplomacy have, in the main, been consistently nationalist in a thoughtful, if narrow, way. The main consequence of this thinking nationalism has been to transform the ruling assumptions of how the world works. This shift of influence was powerfully demonstrated in four closely linked events or developments: the Plaza Accord, Japanese super-industrialism, the Maekawa Reports, and the SII talks. It is here that one may uncover the main public policy lessons of the 1980s.

All these issues affected the relationship between the world's two largest economies. The germination of an unprecedented degree of mutual dependence between the United States and Japan during the 1980s encouraged some commentators, especially in Japan, to view the two economies as a single unit; hence the Japanese coinage '*Nichi–bei keizai*' or the 'joint US–Japan economy'. But the decade that began with a recession and liberal hopes for freer trade ended in bitter recrimination and rising fears of protectionism. One result was a limping campaign in favour of more open markets, reflected in the troubled Uruguay round of GATT, and greater managed trade, which has become a significant feature of trade ties between the USA and Japan.

For the student of politics and foreign policy, the 1980s was a decade of arm-wrestling between Washington and Tokyo over the future shape of the world economy and Japan's place in this new order. One has to be neither American nor Japanese to grasp the central features of this story of the decline of the post-1945 world hierarchy, a parable clearly illustrated by the struggle between America and Japan. Hence the need to put into intellectual order the long trail of policy conflicts and compromises which began in the trade tensions of the early 1980s and ended in the humiliation of President George Bush during his 1992 visit to the Japanese capital. The success of the Clinton administration in the Pacific will be determined by how well it picks up these pieces.

The road to the 1992 'Tokyo primary' has its origins in the trade frictions ignited by the expanding US trade deficit with Japan in the early 1980s: what C. Fred Bergsten, writing in *Foreign Affairs* in 1982, described as the third episode in post-war economic conflict between the USA and Japan since 1970, the earlier ones having taken place in 1970–1 (the 'Nixon shock') and 1977–8.[1] In 1983, America's deficit with Japan reached the record level of $19.3 billion. At the end of 1991, the figure stood at $43.4 billion. Such statistics offer evidence that the crusade to reduce America's trade deficit with Japan, a key goal of Reagan–Bush foreign policy, ended in tears. Neither did the administration manage to tame the growth of protectionist sentiment at home nor to maintain good relations with the Japanese. This triple failure was one of policy as well as of ideas.

Looking back over a decade of flawed policy initiatives and accords, it is plain that neither the Reagan nor the Bush administrations understood the nature of their contest with Japan. American officials relied either on that elusive saviour, market forces, or on misconceived nationalist swagger. In the end the two Republican administrations proved to be neither consistent free-traders nor effective defenders of US national interests. Most important of all, Reagan and Bush, or their key policy advisers, failed to grasp that at each significant policy juncture – the 1983 agreement to liberalize Japanese capital markets, the 1985 Plaza Accord, the 1986 semiconductor market-share pact, the Tōshiba sanctions of the same year, the Maekawa Reports of 1986-87, the 1989

FSX jet fighter fiasco, the Structural Impediments Initiative of 1989–90, the dispute over Gulf War financing, and the ill-fated Bush state visit of 1992 – power was slipping from Washington's hands into Tokyo's. In 1983 Treasury Secretary Regan won what he thought was a victory in the capital markets agreement. In 1992, President Bush, once again attempting to play 'hardball' with the Japanese, came away with little. This altering balance of power defined US–Japan relations during the 1980s, and this change is one that a free-market model cannot explain.

THE PLAZA ACCORD

The two rounds of negotiations in 1983 and 1984 over liberalizing Japanese capital markets were supposed to be triumphs of American diplomatic will. But economists disagree about what was actually achieved by the agreements when viewed against the public policy goals of the Reagan administration. Furthermore, the policymakers themselves have appeared to alter their expectations in response to subsequent market developments. One warning in particular proved prophetic. In his testimony before a US Senate subcommittee, C. Fred Bergsten remarked that 'the recently announced US–Japan "yen agreement" will make the [exchange-rate] problem worse, at least in the short run, by encouraging more capital outflow from Japan.'[2]

The capital inflows that resulted would exacerbate all the other tensions that plagued US–Japan relations, and for years to come. What a different complexion the US federal budget problem might have worn if such capital inflows had been smaller! More important, from the vantage of trans-Pacific policymaking, the capital-market agreements signalled the initial decline of the perceived effectiveness of free-market policy tools, as opposed to free-market goals, in Washington. This mattered over the course of the 1980s because the decay of free-market 'means' would eventually result in the decline of free-market 'ends' as well. Bergsten's warnings were vindicated when the Reagan administration took its next major gamble: the Plaza Accord of September 1985.

Until 1985, the Reagan administration policy line had been that the strength of the US economy had created a strong dollar and high interest rates. There were always dangers in the Reagan policy mix of tight monetary policy and expansionist fiscal policy. Despite this obvious contradiction, the administration was taken at its word by investors at home and abroad because so many market signals, such as the US real growth rate in 1984 of 6.4 per cent, seemed to confirm the optimistic outlook of the proponents of Reaganomics. Japanese officials were therefore bemused when the Reagan administration abruptly reversed its diagnosis of America's economic problems in 1985.[3] In a total break with its previous stance, the Reagan administration now began to insist that 'a strong U.S. economy has not brought with it high interest rates and a strong dollar; rather, these high interest rates and the dollar's strength were weakening the U.S. economy as industries in the United States lost international competitiveness.'[4]

To alleviate the problems of American firms in trouble in overseas markets, US treasury officials browbeat the other finance ministers of the G-5 countries, principally the Japanese, into agreeing to co-operate in devaluing the dollar against the yen and other currencies. The signal sent to overseas investors in the US economy was unambiguous. Their confidence in Reagan boom policies had been misplaced. The dollar tumbled. Within ten months it had dropped in value from ¥240 to ¥150–60. To this degree, market forces appeared to work in textbook fashion. But the policymakers were thwarted in their central aim. Peter Drucker has spelled out the crisis for free-market theory that resulted from the Plaza Accord:

> A sharp devaluation of a currency *must* – according to all theory and all experience – sharply increase a country's exports and sharply decrease a country's imports. U.S. exports did rise, and sharply, though not until a year and half after the dollar's devaluation. By the end of 1988 the rise in exports of U.S. manufactured goods had narrowed the trade deficit by the one-third that can be considered to have been caused, in the first place, by the earlier dollar devaluation. But industrial imports into the United States – which according to all theory and all earlier experience should have all but disappeared – kept on increasing![5]

Drucker points to the new importance of investment as the main factor which determines the direction of traded goods. It is the new weight of investment, rather than traditional 'factors of production', that may explain why foreign investors continued to pour their money into the US economy after they recovered from the shock of the Plaza Accord, and why US firms kept investing heavily overseas with their devalued dollars. Other large issues – the huge federal deficit and America's new status as the world's largest debtor nation – loomed in the background. But the failure of the Plaza Accord to stem the flow of Japanese manufactured imports, a key objective of the Reagan strategy as reflected in the 1985 devaluation of the dollar, marked a major transition: henceforth market manipulation alone was effectively abandoned as a sovereign remedy for the troubles of the US–Japan relationship. At the same time, and for the same reason, policy initiative in tackling these problems began to shift to Tokyo. Japanese methods and approaches would now increasingly dominate the policy options of the *Nichi-bei keizai.*

SUPER-INDUSTRIALISM

The 1980s revealed that capital investment may be the major determinant of market share. Investment-led growth depends on a society's ability to save, and therefore has important public policy implications. There is also evidence that the massive Japanese capital investment of the 1980s helped to mitigate the effects of the Plaza Accord. This is the story of one of the most extraordinary phenomena of the 1980s: Japanese super-industrialism *(chō-sangyō-shugi).*[6]

The Plaza Accord delivered a major blow to the Japanese economy. The high-yen *(endaka)* recession of 1986 confirmed the view held by many business commentators at the time that Japanese manufacturing had been, in effect, doomed to follow the path previously taken by American and British manufacturers towards 'hollowing out' and decline. The Japanese steel industry had been for years a prime candidate for the unhappy tag of sunset industry *(shayō-sangyō).* In the mid-1980s, more than 30 per cent of its output was targeted for export. The sudden devaluation of the dollar reduced to tatters the industry's assumptions about production costs and pricing. Overseas markets were threatened and operating costs soared. Japan's five largest blast furnace operators reported some ¥400 billion in losses in fiscal 1986.

But the recession was masking a new trend that Drucker has rightly identified as decisive: investment-led business growth. Even before the Plaza Accord, Japanese private sector domestic capital investment had been expanding at a rate twice that of the Japanese GNP. Under the lash of the *endaka* recession, Japanese industry began to make war on fixed costs while investing in new plant and equipment on a scale never witnessed before in business history. Nippon Steel, for example, publicly announced its intention to cut fixed costs by ¥1 trillion, or 30 per cent, between 1987 and 1990. Company wages were slashed; excess blast furnace capacity was cut and other production facilities rationalized. By the end of fiscal 1987, Nippon Steel had achieved 40 per cent of its rationalization-drive target. By the end of 1988, the figure was 60 per cent. As a result of counter-measures throughout the industry, Japanese steel regained its ability to lead prices. Exploiting its large share of world markets, the industry crimped supply and global market prices soared in response. A ton of crude steel which might have cost $422 in the lean year of 1986, the height of the *endaka* recession, stood at $750 by the winter of 1988–9. On the shoulders of increased profits, Japanese industry bounced back with new vigour. A similar reversal was seen in other Japanese manufactures: chemicals, non-ferrous metals and paper, for example.

Behind this transformation was a return to capital investment levels that Japan had not experienced since the era of high-speed growth. Capital investment as a per centage of GNP had peaked before the first oil shock at 18.8 per cent in 1970. In 1987 Japanese industry broke this record when it invested 19.5 per cent of the country's GNP in new plant and equipment. Since the sudden ending of the cheap-yen era, investment-led growth has come to dominate the managerial agenda of Japanese manufacturing. During fiscal 1988, Matsushita Electric plunged ¥364 billion into capital investment, half in the vital semiconductor field. In the same year, Hitachi Ltd, one of Japan's major producers of heavy electrical machinery, invested ¥190 billion in plant and equipment, a figure which represented an 85 per cent increase over 1987.

Japanese super-industrialism, with its high rates of investment and determined drives to cut fixed costs, was not a temporary phenomenon. Capital investment roared along at a double-digit pace into the 1990s. In fiscal 1990, Japanese capital investment as a proportion of GNP topped 25 per cent, the first time such a level has been reached by any OECD country. The American figure may have been only half as much. Even if Japanese figures are somewhat inflated by the way accountants there tend to lump together spending on new equipment and new buildings, the overall impression is clear. Japanese manufacturing will remain strong in its home base as well as abroad. The Japanese trade imbalance with the USA, much of it accounted for by manufactured goods, provides an accurate measure of the success achieved.

To the degree that the primary motivation of the Reagan economic policy, as reflected in the Plaza Accord, was to deflect Japanese manufactured imports (much the largest source of the trade deficit), the administration and its noisy advocacy of free-market methods was routed by the forces of Japanese super-industrialism. Never again would the administration turn in confidence to the tools employed with such little success in its attempts to finesse the effects of Japanese competitive ambition and drive. Both the Reagan and Bush administrations continued to insist that free-market principles should define co-operative efforts between Washington and Tokyo, but 'means' would hereafter be left to the Japanese, who in any case have never been as keen as Americans on abstract economic theory and its policy imperatives.

In what sense, then, was this defeat of the Plaza Accord also a disappointment for Japanese policymakers? Plainly the recession was a blow. A permanent higher value for the yen, which was certainly the result of the Plaza Accord if short-term currency fluctuations are kept in perspective, was a major burden for exporters. Cheaper prices for imported goods, services and, most importantly, raw materials was poor compensation for damaged export markets. But there was a broad consensus within the Japanese government that something had to be done to help the Reagan administration, even if it was not clear that what the administration wanted today could be squared with what it might demand tomorrow.

MITI's position on the question of Japanese manufacturing reflected nationalist concerns. If firms had proved unable to ward off the pressures inflicted on the Japanese economy by the Plaza Accord, then MITI's panoply of sunset industry counter-measures would have been dusted off. But there was always the hope that Japanese manufacturing would rise to the new challenge, as it had to others in the past. This Japanese industry did in stunning fashion. No one was more pleased with this result than MITI bureaucrats who took the long view. After all, it was exactly the kind of campaign to invest massively in the future with which reform-minded bureaucrats have punctuated the history of Japanese public policy since the late Meiji period. The founding concern of Japanese industry policy in the mid-1920s was economic rationalization. Fostering the growth of national savings and devising means for their effective investment in industry has been the target for nearly three generations of public policy propagandists. Super-industrialism was a MITI vision come true. Granted, those officials who negotiated the deal with the Reagan administration at the Plaza Hotel in September 1985 were outflanked by Japanese industrialists. But it was like a mother being beaten at tennis by her daughter. The mother cannot lose because it is her child who has won.

THE MAEKAWA REPORTS

The failure of the Plaza Accord to ease America's trade imbalance with Japan, particularly in manufactured goods, spawned a variety of policies. In response to the early-1987 climb in the value of the yen, the G-7 finance ministers, minus the Italians, met in Paris to cope with this new crisis. The result was the Louvre Accord of February 1987. The ministers agreed that further improvements in current account imbalances could not be left to adjustments in exchange rates, thus burying the key Plaza Accord policy tool. Rather, relief must be sought in demand expansion from Japan and Germany, while the USA was to cut its ballooning federal deficit. Despite repeated declarations of intent, some expressed in legislation, the Reagan administration and its successor were unable to meet the hopes set out in the Louvre Accord. Henceforth, American policymakers were reduced to boisterous cheer-leading from the stands, as US policy hopes more often than not came to be the responsibility of officials in Japan and Germany.

Instead of making policy, US administration officials threw their efforts into diplomacy, backed by increasingly hawkish trade legislation from the Democratic-controlled Congress. The result was a series of agreements with the Japanese, of varying quality and effectiveness, in areas of trade as diverse as semiconductors and oranges. Voluntary restraints on major Japanese-manufactured imports, managed trade in everything but name, were enforced. But none of the bouts of trade diplomacy or congressional trade legislation (the '301' and 'Super 301' laws included) had any significant effect on the greatest source of American irritation: the trade imbalance.

After the Plaza Accord, the US trade deficit with the rest of the world climbed until it peaked in 1987 at $150 billion. Since then the deficit has fallen, at first slowly, and then more quickly under the influence of recessionary pressures. It 1992, it was down to $66.2 billion. What did not change much was the American deficit with Japan. Since 1985, Japan's surplus with the USA has fluctuated between $40 and $60 billion. In 1991, the Japanese trade surplus with America stood at $43.4 billion, and made up two-thirds of the US trade deficit with the rest of the world.

Japan's surging success in world markets was unprecedented. In 1986, her external trade surplus reached $101.4 billion, nearly twice the figure for West Germany. No nation in history has ever before achieved a $100-billion surplus. A source of pride at home, this colossal figure made Japan a target of foreign criticism, especially in America. The US government, poorly led and frustrated by outraged feelings of economic nationalism, but still trapped in the straitjacket of orthodox free-market theory, was paralysed. So the burden of tackling the deficit fell on the shoulders of Japanese policymakers. One short-term response was the 1986 Nakasone 'action plan', an emergency call to the nation to import more foreign, that is American, goods.

The only long-term answer, consistent with Japanese interests and goals and, just as important, also within in the reach of Japan's repertoire of policy tools, was structural change. This perception led to the Maekawa Reports, arguably the most important, and certainly the best known, statement of public policy philosophy to emerge from Japan's corridors of power since the end of the US Occupation in 1952.

The three Maekawa Reports were a series of policy papers published during 1986 and 1987 by a private think-tank working for Japanese Prime Minister Nakasone Yasuhiro. They reflected an attempt, at the senior levels of the Japanese public policy establishment, to address one of the most crucial issues facing the global economy: Japan's $100 billion annual trade surplus with the rest of the world.

The reports were written by an influential group of Japanese experts headed by Maekawa Haruo, a former governor of the Bank of Japan. The First Maekawa Report was issued in advance of the conference of the leaders of the world's leading industrial democracies held in the summer of 1986, the Tokyo G-7 economic summit, and was a focus of discussion. The same study group issued an interim report in December 1986, and then the New Maekawa Report was published in April 1987 in preparation for the Venice G-7 economic summit.

Although no complete English translation of the three reports was ever published in book form, the debate about these reports made the name 'Maekawa' part of the vocabulary of international public policymaking in the 1980s. For the student of Japanese public policy, the Maekawa Reports offer an unmatched window on the most significant Japanese policy debate of the late twentieth century. In essence the Maekawa Reports ask but a single question: How can Japan change?

The goal and means both turned on structural change, Japanese style. Structural reform is one of most complex of all peacetime public policy exercises. The three reports are in their own way small miracles of concision. But they were written in a kind of bureaucratic shorthand by and for policy insiders, so it is little surprise that when they were finally published in book form in Japanese, the editors at the *Nikkan Kōgyō Shinbun*, the Japanese-language industrial news daily, felt it necessary to add 160 pages of commentary.[7]

In the West, both at the time of the issue of the reports and afterwards, the Maekawa effort was the object of considerable criticism. The First Maekawa Report was regarded by some as Nakasone's attempt to dupe America into lowering its guard. To dismiss the reports as a Japanese confidence trick therefore became a cliché, especially among those who had not read them. To meet such criticism, the table of contents, not as set out in the reports themselves, but in the Nikkan Kōgyō newspaper book on the Maekawa Reports, is reproduced here.[8]

This is important on two counts. First, the Nikkan Kōgyō book was never intended for translation and therefore could not have been designed to dupe Westerners. Second, the table of contents alone illustrates the comprehensive nature of the policy proposals the Maekawa group discussed between 1986 and 1987.

Chapter one: Why is structural change necessary now?
1 Mounting criticism of a mounting surplus
2 Structural change: a painful process
3 Opening the door: policy beginnings

Chapter two: Ways of expanding Japanese domestic demand
1 Escaping the rabbit hutch
2 Building social capital
3 Solving the land problem
4 Capital investment to promote structural change
5 Expanding domestic consumption

Chapter three: An industrial structure consistent with international harmony
1 Industrial restructuring: beginning the battle
2 Great expectations: foreign direct investment
3 Improving national efficiency
4 Expanding imports and improving foreign access to Japanese markets
5 An agricultural policy consistent with internationalization

Chapter four: Cutting working hours, maintaining jobs
1 Towards Western standards in the Japanese work-place
2 The 1800-hour work-year
3 Coping with problems in employment
4 Changes in the structure of employment and the imbalance in labour market supply and demand
5 In search of a comprehensive national labour policy
6 Redistributing work opportunities
7 Jobs and the older citizen
8 A jobs policy for older citizens

Chapter five: Policies for the regions
1 Coping with structural recession in the regions
2 Placing the emphasis on regional cities

Chapter six: Contributing to the world – Japan's new role
1 What Japan can do
2 Internationalizing the yen
3 Economic co-operation
4 International exchange

Chapter seven: The shape of Japanese industry after structural change
1 The structure of Japanese industry
2 The structure of Japanese employment

Chapter eight: Realizing a vision – the difficulties that must be overcome
1 The need for firm political leadership
2 The decisive challenge: overcoming the opposition to structural change

It was to their credit that America's trade negotiators took the Maekawa message, at least in part, to heart. It influenced the main assumptions on how to change Japan (not in which direction) in the Structural Impediments Initiative (SII), launched in 1989. The Maekawa Reports formed the indispensable subtext during the long, rancorous SII talks themselves. When the results of the SII agreements later appeared to be less than effective, the word 'Maekawa' figured prominently in the Bush administration's headline-winning complaints.

Unlike the Plaza Accord, the Maekawa idea had some chance of success because it addressed itself to Japanese methods and Japanese interests, not as the Bush administration interpreted them, but as the Japanese themselves understood them. This made the whole business that much more plausible. It smelt of the real world, of Japanese reality.

Leon Hollerman has suggested in *Japan, Disincorporated* that the reports were 'ingenious' for the effective way in which the authors managed to square American demands with the circle of Japanese needs.[9] But where Hollerman, in this provocative, valuable book, sees cynicism, it is important to stress the realism of the Maekawa proposals, which sidestepped the very issues – *keiretsu* exclusiveness, government procurements, and Japanese opposition to foreign subcontractors – over which the SII talks would falter. The Maekawa Reports were couched in an awareness that structural change is possible but enormously difficult to achieve. That last chapter of the Nikkan Kōgyō summary is a bow to this obstacle. It was precisely the way Maekawa-style reforms proposed to pinch some vested interests that explains, to a large degree, the criticism of Nakasone's Maekawa initiative in Japan. The failure of the Bush administration to accept the scale of the difficulties involved with structural reform would prove to be the undoing of its SII effort. Meanwhile, at each stage of the process, power was shifting into Japanese hands, making it that much more unlikely that Washington could enforce its demands without regard to Japanese opinion.

THE SII DEBACLE

The first thirteen months of the Bush administration (January 1989 to February 1990) saw the end of the Pacific Raj that America had created in 1945. Within months of Bush's taking office, the Cold War and trade certainties that had given Reagan policies towards Japan a coherence unravelled. In spring 1989 the rout of the Pentagon in its turf battle with the Department of Commerce and its new agenda of economic nationalism signalled the death of those certainties. The question at issue in the FSX squabble was the transfer of technology to Japan, the centrepiece of the FSX jet-fighter technology deal that the Reagan administration had previously agreed with Tokyo. In a way that exposed the new administration's lack of confidence in US technological prowess, Bush officials clawed back some of the 'advantages' that Commerce Department officials accused the Pentagon of giving away to America's most formidable economic rival. In the long hard-fought debate between the congressional trade hawks and White House free-traders, the FSX affair made clear that the Democrats had won.

The FSX wrangle also sent an unambiguous message to the Japanese. Just as the Reagan administration had admitted the failure of its Keynesian-Friedmanite mix of economic policies in the debate over the Plaza Accord, now the Bush administration revealed a sharp retreat in Washington's power in the military field. In this juxtaposition of defence and economic policies was the secret of the importance of the SII and what it said about the shifting balance of power in the Pacific.

The American effort to impose a solution to the trade deficit on the Japanese was made easier in 1989 by the scandal-ridden state of LDP politics, still reeling from the Recruit fiasco. Uno Sōsuke, Takeshita's hapless successor, formally agreed to the SII round of negotiations at the 1989 Paris summit. The talks began in September. The pressure on the Japanese was made tighter by Congressional-mandated progress on the opening of Japanese markets in three targeted product areas: super-computers, satellites and lumber products. Trade sanctions against Tokyo were threatened by Capitol Hill trade hawks if the Japanese proved unco-operative. American progress towards its goals was helped when Kaifu Toshiki succeeded Uno, who had been forced from office in part because of an absurd sex scandal. Kaifu was a minor player, totally dependent on his performance and LDP barons for his job. Kaifu's anxious weakness encouraged the Bush administration to overestimate the degree of leverage that it could exert on the Japanese in the SII bargaining.

The main objects of attack by US negotiators included:

1 Japanese laws restricting the size of retail stores in urban areas, which were thought to conspire against import sales;
2 Japan's hesitancy to increase spending on public works to 'suck in imports';

3 the high price of living space in Japanese urban centres which was viewed as a barrier to greater consumption of imports;
4 the exclusionary practices of Japan's main corporate groups or *keiretsu*, which work, in the American view, against foreign penetration of the Japanese market;
5 the widespread practice of manufacturer rebates to retail distributors;
6 the pervasive web of business cartels and *dangō*, secret bidding agreements to influence public procurements, which also disadvantage foreign importers;
7 the feeble enforcement of Japan's laws against monopolistic trading practices.

The reforms that Bush administration negotiators demanded in all these areas reflected the belief that a modest and symbolic (no administration official ever dared promise more) improvement in the US–Japan trade deficit could be effected only if the Japanese stopped such practices. On the macroeconomic level, the American aim was to win a massive reduction in Japan's savings rate, and therefore to limit its ability, among other things, to sustain phenomena such as super-industrialism and huge capital investment programmes. The disparity of wishes is notable. On one level, the Bush administration was demanding a set of politically expensive changes in Japanese economic practice that would not right the imbalance. On the other, these SII policy intellectuals sought to bask in the dream of total and costless change by evoking the magic of macroeconomic manipulation. The trade imbalance would be wiped out overnight if only the Japanese could be forced to stop saving so much.

The Japanese knew better. The only cure was structural change, which is a much more substantial undertaking even than the contentious tinkering proposed in the 240 reforms of Japanese business practice demanded by the American negotiators. But structural change was vastly more difficult to achieve than the daydream of macroeconomic revolution that was indulged in by the economists on the Bush team. In the SII documents there was a nod to parity – Japanese change for American change – but all sides agreed that this was a polite fiction. Only Japanese change was at issue. The Americans would not, could not, and did not want to contemplate the structural revolution of the US economy. Such massive intervention in the marketplace by the state, and that formed the core of the SII idea, had to be carried out by Japanese bureaucrats. No American civil servant, dressed in the immaculate white gloves of free-market orthodoxy, would dirty his hands at home with structural policies. This was a job for foreigners.

Such constraints point to the importance of the Maekawa lesson. The secret of national success in the post-American century, which has been thus far more the century of Friedrich List than of Adam Smith, is constant structural change. Any economy unwilling or unable to undertake it will be left behind by its competitors. It is the permanent revolution of directed, force-marched structural change that the Bush administration negotiators in the SII talks, and their masters back in Washington, refused to contemplate at home. It is here, as in the persistent Japanese trade deficit with America, that the chief truth of the SII débâcle is to be found.

There was one other. The scale of the American demands have been compared with the reforms imposed on the Japanese by General MacArthur during the US Occupation (1945–52). But with one crucial difference: unlike MacArthur, the Bush administration had lost the competitive struggle with the Japanese, not won it. The new realities of power were laid bare at the most sensitive moment in the SII process, when the third round of the talks, held in Tokyo, broke down in February 1990. That very week, American defence secretary Dick Cheney was conveniently in Tokyo to deliver a quiet, and obviously embarrassed, public warning to the Japanese. Cheney hinted that, unless the Japanese made concessions in the SII talks, the US–Japan Security Treaty, America's nuclear and conventional umbrella, might be withdrawn. In this act, the Bush administration played its last card. Kaifu caved in at the Palm Springs summit.

But within months the Soviet Union began to dissolve, and the security pact was never again likely to matter as much as it did in early 1990. Japan's complex and pained response to the Gulf War reflected the future as well as the past. The old dance of 1945 could not go on. When President Bush attempted to continue it in Tokyo in January 1992, he stumbled over the new realities of Pacific power.

Things might have been very different had the Reagan administration sought structural change of the Japanese economy while America was still indisputably in charge in the Pacific, as it so evidently was back in 1981 when Reagan took office. By the end of the decade, the power equation had been reversed. This suggests that the policy intellectuals who designed the Structural Impediments Initiative should have spent a little less time reading Adam Smith and a little more reading Friedrich List: less economics and more politics.

6 The Ministry of Finance and the Japanese miracle

First things first

One of the longest works in the literature of Japanese public policy is *Ōkura-shō* (The Ministry of Finance), by Kuribayashi Yoshimitsu, the first volume of which appeared in 1988.[1] The theme which gives this huge work much of its coherence and sparkle is the threat posed to Japan's financial and commercial structure by the liberalization of global financial markets. In contrast with much commentary in English, Kuribayashi understands such liberalization, and he is fairly consistent on this point, as an inevitable process, but a suspect one because liberalization gives opportunities for foreign firms to penetrate Japanese markets.

No Japanese reader would find this nationalist theme worthy of special comment in a volume on finance. It has been repeatedly argued in this book that Japan is best understood as a nationalist polity, and for many reasons, but one of the most important is that this perception may encourage the right expectations in the Western reader who turns to writings about the Japanese economy, business and public policy by the Japanese themselves. Nothing has interfered with the sound grasp of Japanese realities by outsiders quite as much as false expectations. This is particularly true when attempting to understand the Ministry of Finance (MOF).

Japanese nationalism and the needs of Japan as a state and nation, as a directed human collectivity, form the leitmotif of Kuribayashi's *Ōkura-shō*. He exploits the disclosure of partially obscured truth. In his analysis of MOF's Banking Bureau, he contrasts MOF's wholesome, if conventional, official obligations with the less orthodox realities that govern the ministry's behaviour. Thus, the author notes that MOF's Banking Bureau is in principle supposed to look after the interests of the depositors in Japan's banking network. This is something that some agency of government must do in any capitalist system of commercial banking. But there is no doubt that in the wake of Japan's defeat in the last war, MOF has had special responsibilities for ensuring that the nation's precious savings were manipulated in ways that aided the rebuilding of what MOF, like the Ministry of International Trade and Industry (MITI), regards as strategic industries. Financing heavy industry, power generation and coal was the bureau's priority concern until Japan overtook its many European rivals in the GNP stakes over the course of the 1960s. Note the time-span: the period of directed investment is far longer than the most positivist economists accept as sound. In many Japanese eyes, MOF's intervention was not temporarily justified by the emergency of the immediate post-war years, or some slightly larger incubation period, for what Alexander Hamilton styled 'infant industries', but a semi-permanent concern synonymous with the national interest.

This crucial task demanded that the Japanese banking system be guarded against most dangers and every adversary, particularly foreign capital. The Banking Bureau's primary official commitment since 1945 has been to keep a watchful eye on Japanese depositor interests, but more important it has served as a protective screen for industry. In Japanese this is called '*gosō-sendanteki gyōsei*' or 'convoy-protection as an objective of administrative control'. Kuribayashi insists that this second goal is the Banking Bureau's supreme responsibility. He calls it '*daiichi-shugi*' ('first things first'). It has been the one post-war policy burden that has overridden all other priorities, including, by inference, that of its duties to the ordinary depositor.[2] In meeting its obligations to this 'convoy' of financial interests, MOF has resembled less a guardian angel than a higher rank of angel: a domination or power.

The suggestion is that Japan's post-war miracle has been powerfully guided, not by MITI alone, but by MITI working in tandem with the other great anchor of Japanese bureaucratic authority, the Ministry of Finance. It may be an issue of some consequence that banking officials at America's Department of the Treasury and Britain's Treasury have not understood their post-war responsibilities for public policy in a similar light.

Stocks and shares

The Ministry of Finance and the Ministry of International Trade and Industry have helped to orchestrate the Japanese economic miracle. To emphasize the role of institutions and the exercise of political will in the advancement of a nation's economy is to embrace some of the key assumptions of what Friedrich List called 'national economy'. His argument persuades because of the powerful contrast he paints between real-world policy practice and abstract economic theory. But the free market has its institutions as well, and none appear more resistant to the intellectual claims of national economics than that supreme embodiment of the neo-classical economic ideal, the stock market.

In a world of 24-hour trading and increasingly global financial markets, a body of practice and theory, such as national economics, must address the institutional challenge posed by the stock market, both as ideal and reality. This should be clear despite the fact that in Germany, institutional practice and economic history continue to conspire against the full exploitation of the potential of free and vigorous dealing in stocks and shares. Certainly the tepid response of the West German financial bureaucracy during the 1980s to the burdens and opportunities of futures markets, for example, reflected rooted doubts about the prudence of such financial mechanisms.

In Britain as well, the recognition that the City is a world institution, not a British one, has fuelled a long debate over the heavy price British industry has paid for London's global ambitions. It is not obvious that neo-classical economic liberalism, as a body of policy, is consistent with the maintenance of a strong *national* manufacturing base. But where does this leave national economics and its relationship to the rigors of the modern stock market?

The answer has an Asian dimension. The debate, for example over the fate of the British Crown Colony of Hong Kong after its reversion to control by Beijing in 1997, is shot through not only with economic ideas but also with assumptions about political culture. Hong Kong's roller-coaster version of modern capitalism is anathema to the mail-fisted old-guard bureaucrats who cling to power in Communist China. To hand back Hong Kong and ask such officials to make a success of it would appear to be as plausible as asking one of these grey-suited mandarins to become mayor of Las Vegas. This East Asian *Kulturkampf* raises the question of how Japan's MOF bureaucrats in the *Shōken-kyoku* (Securities Bureau) have managed to fine-tune the world's largest stock market: Tokyo.

The sharp fall in the Nikkei index at the end of 1991 and the beginning of 1992 produced a flurry of stories of Securities Bureau officials burning the midnight oil in a desperate search for a mix of policies that would help to stiffen market confidence. Before the securities house scandal came to light in the summer of 1991, MOF would have joined hands with the 'big four' Japanese securities houses – Nomura, Daiwa, Nikkō and

Yamaichi – to prevent a major fall in market prices. But the the waves of foreign anger provoked by revelations of gross manipulation of stock prices, and apparent MOF acquiescence in this arrangement, temporarily tied the hands of the Securities Bureau during the 1992 downturn. Some Western business commentators jubilantly welcomed the liberation of the Japanese stock market from government interference, but they also worried over the global impact of a possible 'Nikkei melt-down'. In the solutions proposed at the time, there was ample evidence of the philosophy, values and policy tactics that had helped the Tokyo market, and other world markets, to weather the October 1987 collapse. This was an example of managed capitalism, and MOF was at the heart of it.

The relationship between the ministry and the main powers in Japan's financial markets has been anything but distant and cool. It has been in the interest of the big four to co-operate with MOF. But this entente with MOF bureaucrats has meant that Japan's largest securities houses have functioned during the liberalizing 1980s, just as they did during the mercantilist 1960s and 1970s, as public policy instruments. One conclusion seems plain: if the 1991 scandal had not hampered the capacity of MOF to intervene via the big four, the 1992 decline in the value of the Nikkei index might never have occurred, or to put it in the kind of language that intimidates free-marketeers in New York and London, it would never have been *allowed* to occur.

This throws fresh light on the much-vaunted rush of foreign investment, estimated at $25 billion, that has been thought to have 'saved' the Tokyo market during the lean months of 1992, after MOF had been forced to administer an official and highly embarrassing slap to the big four by requiring them temporarily to suspend operations in the autumn of 1991. Foreign saviours played a significant role in the Tokyo market as a result of the scandal, but MOF's reluctance to intervene will not last. The Tokyo stock exchange is a Japanese show, and it will be run on Japanese principles. Examples when MOF has hesitated to intervene reflect its reluctant surrender to economic liberalism; but its heart is not in it. If the big four can learn to make such wayward investment return a stable profit, then the market will prosper. But gyrating markets are not welcome.

The main source of Tokyo's stability has been artful manipulation by the main private players. But this effort would be futile if the 'fundamentals' of the Japanese economy were not so sound. Three pillars are involved: Japan's ¥1 trillion ($750 billion) in assets held by private individuals; the rock-solid fundamentals that are sustained by Japanese industry, also asset rich; the system's capacity to manage itself, not by regulation but by manipulation. All three pillars are in part the product of two generations of hard labour by the Ministry of Finance. *Pace* Adam Smith, this has been the work of visible hands.

Up close and personal

The most abused and misunderstood word in writings about the Ministry of Finance is 'deregulation'. The Japanese use the term '*jiyū-ka*' (liberalization rather than deregulation) to describe the policy changes that the 1980s brought to world bourses, but the '*jiyū*' (liberal) in '*jiyū-ka*' has no more positive resonance in Japanese ears than the '*jiyū*' in '*jiyū-minsha-tō*' or Liberal Democratic Party, the corrupt but effective political cartel which presides over the Diet. Aside from a small camp of economists, all belonging to the Anglo-American school of 'modern' economics, and the more free-market-minded of business pundits, most Japanese feel that there is little liberation in liberalization. The same strictures apply to the term 'free trade' ('*jiyū boeki*'), which stands, in many minds, for the disagreeable intrusion of foreign goods and practices into Japanese society.

The word 'deregulation' is inappropriate in other ways. The idea that modern Japan is a post-Confucian state has been overworked in recent Western writings on Japan, but this insight should not be totally discarded. There is no question that traditional Japanese statecraft has, partly under the press of Chinese Confucian influence, been informed at numerous points by the assumption that authority is to be deferred to and that the highest political values are naturally superior to the highest economic motivations. In the Japanese social system, the nation is superior to the market. The doctrine of free enterprise and the rights it confers on the businessman do not have the commanding place in Japanese consciousness that they appear to have in American thinking. The benefits of competition are recognized, but so is the price of corporate greed. Nowhere in East Asia does the pursuit of personal gain benefit from moral dispensation. Liberalization and deregulation are viewed in Japan, as elsewhere in post-Confucian Asia, not as a return to pristine normalcy or a preordained harmony, but as the unleashing of some of the worst human passions and dispositions. This is the chief moral drawn from the scandals that have been characteristic of the LDP's reign since 1955.

If 'deregulation' is suspect as a concept when applied to Japan, so is the term 'regulation'. Part of the problem turns on the way authority is regarded in Japan. In *Politics in Modern Japan*, Kishimoto Kōichi offers this able gloss as if it were almost a fact of nature. He cites the long Japanese tradition of 'the subordination of the individual to the social unit' and 'Japan's long pre-modern history of nonrepresentative, authoritarian government':[3]

> Under the Meiji government the deeply ingrained tendency to subordinate the common people to the members of the officialdom survived intact. Like the policies of the *baku-han* system, the task of modernization was left to the *okami* – literally, 'those above.' The *okami* of the feudal era, the samurai, were simply replaced by the bureaucrats, and the ordinary people easily transferred the formula for survival in feudal times – 'yield to the powerful' – to the context of modern government.[4]

The hierarchic assumptions at work in the notion of '*okami*' are not totally absent from the concept '*ōyake*', which is the traditional term for the imperial court, the nobility and the bureaucracy, and, by extension, their powers. This nuance of the word '*ōyake*' should be kept in mind because it is also the Chinese character '*kō*' in the Japanese term *kōkyo seisaku*, or public policy. '*Kō*' is correctly rendered as 'public' in a sense close to the English meaning ('open', 'public', 'fair'), but behind this surface similarity lurk the old rigours of imperial hierarchy and official power.

In the high Confucian tradition, mandarinate superiority and power must be balanced with humaneness. This explains the paternal quality in Japanese administration. It is not merely an anthropological issue. In *Genzai Nihon Kanryo-sei no Bunseki* (The Japanese Bureaucracy Today: an Analysis), Itō Daiichi, discussing Max Weber's classic reflections on bureaucracy, suggests that there is an important contrast to be developed between what he calls the Japanese and the Western 'models' of bureaucracy. Itō notes that:

> In Japan, it is commonly observed that while there is an official policy for dealing with farmers, there is no such policy for dealing with agriculture. This insight is very much to the point. The operational focus of the administrative apparatus of the Japanese Ministry of Agriculture and Forestry is neither the farm industry, nor its business, nor its economic functioning, but farmers and the family communities themselves. These form the objectives of policy, and the implied link is personal and direct.[5]

The benevolence that the high-minded bureaucrat has been urged by tradition to show to the peasant masses does not describe the relationship between the Ministry of Finance and the centres of Japanese business and commerce, but links at once 'personal and direct' do. The senior officials of MOF, like those of MITI, share the values, outlook and educational backgrounds of their counterparts at the most senior levels of Japanese finance and manufacturing. Japanese public policy aims to affect people directly. The contrast with the Western approach, which stresses impersonal objectivity (administrative fairness) and indirect influence on economic actors via marketplace regulation, reflects a different state philosophy. There is not a single textbook of economic principles, in English, that does justice to the personal and direct Japanese relationship between the state and business. In the Japanese context, terms such as 'deregulation', 'liberalization' and 'internationalization' refer not to the freeing of entrepreneurial energies from misguided government controls, but to the erosion, even destruction, of a way of life. It should surprise no one that the Japanese ministries most concerned have fought so sustained a rearguard action against these changes, and had so much help from Japanese businessmen and politicians in doing so.

BANKING ON JAPAN

The liberalizing of world financial markets has forced the greatest revolution in Japanese banking and finance since the early reforms of the Meiji state in the 1870s and 1880s. The current changes are even more drastic for they reflect an attempt to end the domination of financial markets and institutions that the Japanese bureaucracy has exercised since it created them. In essence, the struggle of the 1980s and 1990s has pitted globalization and market-driven competition against the old order of dynamic state-led mercantilism that fostered Japan's economic advance after 1868. It has brought great pressures to bear on the cosy elite alliance which worked the post-war miracle. The heart of this battle is about institutions, not markets.

It is consistent with the Japanese preference for the political over the mere economic that the key issue is about power, not money. The liberalization of Japanese financial markets would be a vastly easier affair if it did not threaten the same organizations which have done the most to augment Japanese power. To describe such bodies as 'special interests' is as absurd as the simplistic employment of the term 'deregulation' in discussing Japanese public policy. Since the late 1980s, three major victims of Western-style liberalization have been identified: The long-term credit banks and the Industrial Bank of Japan (IBJ) in particular; Japan's smaller security houses; and the Ministry of Finance itself.

In this battle of the titans over the destiny of MOF and IBJ, brokerage commissions and the right to open new provincial branches are the currency of the struggle, not the goals.

The Japanese suspicion is that the introduction of universal banking on the Anglo-American model may leave no place for these key components of Japan's GNP machine. City banks such as Dai-ichi Kangyō may thrive; securities houses such as Nomura may prosper; but, as the 1991 securities house scandal showed, the interests of the banks and the investment houses are so interlinked with the bureaucracy that sensitivity to the new changes, which all regard as irresistible, is ubiquitous in Japan's centres of power.

One of MOF's greatest worries is the future fate of IBJ. It is this issue, as much as any other, that has slowed progress in the painful and complicated business of designing what a key 1989 MOF interim committee (*chōsa-kai*) report described, without enthusiasm, as 'a new financial system' for Japan. Reports from MOF's deliberative council (*shingikai*) followed. The road towards a consensus, and therefore a final decision, has since been obstructed by the struggle of conflicting interests and a 1991 scandal involving the senior officials of IBJ itself. This delivered a shock to the consensus-building process because of IBJ's close identification with national goals and its high reputation for astute management and sober banking. But sooner or later MOF will hammer out a solution that serves the nation's interests, hierarchically defined.

This suggests a lack of enthusiasm for the much advertised benefits of financial reform. It was not the benefits of change that persuaded Japanese policymakers to embrace reform, but rather the view that internationalization is almost a Hegelian necessity, forcing the pace of global integration. This lack of Japanese keenness should call attention to the contrasts, not the similarities, between the Japanese reform effort and the American endeavour to overhaul the Glass–Steagall Act or, for that matter, the 1992 reforms proposed for banking within the European Community.

Having stressed the price of reform, it should not be denied that the Japanese system has some built-in inefficiencies that demand change. All the main players accept the need for reform. But it is also clear that the battle over changing the system reflects a fundamentally different approach to national goals and state-led banking.

As elsewhere, the tide of financial liberalization forced officials at the Banking Bureau to begin in 1985 the sensitive business of redrawing the legal boundaries between city banks, long-term credit banks, trust banks, regional banks, and mutual banks. This complex division of labour in the financial industry is rooted in the history of Japan's drive to build a strong national economy since Meiji, and in particular, the burdens of post-war reconstruction after 1945.

Throughout almost its entire modern history, the Japanese state has been hampered by a relative shortage of investment capital. Japan's wartime effort in part faltered because of a lack of finance. In the wake of the Second World War, the perennial problem became a national crisis. Post-war reconstruction presented the country with pressing short-term and long-term capital needs. The banking system was rebuilt to meet those needs. But more important than the design were the results. The new system worked beautifully. It was MOF's greatest contribution to the Japanese miracle.

The successes achieved made the costs of the system worthwhile. It is a hallmark of Western economic criticism of Japan's financial system to stress the costs while ignoring the gains, but then positivist economic analysis is like that. One node of criticism was the argument based on market 'efficiency'. The MOF approach to banking ignored inefficiencies that were the result of the MOF's 'escort duty' for the 'convoy' of the Japanese financial sector and its special needs. This system – referred to as '*goei-sendan-hōshiki*' or '*gosō-sendanteki gyōsei*' – paid a price for its success, as all systems must.

In the MOF convoy system, the main corollary to the principle of 'first things first' has been that no important financial institution should be allowed to fail. This meant that the entire 'convoy' could be allowed to proceed only at the speed of the slowest ship – the least competitive company. This constraint on the industry rested on a historic compromise: the financial sector willingly endured close and detailed bureaucratic policy controls, but all financial institutions, in bad times as well as good, were protected by MOF's arsenal of policy powers.

In an era of 24-hour markets, this convoy system has become unworkable. It may be seen to stand in the way of progress. But in Japan the old order is not the banking world's answer to 'rotten boroughs'. Quite the contrary, it was the system that financed the greatest economic advance the world has ever seen. There were 'economic inefficiencies' that liberalization will now ease or eliminate, but the larger point must be that the so-called costs of these inefficiencies were a price worth paying because Japanese public policymakers and industrial leaders achieved for their country what they felt was most important: the status of the world's leading industrial power and the domination of global financial markets. What other system has achieved as much during the post-war period? No wonder MOF is concerned about IBJ; it has aided Japan's economic success in a way that no Western bank has aided its own country. Tub-thumping about market inefficiencies misses the point.

7 Japanese industrial policy

The great debate

PLURALISM AND DOGMATISM

Nothing in the Western concern with modern Japan engages the intellectual passions quite like the issue of industrial policy. Japan's public policy practice in the industrial sphere strikes at first principles. It overturns foundations, altering not only political behaviour but also how we regard what we do when we make policy.

Industrial policy, its nature and ramifications, is complex, almost an intellectual universe in itself. But in its complexity it embraces what Henry James might have called a 'stupendous fragmentariness'. This explains why the phenomenon of Japanese industrial policy resists easy summary, and, at the same time, touches almost every chapter in this book. Thus, in Chapter 2, the meaning of 'economic structure' and something of its importance to the Japanese industrial policymaker has been surveyed. In Chapter 4, the role of the Japanese bureaucrat, the principal maker of industrial policy, was examined. All the lessons of the 1980s set out in Chapter 5 have direct bearing on any rigorous understanding of how Japanese industrial policy works. Chapter 10 attempts to put the Germanic roots of industrial policy into historical perspective. Just as microeconomics, as an idea, is insufficiently flexible to comprehend the broad institutional concerns of the Ministry of International Trade and Industry (MITI), so the mission of the Japanese Ministry of Finance (MOF) reaches beyond mere macroeconomic concerns. This issue was perused in Chapter 6. Here, all the different strands of the argument will be brought together to form the essential backdrop to the Western debate over the nature and meaning of Japanese industrial policy.

What are the main questions at issue? Because much of this book is animated by a sceptical view of the explanatory powers of the economist who is almost always a positivist, it may be appropriate to let a distinguished economic historian, albeit a scholar who gives attention to institutional factors, set out the larger features of the discussion.

In his article in *The Cambridge History of Japan, Volume Six*, 'Industrialization and Technological Change, 1885–1920', E. Sydney Crawcour of the Australian National University, observes that:

> The Japanese government is widely credited with having played a large part in Japan's economic growth. Except during the Sino-Japanese and Russo-Japanese wars, the government's current and capital expenditures, including military expenditures, were between 7 and 11 percent of gross national expenditures, a rather modest proportion by today's standards. The government's role in capital formation, however, was much larger. From 1897 until the private investment boom during World War I, the government was responsible for 30 to 40 percent of all capital investment. Government investment was, moreover, heavily concentrated in the strategic heavy and engineering industries and in facilities such as railways which contributed in a number of crucial ways to the development of modern industry in Japan.[1]

The impact of the Japanese state on the early 'take-off' stage of the Japanese economy is duly recognized in this passage, diluted only by the nod to intellectual consensus contained in the phrase 'is widely credited'. This qualification must be taken to heart by the 'miracle-man school' in Japanese political science; the rest of the passage speaks volumes to the neo-liberal economist determined to believe that government can do nothing, and that everything that might be done must be done by unsoiled market forces.

The other salient feature of Crawcour's summary is how relevant it is to Japanese industrial policy after 1920. The strategic industries so lovingly cultivated by the industrial policymakers of the Meiji and Taishō eras received even more fruitful attention from Japanese bureaucrats during the whole period between 1930 and 1970. What has altered since the first oil shock is the target of 'sunrise' industrial policymaking. As the commanding heights of the world economy have shifted, so have Japanese policy targets. What has remained unaltered, in years of victory or defeat, success or failure, is the state goal of commanding those heights.

What then of the private sector's role in this industrial policy success story? Here, again, Crawcour aims for balance and objectivity:

> Depending on the relative importance ascribed to public and private motives, Japan's experience has been described as either 'growth

from above' or 'growth from below'. These two views should not be regarded as mutually exclusive. The production of goods for domestic consumption, for example, was in general the result of individual decisions and market behavior, but it was also influenced by public decisions about the rate of investment relative to consumption and official encouragement to retain traditional Japanese ways of life. Government decisions on defence and defence-related industries, foreign trade and payments, and education affected both the pace and the direction of industrial development. . . . Leading entrepreneurs like Iwasaki Yatarō may have been as devoted to personal profit as were their counterparts elsewhere, but that profit depended heavily on the good-will of the government. . . . Irrespective of judgments about the motives, methods and outcomes of public policy in Japan, to explain its economic development without referring to these factors would be to tell only part, and probably a misleading part, of the story.[2]

This is a picture of the Japanese economy and of the interaction of the Japanese state and the private sector which the political scientist who does not subscribe to 'public choice' theory will find persuasive and faithful to his research findings. Again, however, as was true of the first passage quoted from Crawcour, there are the nicely judged quali-fications which the state theorist needs to keep firmly in mind, notably the warning contained in the phrase 'depending on the relative importance ascribed to public and private motives'. This is not a final determination of which view is correct, only a caution that the economic literature has been decisively influenced by the perspective that the commentator or researcher brings to the facts. Nevertheless, from the point of view of the student of Japanese politics, Crawcour's description of the influence of Japanese public policy provides exactly what is required: a conceptual space, free of neo-classical economic dogmatism, where a strict understanding of the state's role in Japanese economic development might be nurtured unburdened, at least in the initial phase of theorizing and data collection, by positivist laws. Why this may be of profound intellectual consequence is suggested by the third and final lesson which may be drawn from Crawcour's expert summary, in which he states the three seminal questions at issue:

Did the Japanese government simply provide an infrastructure and a business climate favorable to economic enterprise, leaving investment and production decisions to be determined by market forces? Or were there important areas in which the government effectively preempted those decisions, overriding such considerations as relative factor prices and demand conditions? Is it possible, in other words, that state intervention brought about more growth than would otherwise have occurred?[3]

Crawcour's own answer is unmoved by the neo-classical view that defines the approach of most Western economists when they turn to Japan. He casts doubt on the belief that *laissez-faire* adequately describes what happened in the Japanese economy between 1868 and 1920, but he makes it quite clear that Japanese public policy 'did not on the whole counteract underlying economic conditions'. Crawcour nevertheless acknowledges that government intervention and manipulation 'enabled a fuller realization of the economy's development potential than would have been achieved without them'.[4]

In this theoretical concession is contained a kernel of freedom that allows the political scientist to nurture an apositivist approach to Japanese public policy. It also should encourage a greater intellectual pluralism within the European tradition of political reflection, for it is against such pluralism that the doctrine of market forces and the 'invisible hand' has in recent years conspired against so effectively.

EARLY STAGES

This chapter is intended also to provide a guide to reading the most important work in post-war Western scholarship on Japan: *MITI and the Japanese Miracle* by Chalmers Johnson. In this study, he traces MITI's previous bureaucratic incarnations back to 1925 when the Ministry of Commerce and Industry was established. But as Johnson himself would be the first to acknowledge, the MCI was not created in a vacuum. On the contrary, MCI bureaucrats were heirs to an extraordinary set of earlier policy experiments. Only two of these experiments – Satsuma's pre-1868 modernization drive and the Meiji government campaign to break foreign domination of Japanese coastal shipping – will be touched on here.

Among the earliest and most influential of these pre-MCI/MITI experiments were the various policy initiatives undertaken by Satsuma *han* prior to the Meiji Restoration. In his biography of Ōkubo Toshimichi, Iwata Masakazu observes that, 'It is interesting to note that the centralization of the Satsuma *han* was in microcosm the basic reform that was to be effected on a national scale after the Restoration.'[5]

Centralization of elite decision-making is one of the key doctrines of MITI philosophy because it assumes rightly that Japan's elite is polycentric. Centralization was only justifiable because of the foreign threat that has been perceived as a constant of Japanese national life since the end of the Edo period. This is how Marius Jansen, in his classic study, *Sakamoto Ryōma and the Meiji Restoration*, formulated the issue:

> The outstanding intellectual and political experience in the formative years of Japan's Restoration activists was the discovery that their society was incapable of successful resistance to the Western threat. In the wake of this realization came proposals for political and social change that were designed to make good the weakness and inadequacy of their country.[6]

To ask whether modern Japanese public policy has its origins in these 'proposals for political and social change' is to arrive at the very heart of our inquiry. It is to suggest that the modernization drive that has defined Japanese national goals since before the Meiji Restoration forms the essential point of departure and intellectual horizon for contemporary Japanese policymaking in the public sphere. Jansen's formulation is strikingly cogent because of its emphasis on the distinctly intellectual dimension of the problem that confronted the founders of the modern Japanese state. The implied dynamic of thought has various stages.

First, for the purposes of the modern Japanese policymaker, the external threat to national life had to be identified with precision. Second, a response which bore exactly on this threat had to be formulated. Third, this response had, in turn, to be translated into a specific set of national goals, whatever their local or private implications. Fourth, such goals, when they touched on the integrity of the polity, had to be translated into state policies. Fifth, policies conceived in the abstract required policy instruments for their implementation; where these have been lacking, they had to be created. Sixth, the nation (*kokumin*) had to be harnessed to achieve these collective ends.

Regardless of the success or failure of the national Japanese enterprise at any point during the past 120 years, this dynamic has defined the core of state policy from the Meiji period to the present. It gives meaning to T.J. Pempel's suggestive phrase 'creative conservatism', and the weakening of this dynamic under the impact of liberalization and structural reform during the past ten years constitutes one of the turning points of twentieth-century Japanese public policy.[7]

The first of the six stages – the identification of the threat – is by far the most important. An example from the *bakumatsu* period (the end of the Edo era) illustrates the nature of the difficulty. Both the intellectually resistant nature of the problem and its significance to national survival ensured that the precise identification of the kind of threat posed by the Western powers to Japan in the middle of the nineteenth century constituted the chief policy challenge facing the faltering ancient regime, the *bakufu* and the strongest *han*.

Ōkubo, the chief architect of the Meiji state and Japan's Bismarck, witnessed the British bombardment of Satsuma in 1863. The response of his *han* suggests that the Western threat was perceived as organizational and technological, a view that seems obvious but was anything but clear to the scholar-mandarins who dominated state policy elsewhere in East Asia. Ōkubo himself apparently helped to persuade the Satsuma daimyō to create a *Kaiseijō*, an academy for the pursuit of Western learning.

Historians argue that at this complicated juncture in Japanese affairs, the 'state', because of its lack of unity, was seen as part of the problem rather than a solution. Less than two years after the British assault, Ōkubo was striving to achieve to enrich his country and strengthen its armed forces (*fukoku kyōhei*), but the objective of *fukoku kyōhei* was not the Japanese nation but Satsuma itself. The roots of the post-war Japanese miracle are at least as old as that.

The second experiment that illuminates the climate of opinion which permitted the creation of the Ministry of Commerce and Industry, MITI's predecessor, was the campaign of the Meiji state to sustain Mitsubishi in its battle with the American Pacific Mail Steamship Company and the British Peninsular and Oriental Steamship Company.

In a step that proved crucial to the building of Japan's modern commercial fleet, the Japanese government in 1874 awarded a shipping contract to Mitsubishi. The government's immediate motivation in breaking with the hesitant approach of the *bakufu* to the development of maritime shipping was the struggle with China over sovereignty of the Ryūkyū Islands. An armed show of strength had to be effected in native-owned and operated ships, and to this end the Japanese government purchased its first vessels of more than one thousand tons. These steamships were then 'entrusted' to Mitsubishi so that it could get on with the job. This emergency provided Japan with its first opportunity to regain commercial control of its waters. Given the nationalist commitments of the Japanese polity, it is hardly surprising that within two years the ships were formally transferred to Mitsubishi control. Indeed, only a nationalist orientation of some consistency allowed Japan to overcome the fractious battle of interests and personalities, let alone the influence of American and British policy players at several levels of the Japanese policymaking and execution effort. [8]

As so often in Japanese public policy, it is not the process that is important but the policy tools and tactics developed and, still more critical, the results achieved. There is a temptation in the summary statement of policy to overstate the degree of cohesion, just as detailed analysis may lose sight of the forest in focusing on individual trees. In some Japanese narratives of policy processes at the national level there is a tendency to retell a tale, such as Mitsubishi's, as a triumph of nationalist success. It was; but the process was anything but neat. This is how William D. Wray describes Mitsubishi's struggle to drive an American firm from its Yokohama to Shanghai route:

> Mitsubishi began the 1875 competition on the Shanghai line by slashing freight rates between Yokohama and Shanghai by one-third. More drastic cuts were made in domestic rates, with second-class passenger fares between Yokohama and Kōbe falling from ten dollars to around two dollars. Though both Mitsubishi and the Pacific Mail continued this severe rate cutting, there is evidence that the competition was not nearly the death struggle that some writers portrayed. The real issue was not who would emerge the 'victor' or whether the 'loser' would 'collapse,' but simply what was to be the price of the American company's withdrawal. Furthermore, it was assumed, in the short term at least, that the price would be borne by the [Japanese] government.[9]

Two questions must be raised about an account that is obviously striving for balance and accuracy. First, the 'price of the American company's withdrawal', to an economic nationalist is not primarily a balance-sheet issue but one of national ambition. It is the stuff of victory. One has only to describe the post-war rout of America's domestic electronics industry as a battle to determine what price the Japanese would have to pay to force US capital to 'withdraw' from the fray to make the point. Second, a free-marketeer will have critical things to say about the Meiji government's subsidy to Mitsubishi, but to the economic nationalist, a List or a Stein, for example, the objective to be won justified almost any cost. The episode, especially when viewed in the perspective that the late twentieth century confers on this piece of nineteenth-century business history, does now take on the patina of a life-and-death struggle; if, but only if, one cares about these things. The point is that the Japanese do care about them.

In Mitsubishi's war with Pacific Mail, the Japanese government sustained the Japanese firm, and then lent it the money ($810,000) to buy the US line when the Americans gave up the fight. But the Mitsubishi story does not end with this victory. In 1876, it earned $139,000 by providing transport for a military venture off the coast of Korea. This money proved indispensable for the firm's next commercial battle, with P&O, after the British firm began operating a service between Shanghai and Yokohama in February 1876. Japanese accounts of the clash between the Japanese and British shipping interests have been criticized, once again, for over-dramatizing the nature of contest. Japanese officials and entrepreneurs are thought to have 'exaggerated the P&O threat because they were unaware of the tentative nature of the British firm's decision to challenge Mitsubishi'. [10]

This is wisdom after the event. It may have been essential to exaggerate the threat to achieve a consensus in Japanese ruling circles. But the fight was not in essence the outcome of market forces or merely a commercial decision to be decided by the flick of the abacus. When P&O raised the competitive stakes, Mitsubishi retaliated by launching a campaign through the press to encourage Japanese travellers to boycott foreign shippers such as P&O. But as Wray rightly concludes:

> Mitsubishi's strongest weapon in the competition, however, was the government, which intervened in 1876 to pass a control law requiring all Japanese traveling on foreign steamships to purchase a pass costing 25 *sen*, without which they would be subject to arrest upon reaching their destination. It is reported that by July 12 Mitsubishi's Shanghai-bound ship was full, whereas a P&O ship on the same day carried only three passengers. [11]

The P&O challenge was beaten back. The very different stories of Satsuma reform and the birth struggles of Mitsubishi's NYK, Japan's largest shipping firm, illuminate the early forms of Japanese industrial policy, understood as a dimension of state-building in which nationalist considerations loomed particularly large. Such an interpretation is sometimes avoided in the name of alternative values and world views. To this problem, we must now turn.

PRIDE AND PREJUDICE

'The concept of industrial policy is regarded in Japan as constructive and is well accepted as a meaningful tool for the promotion of the national economy.' [12] This is the thoughtful conclusion of two members of the Japanese elite, writing from positions at the very heart of the Japanese bureaucratic-industrial complex, not during Japan's post-war emergency or the era of high speed growth, but in 1980. The two authors were Hosomi Takashi, then an adviser to the Industrial Bank of Japan (IBJ) and a former Ministry of Finance (MOF) bureaucrat, and Okumura Ariyoshi, then a member of IBJ's prestigious industrial research department (*sangyō chōsa-bu*). It would be a rare American or British banker, in a position of similar prestige, who would accept such a conclusion, however reflective of Japanese circumstance, as intellectually sound.

This gap in perception conspires against an understanding of industrial policy, one of the most debated features of post-war Japanese public policy, by anyone who would attempt to think through this question in the English language. This perception gap may be rooted in an empirical (factual) or conceptual misunderstanding, but first it reflects a linguistic divide. In 1968, the *Shūkan Tōyō Keizai*, the Japanese economic weekly, ran a cover story on Japanese industrial policy (*sangyō seisaku*). The commissioning editor, as is *Tōyō Keizai's* practice, wished to include a decorative foreign-language term on the cover, and began to search for an English equivalent of *sangyō seisaku*. In the end, he made do with the French *politique industrielle*. This French compromise was not surprising. According to Tsuruda Toshimasa, the first example of international recognition of the term 'industrial policy', as acceptable English, may have been its employment in a policy document published in 1971 by the OECD titled 'The Industrial Policy of 14 Member Countries'.[13]

Why then has it long been possible to discuss 'fiscal policy', 'monetary policy', 'trade policy', 'farm policy' and even, in the wake of first oil shock (1973–4), 'positive adjustment policy' without violating the canons of English common sense, but not 'industrial policy'? The answer may be that the very notion of 'industrial policy' is seen to offend against the best-grounded assumptions of British and American economic policymaking in the public realm. These assumptions are modern. England's long struggle against Holland for commercial supremacy during the seventeenth century depended on mercantilist trade policies which may be usefully compared to the spirit and intent of twentieth-century Japanese industrial policy, if not its substance. The long series of Navigation Acts, most notably Cromwell's of 1651, formed the core of England's approach to economic competition. Aimed at the Dutch, such legislation was kept in force until the mid-nineteenth century, when Britain's commercial and industrial supremacy was unchallengeable. Such acts, which required that imports could not be brought to England in third-party ships nor English exports carried in any but English ships, were applied also to England's dependencies, provoking protest in Ireland and revolution in the thirteen American colonies.

There is a direct intellectual link between the American critique of the English Navigation Acts and Alexander Hamilton's advocacy of national protection and encouragement of 'infant industries'; and it stretches from Hamilton to the economist Friedrich List and the German historical school, and from List to the inventors of Japanese industrial policy. It is no accident that the industrial might of the four greatest manufacturing powers of modern times – Britain, Germany, the

United States and Japan – was built behind formidable protectionist walls. In this sense, the absence of the term 'industrial policy' from contemporary English reflects a selective amnesia.

This loss of memory has been encouraged by the rise of classic economic liberalism to its contemporary place as the ruling economic and political dogma of the Anglo-American mind. The recent character of this apotheosis cannot be over-emphasized. Adam Smith published *The Wealth of Nations* in 1776, David Ricardo's *On the Principles of Political Economy and Taxation* appeared in 1817, John Stuart Mill's *Principles of Political Economy* in 1848, Alfred Marshall's *Principles of Economics* in 1890–1, and *Credit and Commerce* in 1919, but the gap between the theory of the great thinkers about economics in the English language and the policy practice of the United States, the greatest English-speaking economic power by 1914, persisted until the Second World War.

In 1940, American tariffs, the ratio of duties paid to value of duty-paying merchandise imported into the USA, still stood at just under 40 per cent, nearly a century after Britain succumbed to the free trade campaign of the Manchester School and repealed the Corn Laws in 1849. It is not obvious that even this British embrace of the virtues of free trade was complete, for despite the warning contained in Ricardo's doctrine of comparative advantage that any restraint on trade was bad, Britain retained the retaliatory provisions of the old navigation acts on her statute books long after free trade has been accepted as national policy.

Cordell Hull, Franklin Delano Roosevelt's secretary of state, concluded that 'free trade dovetails with peace', but only after America and its allies had established that peace by force of arms. It is said that industrial policy demonstrates a willingness to render to Caesar what rightly belongs to Adam Smith. But the great English-speaking peoples have taken this belief to heart only when economic ascendency has made anti-protectionism relatively cost-free. Indeed, since the departure of Ronald Reagan from office in 1989, America's post-war commitment to free trade has steadily eroded. It was doomed by a competitive challenge from East Asia that George Bush tried to ignore and that Bill Clinton cannot.

What then is one to make of those Japanese economists who are among the most vigorous critics of Japanese industrial policy? There is for example the substantial volume edited by Komiya Ryutarō, Okuna Masahiro and Suzumura Kotarō titled *Nihon no Sangyō Seisaku* (1984), published in English translation under the title *Industrial Policy of Japan* in 1988.[14] This often critical assessment of Japanese post-war industrial policy should not be ignored. Nevertheless, given the thrust of Anglo-American prejudice in favour of classical theory and against the human potential to make society work without scrupulous attention to positive economic laws, Western readers must proceed with care when they turn to studies which play to their common-sense prejudices.

Positivism versus empiricism

First, it must be stressed that the impact of free-market theory on the practice of Japanese industrial policy has been slight. This has meant that economists who have taken a rigidly neo-classical line have rarely, if ever, been key players in this paramount field of public policy. Far more frequently, these neo-classicists have composed an ivory-tower outpost of what is to most Japanese – policymakers, politicians, business leaders, white- and blue-collar workers and consumers – an alien doctrine redolent of foreign authorship.

One result is that Japanese economists in the Anglo-American mould often appear to be more in touch with current Western theory than with ruling Japanese values and practices. These economists have come to exert a special influence on Western economists by encouraging such scholars, who are seldom able to read Japanese and are thus unable to consult any documentary evidence except in translation, not to take Japan seriously. Like some errant bishop, many Japanese economists would confirm our intellectual prejudices.

Second, there is the problem posed by modern economics itself. This provides one of those rare occasions when recourse to scientific jargon helps to clarify rather than obscure a problem. Two words are of particular importance: 'positivism' and 'empiricism'.[15] Positivism, an abbreviation of the term 'positive philosophy', is usually traced back to the writings of David Hume and Auguste Comte. In essence, this doctrine urges the student of human society to be scientific in approaching his subject. Behind such urging stands the model of the natural sciences, devised and applied by the modern heirs of Francis Bacon, Galileo and Newton. It was the perceived success of the modern physical sciences, particularly mathematical physics, that so influenced the European Enlightenment and its nineteenth-century followers. This tradition underwrites much practice in the social sciences today.

But how scientific must a discipline be to win acceptance as a science? Compared to the achievements of physics or chemistry, the modern historian or political scientist has consistently been viewed as a poor relation. Among students of society, only the economist has demonstrated the kind of progress required. This is because modern economics

– especially since William Stanley Jevons, one of the first economists to employ the concept of 'marginal utility', as well as the great Alfred Marshall – is anchored in positive laws, formal insights into human nature that are universal and predictive of future human actions. A great deal of twentieth-century research in almost every branch of social studies, to employ the term used by those who feel that their disciplines have yet to become sciences as physics is a science, has been a valiant effort to generate positive laws in sociology, political science and other apparently benighted disciplines; but only economics is held up as a contemporary model of genuine scientific success. But no one denies that the historian or political scientist or anthropologist is engaged in empirical research.

'Empiricism, in general, maintains that the only way to ensure that knowledge of matters of fact is sound or scientific is to base it on observation or, more generally experience.'[16] Political science and history, to take the two fields most relevant here, are both empirical sciences in this sense: they are grounded in observation, and by extension, experience. But no political scientist writing on Japanese politics today, certainly none of the political experts cited in this book, is trying to invent or discover or prove a positive law. Such political scientists are empiricists, not positivists. Neither physics nor mathematics offers them a model for their research. The importance of this distinction for the debate over the true nature of Japanese industrial policy can scarcely be exaggerated. Critics of Japanese industrial policy all fall, more or less, into one of two camps: positivists or empiricists. Thus the vigorous attack on Chalmers Johnson's thesis, 'Japan as a Developmental State' in David Friedman's *The Misunderstood Miracle* (1988) is grounded almost entirely in empiricism.[17] It is a factual critique, with hardly a reference to positivist laws. This is entirely in keeping with the fact that Friedman is more a political scientist than an economist. His approach contrasts sharply with the assaults on the claimed effectiveness of industrial policy contained in Hugh Patrick and Larry Meissner (eds), *Japan's High Technology Industries* or Komiya Ryutarō *et al.* (eds), *Industrial Policy of Japan*, which are almost wholly dependent on arguments based on positive laws.[18] Of more general interest is the fact that the denunciations of industrial policy in *The Economist* and *The Wall Street Journal* are more frequently than not dependent on the argument from positive laws. The first question therefore that the student of Japanese industrial policy should ask himself is whether the critique he is reading is by a positivist or an empiricist. But if positivism and empiricism are more or less the same, and this is the most widely held view, why should this distinction be important? The answer turns on the facts.

The universal laws of the positivist are just that: universal. The 'law of supply and demand' or the strictures of 'price theory' apply everywhere, all the time, without distinction, in Britain or Japan or Timbuktu. Armed with positive laws, the would-be student of Japan can travel there and be confident that he has a theory in his pocket that explains all he surveys. Or better yet, ensconced in his study back home with any introductory textbook to positive economics, such as Samuelson's *Economics* or Richard G. Lipsey's aptly titled textbook *An Introduction to Positive Economics* at his elbow, this positivist has no need to go to Japan at all.[19]

The economist committed to positivism believes that he already knows how Japanese society behaves in the economic sphere because it is exactly the same way that profit-maximizing individuals behave everywhere. This situation could not be otherwise, because if Japan were different then universal positive laws would not be universal. It follows also that the need to learn the Japanese language will not be strongly felt by the modern economist because, aside from the raw data, knowing Japanese has, by definition, no substantive implications for the working of positive laws. Confident in their scientific positivism, some economists have even called for the abolition of political science, including the study of Japanese government, because it is not a positive science.[20]

But the question must be asked: What if economists are wrong? The deepening impact of mathematical economics is felt to be a threat even by those few economists who know Japan and the Japanese language. Institutional economists, such as Oxford's Jenny Corbett, are not sanguine about the lack of real-world experience of their students, who arrive in Japan heavy-laden with theoretical doctrines and an emotional commitment to empirically insensitive, positivist models.

This matters because positivist economists hold that Japanese industrial policy cannot work in practice because it cannot work in principle. The very notion of an industrial policy violates the main tenets of economic theory. In contrast, the empiricist does not argue from first principles, but from groups of individual facts that challenge or confirm the importance of Japanese industrial policy. To insist that industrial policy, Japanese or any other, cannot work, is to say something very different from the theory that industrial policy might work but does not. The positivist eliminates irritating 'Japanese' facts before he starts; the empiricist makes these same irritating facts the object of his inquiry. The two methods could not be more different. Because positivism is often anti-empirical, the radical empiricist who knows Japan well would probably discourage the student of Japanese government from tackling *any* positivist assessment of the workings of the Japanese economy until the student had a good grasp of the facts about Japanese politics.

The divide is a sharp one. Even Western writers unsympathetic to orthodox economic neo-classicism, such as Chalmers Johnson and Daniel Okimoto, still feel compelled to discuss Japanese industrial policy in terms of 'market-conforming' legislation and approaches. But what is really required is a new language that permits the analysis of economic activity without resort to positivist abstractions. The problem is that positivist economics is like the medieval theology of the schoolmen that Francis Bacon so derided: their systems form a whole; one cannot borrow selectively from them. To get an egg, one must buy the farm. This, for better or worse, describes the essential nature of the positive approach in economics, an approach which has in so many other ways been fruitful.

One consequence is that the novice student of Japanese industrial policy should be warned that any book on Japan with a title that includes the term 'political economy' is likely to be an attempt to marry two warring approaches, political science and positivist economics, and may therefore result in intellectual confusion. That is because such works, otherwise respectable, are often attempts to blend empiricism with pure positivism. This is a recipe for a 'mixture' not a 'compound'.

Two-edged sword

Three charges have thus far been pressed against the critics of Japanese industrial policy who dominate the discussion of this topic in the English-speaking world: empirical neglect, historical amnesia and intellectual dogmatism. Such charges have not been lost on the social democratic critics of neo-conservative business interests and free-market liberals ('neo-conservatives' in American parlance).

One result has been a rush to endorse the lessons of Japanese industrial policy success by American Democrats and British supporters of the Labour Party. *The Economist* is representative of English-speaking business opinion in its constant attacks upon the European weakness for industrial policy, principally among socialists such as French President François Mitterrand and Jacques Delors, president of the EC Commission since 1985. This parallels the row in the United States between the editorial writers for *The Wall Street Journal* and advocates of an American industrial policy, such as Clinton's adviser Robert B. Reich. He was one social democrat who may have had a significant impact on the economic policy proposals, including an industrial policy, of Walter Mondale, the 1984 Democratic candidate for president. Now Reich's candidate has captured the White House. A parallel strand of argument may be found in the writings of Cambridge University economists such as Sir John Eatwell, adviser to the Labour Party, and a proponent of an industry policy which nods at the MITI model.

Economic liberal scepticism towards would-be industrial policy-makers in the social democratic camp is often well founded but for the wrong reasons. The problem is not that the social democratic conception of industrial policy frequently involves violation of positive laws, which it does, but rather that few West Europeans and Americans recognize just how demanding an effective industrial policy is in practice. Falling back on economic-textbook positivism is in any case almost always wrong because the abstractions and reasoning chains involved are too rigid and misleading to be of much use. Such laws are biased against most forms of economic intervention, and sensible discussion of the rigours of industrial policy, as practised by the Japanese, invites the conclusion that the arguments of economic positivists are less helpful than they sometimes appear.

But the point about rigour stands, and the position of the British Labour Party more clearly illustrates what is at stake than, for example, that of America's Democratic Party. This is because Britain is a unitary state in which Parliament is constitutionally supreme. The US constitution is designed to prevent sustained economic reform in the Japanese manner. If market forces cannot reverse American decline, the Japanese model cannot save her without substantial constitutional change. American neo-conservatives should derive no comfort from this because the evidence from the long era of neo-conservative control of the White House suggests that market forces alone will not prevent Japan from overtaking the USA as the world's largest economy. Only one model of economic reform is available to her, and it does not appear to work. This may be Clinton's tragedy and America's. What then of Britain? If the Labour Party had a large majority in the House of Commons, nothing but common law could stop it from introducing a set of industrial policies every bit as revolutionary as those imposed by successive Thatcherite governments between 1979 and 1990. The Labour Party has well-advertised commitments to strengthening Britain's manufacturing base, with both investment and training programmes, which draw discreetly on the Japanese or German models. Such proposals have parallels in America, but the difference is that the British have a system of government which allows their rapid implementation as law.

Labour would also benefit from the absence of some of the defects of Britain's European competitors. The British workforce spends much longer in their factories and offices than the Germans, and the British have yet to import the French *vacance*. The British have also a strong engineering tradition. But the critic raised on the clear-sighted rigour of the Japanese approach will point to some perhaps fatal weaknesses. Worker discipline is one. It is not just a question of strikes, which the Tories have tamed during the 1980s and early 1990s with unemployment and recession, but of the pace of the workday. Under the most favourable conditions possible, Nissan and Toyota have been able to demonstrate that they can raise British productivity in automobile manufacturing to levels almost unimagined elsewhere in British industry, but this is the exception that proves the rule. It would take a social revolution unprecedented in British history to reach and *permanently* to match East Asian standards.

But any lapse into the kinds of work-place complacency cruelly caricatured by Peter Sellers in the 1959 film *I'm alright Jack* would make it impossible for a Labour industrial policy to deliver the kind of improvements needed to match world standards. It is not obvious that either British management or workers or, for that matter, British consumers are anything like demanding enough of themselves or other groups as economic performers to ensure the success of Labour plans. More damning still, Labour leaders are at heart ambivalent about the real world of capitalist competition, let alone the level of international competition necessary to beat back the manufacturing challenge from East Asia. The old-guard socialist advocacy of 'import controls' and protectionism bears no sensible relationship to Japanese and East Asian practice.

Labour's *naïveté* on this count is also demonstrated in its philosophy towards education. The 'child-centred' approach so admired in left-wing circles in Britain during the 1960s is far too flabby a notion to be relevant to an effective industrial policy. It has provided no match for the relentless nationalism, group discipline and competitive tenor of the Japanese classroom, and by extension, work-place. Talk of 'technology' may also be misleading. In the contemporary world, investment-led growth is all about descending one learning curve after another – in never-ending succession – as quickly as possible. Technology may be glamorous, but the schoolroom and laboratory realities of East Asia emphatically reject the notion that children should develop 'at their own pace'.

The bureaucratic powers that must be concentrated in institutions beyond the reach of party politicians also contain a stark challenge for

Labour or US Democrats, and one that casts a raking light on Japanese administrative guidance (*gyōsei-shidō*):

> Bureaucrats draft most statutes in Japan, and they do so with the goals of maximum discretion and broadest scope of authority foremost in their minds. Nor is it in any way remarkable or surprising in itself; equally broad delegations of power are common in U.S. economic legislation. What distinguishes MITI's position from similarly situated American agencies is more the doctrinal matrix that restricts judicial review of administrative action in Japan, particularly doctrines of justiciability, standing and scope of discretion, that is the lack of statutory standards.[21]

Frank Upham's conclusion is straightforward: 'Under this definition, most of industrial policy is beyond review. MITI almost invariably acts informally in a legal sense, and only a final and legally formal act directly creates legal rights and duties'. This is 'No, Minister' with a vengeance, but the long arm of Japanese administrative discretion reaches still further:

> It is not just informal actions that escape judicial scrutiny. Supervisory orders, permissions, approvals, or regulations within an agency or even among agencies and public bodies like *shingikai* [committees for bureaucracy-industry policy discussion], no matter how formal or final, are not reviewable because they are considered internal government behavior that does not directly affect the legal rights and duties of private citizens.[22]

When students of Japanese industrial policy insist that the bureaucracy rules while the party politicians reign, this is not idle phrase-making. The implications for Western politics and policy practice are unambiguous. British Tories may believe in market forces, but the pace of British industry may be too stately to generate the needed productivity levels on its own. The Labour Party thinks that industrial policy is attractive, but has not begun to grasp the shop-floor revolution implied. In short, the kind of surging frenzy of economic rationality that characterized the burst of Japanese super-industrialism (see Chapter 5) is probably beyond the reach of Britain and its European partners. This means that domestic manufacturing within the EC will not flourish, as French and Italian bureaucrats recognize, except behind protectionist walls, and this is Europe's tragedy.

8   Politics and policies since the bubble

The worldwide recession of the early 1990s put many of the arguments offered in this book under fresh and invigorating pressure. This chapter is an attempt to put these larger changes into perspective. But the Japanese crisis of confidence of the 1990s does not overturn the truth of Verdi's call, quoted in Chapter Two: 'Let us return to the past; it will be a step forward.' In the new Japan so obviously taking shape in the 1990s, the past blossoms long. Nevertheless, events during the 1990s suggest that Japan's post-war economic structure has been experiencing one of those benchmark transformations, perhaps one of even greater importance than the transitions that she underwent between the collapse of the Bretton Woods system and the first oil shock in the early 1970s or between the 1985 Plaza Accord and Japan's surging recovery from the high yen (*endaka*) recession. If Japan today faces the greatest turning point in her history since 1945, or even 1868, then we must rethink the two-stage chronologies (post-war mobilization followed by liberalization) which anchor the analyses of post-war Japan's economic policy even in such admired works as Chalmers Johnson's *MITI and the Japanese Miracle* (1982) and Suzuki Yoshio's *The Japanese Financial System* (1987).[1]

The 1990s may prove decisive in a way untrue of the 1970s and 1980s, which should be understood as extensions of what went before rather than as radical departures from the post-Meiji model of nationalist development. While it is true that each decade since the 1950s has been relatively more liberal, in economic terms, than the decade before it, nationalism has defined the Japanese enterprise as a whole. Looking back now the remarkable feature of the post-war era, from 1945 until the post-bubble earthquake of the 1990s, has been the continuity of beliefs, institutions, practices, attitudes (such as the nationalist concern to blunt liberlization with cross-ownership of shares), and most radically of all, public policies that sustained Japan's economic miracle in its successive incarnations.

In contrast, the 1990s signalled the arrival of Japan's own 'liberal hour', one that is both social and economic. Evidence for this view is to be found in the first court judgment, in 1992, against a firm for the sexual harassment of a female employee, in the creation of support groups to defend the rights of not only legal but also illegal Asian immigrants, and in the decision by education officials in Hokkaidō, mindful of the island's Ainu minority, actively to counter in the classroom the well-established doctrine of post-Meiji Japanese education that the country is racially and culturally homogeneous (*tan-itsu minzoku*).

Then there was the 1992 decision by the government of Osaka to allow non-Japanese university graduates to sit the local government employment examination. This appears to have generated considerable impetus towards the ending of exclusionism in hiring by local government bodies and agencies. The main beneficiaries of this new dispensation are likely to be Japan's large Korean minority, some 687,940 people or 64 per cent of all foreigners legally residing in Japan at the end of 1990.[2]

This may prove to be one of the first indirect steps towards evolving a concept of Japanese citizenship not grounded in presumed blood purity. The recent Western European struggle to free itself of blood- or racial-ethnic concepts of nationality reflects a parallel set of developments, and one that may have as its goal the American model, where a classless and colourblind definition of citizenship is aimed for, if not always attained.

Such relaxation of bans on foreign participation in formerly closed areas of Japanese public life has been anticipated by the internationalization of the Japanese firm, both in companies with a substantial presence in foreign markets (where local business practices have been adopted) and by easing old barriers against foreign hiring inside Japan. This also hints at a significant change because it is the racial-ethnic definition of the Japanese citizen that made the 'Japanese company' a recognizable entity that benefited from state protection and encouragement as well as public policy management. The Japanese bureaucrat has never been in doubt about what constituted a Japanese export or a foreign import. The contrast with the understandably confused 1990s debate among US unions over whether to support nominally American firms which manufacture overseas or Japanese firms which manufacture in the United States is striking.

Common opinion holds that this liberal hour is irreversible, but the sharp economic recession of the early 1990s generated temporary and permanent changes which will erode nationalist certainties. These changes threaten both the institutions and the values that have sustained Japan's post-war advance. The bursting of the great economic bubble during the early 1990s also challenged the Japanese public policymaker. The Western view is that liberalism must be 'created' in Japan, whose model of civil society is obviously flawed. The recession of the the early 1990s has sparked a crisis of confidence in business and the economic bureaucracy. The headline economic stories of the decade paint a picture of a political system in radical transition, but concrete change may come only slowly.

The bubble phenomenon in the Japanese economy was the consequence of excessive banking liquidity, low interest rates, and the erosion of conservative banking standards and practices. These conditions encouraged an unprecedented bank lending spree and fuelled the greatest property boom the world has ever seen. A part of this investment has now been lost as a result of falling land and share prices. Japanese banking's carefully nurtured reputation for sobriety and soundness has been dented in what some have seen as an orgy of greed and incompetence.[3] In March 1992, losses from securities transactions by Japan's eleven city banks were estimated at ¥831.7 billion. In the previous year, the figure had been ¥167.4 billion.

Observed more closely, the series of unedifying financial scandals of the late 1980s and early 1990s – the Heiwa-dō group and its dummy companies, Tokyo Sagawa Kyūbin and its notorious gangster connections, Kokusai Kōgyō and its shady share deals, the embarrassing bank loans in the Itoman and Kyōwa affairs, and the indefensible loans made on the basis of forged deposit certificates to an Osaka restaurateur in the Tōyō Shinkin collapse – appear to have been the product of excessive competition between Japanese banks as well as sectional and personal rivalries within the banks themselves. These six scandals reduce to nonsense the assumption made by some Western academics that the Japanese bureaucracy is unique in being compromised by inter- or intra-organizational conflicts (*nawabari arasoi*).

In the wake of recent private-sector excesses and market-generated chaos, it is the Ministry of Finance (MOF) to whom all turn in the effort to restore order.[4] This is consistent with the main thesis set out in the volume on the Banking Bureau of Ministry of Finance in Kuribayashi Yoshimitsu's massive study *Ōkura-shō* (The Ministry of Finance) discussed in Chapter 6. Kuribayashi insists that the principal obligation of the Banking Bureau, as the bureau sees it, is the protection of all the firms which compose the Japanese banking system. During the post-bubble pinch, this obligation has become particularly onerous.

Part of the difficulty has been the gradual erosion of MOF's powers to control the Japanese financial system, a process begun by the gradual liberalization of the country's financial markets under foreign pressure in the early 1980s. But there has been a parallel decline in the ability and willingness of Japan's major corporate groups and main banks to maintain order in their separate fiefdoms. It has been left to MOF to clean up the mess of private sector mismanagement and corporate greed.

MOF's difficulties are illustrated by the chorus of protest that has greeted the tough anti-bubble line taken by Bank of Japan Governor Mieno Yasushi. As the value of shares on the Tokyo Stockmarket continued to fall during the spring of 1992, a noisy press campaign was organized by the floundering end of the finance industry, including many major investors, to force the Bank of Japan to reverse its course.[5]

Spokesmen for the Japan Securities Dealers Association, representing 1.6 million shareholders, desperately urged the implementation of a government plan to revive the value of Nippon Telegraph and Telephone (NTT) shares to lift the market. This was because MOF's sales of NTT shares are a significant factor in determining the value of the market's most prominent stock. Critics of the government's anti-bubble stance frantically quoted projections by foreign economists that the Japanese recession might last until 1994 or 1996. But there was more than economic analysis at work in these calls to refloat the Tokyo stockmarket. Behind the scenes, ruling party politicians attempted to exert pressure on behalf of their desperate corporate donors who had exploited the fat bubble years, but who now faced a leaner future. Mieno's hardline approach reflects a wide consensus within the Ministry of Finance that the bubble must not be allowed to reinflate (to 're-bubble' in Japanese) despite the vigorous press campaign of pressure groups allied with LDP party bosses.

Two features of this interest-group crusade to reinflate the Japanese bubble merit comment. First, and perhaps predictably, the press campaign reached an important peak just as a broad elite consensus, particularly in the economic bureaucracy, was forming in the spring of 1992 that the Tokyo stock market had bottomed out and that an economic recovery was likely before the end of the fiscal year. Because policymakers and economists had been ambushed by the unpredicted downturn during the last half of fiscal year 1991 (September 1991 – March 1992), the new optimism was quietly asserted. Second, the calls for public policy measures to reinflate the bubble demonstrated the strength of the Japanese belief, even among institutional investors, that the bureaucracy remains the redoubt of the Japanese nation. It is revealing that the anti-deflationary protest mobilized by the tabloid press has decried the policy line of the 'three Ms': Mieno Yasushi, governor of the Bank of Japan, Matsuno Toshihiko, MOF's Securities Bureau head, and Miyazawa Kiichi, the prime minister and a former MOF minister.

The Banking Bureau's commitment to defending the national interest and the soundness of the foundations of the banking industry also reflects an astute reading of MOF's political needs. Just as the Budget Bureau's first commitment (*dai-ichi-shugi*) is to maintain a balanced budget because an unbalanced budget makes the ministry more vulnerable to unseemly meddling by LDP's factional leaders, so a sound industry flourishing within the restraints of law and sobriety is the only guarantee the MOF has against interference by special interests in the formation of financial policy. The large point must be that whatever the powers of the LPD, it is so obviously corrupt, so obviously the pawn of special interests, that it is incapable of taking on either the kind of development-state leadership role exercised, for example, by Singapore's Peoples Action Party, or bearing the burdens of responsible day-to-day administration demanded in the public policy sphere. This must be the lesson of the Sagawa Kyūbin scandal, which like the Recruit scandal of the late 1980s, involved bribery of senior Diet politicians on a vast scale.

Then there was the unprecedented intervention of MOF in the Tōyō Shinkin affair. Tōyō Shinkin was an Osaka-based bank which became the centre of a massive fraud. Some $2.6 billion in forged certificates of deposit (CDs) were issued by Tōyō Shinkin, allegedly to Ms. Onoue Nui, a remarkably well-connected Osaka restaurateur and stockmarket speculator, who used them to borrow ¥179 billion from other financial institutions, apparently to manipulate the market. Other victims of Ms. Onoue included such pillars of the Japanese financial system as Fuji Bank and the Industrial Bank of Japan (IBJ). The latter reportedly lent her ¥90 billion. Both banks agreed to write off, with MOF's permission (as is required in Japan), some ¥11 billion in bad debts. IBJ Lease, the bank's affiliate, was forced to write off a still larger sum (Japan's nonbanks were the great victims of the 1991–2 economic slowdown). Sanwa Bank, Tōyō Shinkin's main bank, refused to shoulder the burden, as post-war convention demanded. It was Sanwa's resistance that ensured MOF intervention with public money to restore investor confidence by putting Tōyō Shinkin out of business.

In a complex rescue package, MOF helped to arrange for employees and branches of Tōyō Shinkin to be absorbed by Sanwa Bank and twenty-two Shinkin Credit Associations in Osaka. To ease Tōyō Shinkin's debts of ¥260 billion, its main creditors abandoned sizeable parts of their claims. The remainder of Tōyō Shinkin's losses, some ¥130 billion, were met either by the sale of assets or low interest loans from IBJ, the Shinkin Bank Association and the government's Deposit Insurance Corp. MOF officials argued that intervention in this first-time dissolution of a Japanese banking institution was necessary to prevent a financial panic. Many banking experts were sceptical of this explanation, but no Japanese bank has failed since 1945, and MOF was right to exploit its full panoply of power and persuasion to keep this record unblemished. MOF is after all the sheet anchor of public confidence in the banking system. Well-placed public confidence in the bureaucracy has sustained Japan's massive post-war savings boom, and this in turn has helped to finance the national economic miracle at every stage of its progress.

MOF intervened in the Tōyō Shinkin affair to meet its policy obligations both to the firms that compose the industry and to the public which deposits its savings in the system. In this sense, a double purpose was well served. Consistent with the convoy principle, it is also clear that MOF was taking care of its own, and those who came to the rescue in the matter were not likely to be unrewarded. This is not to deny that MOF's intervention combined a policy mix of penalties, rewards and reforms.

This episode illuminates another dimension of the struggle to reform Japan's financial system discussed in Chapter 6. The financial scandals of the 1980s and 1990s encourage closer attention to the rumours so often repeated in Ōtemachi, the Tokyo home to many of Japan's largest companies, that the weakness of Japan's securities firms offered an opportunity for banks, such as IBJ, to exploit. One result is growing prospects that, despite the post-bubble downturn in the market and the troubles of Japan's largest banks (the eleven city banks, the three long-term credit banks, and the seven trust banks which hold 70 per cent of Japan's banking assets), the birth of an 'IBJ Securities' may be on the cards. As the Japanese bureaucracy does not indulge in *blitzkrieg*, this sensitive realignment of institutional power will inevitably be a gradual business.

Whether MOF's hopes to curb Nomura Securities' formidable powers to manipulate the Tokyo stockmarket would be helped by the simultaneous birth of a 'Nomura Trust Bank' is another matter. But either way, the twin birth of an 'IBJ Securities' and a 'Nomura Trust Bank' would represent an appropriate outcome of MOF's struggle to reform Japan's financial system in a way consistent with the triumphs of the past and the needs of the future.[6]

Nomura's huge market presence is the exception. The collapse of the bubble has wounded Japan's other major securities houses while bankrupting many smaller firms. This has forced retrenchment on larger firms, and threatened Yamaichi Securities, one of the 'big four', with restructuring (i.e., bankruptcy). All this has confirmed the status of Japan's securities companies (Nomura excepted) as junior partners in the financial system centred on MOF. The vulnerability of the securities industry points to the staying power of the pillars of the old regime. Despite the appalling examples of financial culpability in the Tōyō Shinkin affair and similar scandals, or perhaps because of them, it appears to be safe to conclude that in the new Japan, MOF's duties as the escort protectors of the country's banking convoy remain important even if the new goal is further liberalization.[7]

This interplay – of nationalist philosophy, the public-private alliance of interests that underwrote the Japanese miracle, and the demands of a more liberal age – defines the high ground of Japanese public policymaking in the 1990s. This interaction puts into sharp perspective the issues at work in MOF's campaign to restore order and respectability to the country's securities industry while the Nikkei index has escaped the discipline of the big four. This dynamic is reflected in the ministry's public stance of horror at the prospect of a securities giant, such as Yamaichi Securities, having to be restructured, and the sustained whispering campaign in Kasumigaseki which hints that few official tears would be shed if Yamaichi encountered real difficulty.

The same concern to further liberalization in order to make the market more manageable has also been cited to explain the challenge posed by the Japanese practice of '*tobashi*'. Sometimes compared to the city bank custom of requiring reserve accounts from loan customers to augment bank income for loans at officially fixed rates, *tobashi* results when a broker arranges sales and repurchases of securities at artificial prices between clients with varied settlement dates. This allows such clients to avoid reporting investment losses on their securities holdings.

Such anti-market impulses are, as Adam Smith noted two centuries ago, a permanent temptation for the businessman or manager, but the systematic violation of market principles in capitalist Japan argues against the easy reform of the country's economy in accordance with strict Anglo-American liberal expectations. But in another sense *tobashi* was a kind of market substitute which introduced some flexibility into a hitherto rigid system of fixed interest rates. It is to transcend such half-measures that MOF has sought to accelerate the liberalization of Japanese markets. Beyond these reforms, punishments and inter-ventions, there is evidence of a gradual revolution of mind about the nature of Japan and its national business goals. As the 1990s have unfolded, policymakers have sought to restructure the Japanese economy in ways that decisively break with the cohesive nationalist commitment to economic growth. The new orientation of public policy during the 1990s offers further evidence of an important shift of national direction. The new Japan is here to stay.

The slow erosion of the old consensus and the gradual creation of a new elite view of Japan's future must be the work of many minds. In the winter of 1992, for example, Morita Akio, the former president of Sony and the deputy head of the Keidanren, the Federation of Economic Organizations which represents senior managerial opinion in Japan's largest companies, made a start. He called for a radical rethinking of the post-war philosophy of retaining earnings for re-investment by Japanese firms. Morita urged a significant rise in corporate salaries to ease the gap between relative corporate wealth and employee poverty that has been one of the distinguishing features and essential mechanisms of the Japanese miracle. Morita's article in the intellectual monthly *Bungei-Shunjū* (February 1992) provoked wide discussion, not all of it critical, but this dissent from the goals of the Meiji state and its Shōwa reincarnation should be seen as another sign of an emerging Japanese consensus which accepts the view that the thrusting nature of the country's GNP machine must be altered.[8]

Similarly, the 1992 *MITI White Paper* (*Tsūsan Hakusho*) placed fresh stress on the need to enhance the material well-being of the individual household, rather than the firm, as the future priority of public policymaking in the traded sector at national level.[9] The 1992 *White Paper* was novel in its relative freedom from the complex defences of industrial policy that have coloured MITI's public statements in recent years and in the ease with which it passed through the various screening challenges, at the bureau, ministry and cabinet levels. Implicit in MITI's new approach was a determination to look beyond the numbers game involved in the zero-sum contest over export surpluses towards new criteria in setting policy goals and in judging policy success. Here, as in the Morita critique, the emphasis is on raising Japan's standard of living. The *MITI White Paper*, by sidestepping, some would say snubbing, the policy pretensions of the Bush administration over the trade question, was also an attempt to finesse the effects of the era of bad feeling in US–Japan relations with a domestic or national solution to the country's international problems. The suggestion would be that Japan is a nationalist regime that may be turning liberal, but on Japanese terms.

PART II
THE PHILOSOPHY

The foundations of the
Japanese approach

9   A Japanese lesson

Language and nationalism

Apples and oranges

Japan is a poor country, but an ambitious one. The theme of Japanese penury, in wealth and resources, reverberates like a drumbeat in assessments by Japanese writers of the conditions that have constrained, and therefore defined modern public policy in their country. Less discussed but more important has been the purposeful cast of the Japanese national ethos. Indeed, national objectives should be seen to stand at the heart of the collective enterprise that has characterized Japan's modern era. Nevertheless, because many countries are poor and few would not be superpowers if becoming one were only a matter of wishing, it is the subtle Japanese blend of ambition and poverty that compels attention. Japan's success points to an important truth: the chief factor in fostering state power as an act of collective will is the fruitful marriage between clarity of purpose and the vigorous creation of the state institutions necessary to achieve the desired goal. The secret of Japan's phenomenal success has many sources, but the striking feature of her modernization drive has been this lucidity of national purpose.

It has helped to foster a national agenda that has been at once comprehensive in scope and capable of precise application. Behind this accuracy of vision and this public policy agenda stands a cohesive set of reinforcing values and assumptions as well as a philosophy of state action and nation-building. The degree of coherence must be neither over- nor understated. The comprehensive scope of Japanese ambitions has been accompanied by a vagueness about means, which has encouraged *ad hoc* policies. Reviewing the progress of the Japanese state since the beginning of the Meiji Era (1868), one must conclude that Japanese policymakers have been just clear enough and just consistent enough to allow Japan to overcome the kind of contradictions and conflicts of interest that necessarily affect any great collective project that is undertaken not by angels but by men. To say as much is to begin the difficult task of comparing political systems. Among students of comparative politics there are two important schools of thought. One is the modern faction which insists that the cardinal intellectual move in comparative politics is to compare like with like, not apples with oranges, but apples with apples. Such modernists reject as unfruitful any attempt to compare and contrast, for example, Mexico with Australia, that is, a classic one-party regime with a pluralist liberal democracy. This school argues that Japan is worth comparing with America only to the degree that both countries are judged to be advanced industrialized democracies. To insist that modern Japan is neither a liberal nor a market-socialist polity but a nationalist one would appear to violate this assumption.

But there is a more ancient school that feeds on great contrasts. Where the modernist might have hesitated, Herodotus boldly compared Greek city states with the empires of Asia Minor in *The Histories* (c.445 BC), the first great prose work in European letters. Even comparisons of Greek states present challenges. It is not obvious that the modern school would have been keen to compare ancient Athens with Sparta. Yet no act of comparative politics has been more important to the Western tradition of political reflection and cultural identity than this classic study in contrast between the unwieldy and imperialist democracy that was Athens and the army-camp discipline of Sparta.

Comparing apples with apples is no doubt the more sober approach, but setting oranges next to apples often poses the more arresting question. The modern economist who would stress the vices of the centrally planned economy will regret the passing of the Soviet Union because of the persuasive lessons that could be and have been drawn, in almost every English-language textbook introduction to modern economics written since 1945, by stressing the contrasts between Soviet communism and American capitalism.

Here a compromise between the ancient and modern schools of comparative politics is proposed. First, it must be acknowledged that Japan is rightfully a member of the Group of Seven (G-7), the umbrella organization that provides a forum for the heads of government and the foreign and finance ministers of the United States, Great Britain, France, Italy, Germany, Canada and Japan to discuss world issues and the management of the global economy. This is not a diplomatic fiction. Japan is the world's second largest capitalist democracy. This is to agree with the modernist view that Japan is sufficiently liberal in its mode of government, its constitution, and its judicial system to qualify as a genuine democracy. It is also to concede that the Japanese economy is open enough, market-driven enough, and emphatically modern enough to bear useful comparison with the political and economic systems of America and Britain. The word 'enough' has its place in this sentence because there remain well articulated doubts about the relative fragility of Japanese democracy and about the mercantilist character of her economy. Common membership in the councils of the Group of Seven does not, in any case, mean that public policy is executed in an identical manner in Italy and Canada or Britain and Germany. But the political systems of these countries appear to be similar enough to allow the G-7 to function. This is surely sufficient to meet the demands of the cautious modernist in search of productive comparisons between similar nation-states as they exist today.

But what about yesterday? Contemporary comparisons of equal comfort and conviction between the experience of the English-speaking democracies and Japan could not have been made in any year before 1868, or even before 1945. Economically, there are numerous reasons for arguing that any insistence on the liberal character of the Japanese system of governance as reflected, for example, in microeconomic policy was vulnerable until as late as 1985. A similar line of questioning might be followed about modern Germany. Precisely when, in the wake of Hitler's fall, did German democracy become persuasively comparable with Britain's? Some sceptics insist that even now neither Japan nor Germany qualifies as a genuine democracy because in neither country would democratic values and liberal practices survive that crucial 1930s test: economic depression.

One may set to one side this futurologist's nightmare and still, in good faith, ask: Is Japan therefore an apple or an orange? The ruling assumption in this book is that Japan is an orangey apple. There are sound public policy reasons for taking this view. Such an interpretation of modern Japanese government turns on the perception that while Japan, like Germany, qualifies today as a liberal capitalist democracy, the path the Japanese have taken to arrive at this state is very different from that followed by Britain or the United States. This is not to claim that Japanese or German policymakers or businessmen had to re-invent the Industrial Revolution, where that elusive phenomenon is defined as a concrete bundle of late-eighteenth- and early-nineteenth-century technologies. But it is to argue that there are different ways to modernize and to democratize a nation employing such technologies.

Such a conclusion may seem little more than common sense. This is anything but the case. If Japanese and German policymakers have discovered an alternative path to democratic modernity, then this is the stuff of an intellectual revolution that would break with the key Enlightenment belief – so active in the writings of Adam Smith and John

Stuart Mill, of Milton Friedman and John Rawls – that truth is one and error is many. Whatever their differences, all these thinkers in the Anglo-American tradition assume, at some level of philosophical intent, that there is but one way for a nation to achieve any degree of political civilization. The Japanese experience of government may demonstrate the radically pluralist nature of Vico's world, the world of man.

To reject the monism of the Anglo-American philosophic and social scientific approach is to insist that students of comparative politics remain open to alternative traditions of public policy. Such openness is especially pertinent when studying modern Japan and Germany. This perception points to an important distinction drawn in Japanese between the the contrasting public policy traditions of 'leading nations' (*zenshinkoku*), such as the US and Britain, and 'catch-up' nations (*kōshinkoku*), such as Japan and Germany. But is Japan, therefore, an apple or an orange? The answer must be that Japan is a distinctly orangey apple.

So to argue that Japan is a nationalist polity which is gradually becoming a liberal one is also to insist that it is the nationalist legacy in contemporary Japanese governmental practice that makes Japan difficult to understand and to influence. This may explain why, when comparing more or less similar polities, the rigorous examination of the differences between liberal capitalist nations may be as useful as the emphasis on their similarities.

WORDS

Japan is a nationalist polity. What then is a nation? The answer is important because the 'nation' is simultaneously the cause, the means and the end of Japan's modernization drive. Understand this complex idea and the door on the mind of the Japanese policymaker will be substantially opened. But the language of nationhood is prodigious and polysemous: there are many key words and they display a resistant variety of meanings. In discussing nationalism, ambiguity and nuance are all.

Thus the nuance of the Japanese word '*kokka*', which can mean 'nation' or 'state' or a combination of these terms, is at once tighter and looser than implied by the definition of the faintly academic English term 'nation-state'. The equivalent of this English idea in Japanese is '*minzoku-kokka*' (literally, 'nation/race/*ethnie*-state). This is an academic translation from English but one which retains the ambiguities of the word '*kokka*'. It conjures up the abstract and alien quality of the word 'state' in British English. There is also the traditional Japanese word '*kuni*' meaning primarily 'country' but used to refer to both the 'state' or central administrative authority as well as one's provincial home. In this last sense, '*kuni*' is redolent of local identity. It is warmer and has more of a native feel than compounds of imported Chinese characters such as '*kokka*' and '*minzoku-kokka*', though '*kuni*' can be written as a single Chinese character.

Such linguistic shadings are important because without a clear answer to this question, 'What is a nation?', it is almost impossible to make sense of modern Japanese public policy. So what do dictionary definitions tell us? The editors of *The New Collins Concise English Dictionary* (1982 edition), for example, draw a crucial distinction:

> nation: n. 1. an aggregation of people or peoples of one or more cultures, races, etc., organized into a single state: the Canadian nation. 2. a community of persons not constituting a state but bound by common descent, language, history, etc.[1]

The Japanese experience of nationhood puts this definition under illuminating pressure. However well the Collins distinction between multi-ethnic nations and single ethnic non-states may apply to other nations and peoples, in speaking of themselves the Japanese would collapse the definitions into a single formulation: the nation is a community of persons bound by common descent, language, history, etc., which is emphatically organized into a single state.

Such singularity is a rare condition in the modern world. There is, for example, not a single English-speaking democracy (not even Wales or Scotland) which can boast the kind of overlapping unities and uniformities that are probably true of the Japanese nation and certainly assumed to be true by most Japanese. However precise the meaning of the word 'aggregation' in the Collins definition, this word shelters the rooted English assumption that individuals exist prior to collectivities. Individuals are the units from which nations are 'aggregated'. No Japanese nationalist worth his salt, no believer in nations as organic unities, would ever refer to his nation and people as a mere 'aggregation'.

The implication would be that, although individual Japanese may have differing interests, they are united by a single national identity, organized into a single state and anchored in the values of a single ethnic culture or what political anthropologists call, borrowing from the French, an *ethnie*. This is not to claim that the Japanese state contains no ethnic minorities, but it is to assert that these minorities are defined by a convenient convergence of state practice and cultural convention as 'non-Japanese', marginal to national life, and, more important, to national identity. This condition sets Japan apart from every other advanced industrial democracy, certainly from every other G-7 nation, among which Japan is the sole non-Western country.

The distinctive character of the Japanese 'nation' gives a particular weight to the otherwise scholarly definition of '*kokka*' frequently found in Japanese writing on the nation. Take, for example, the definition of '*kokka*' contained in the *Kojien* dictionary, the standard and widely used authority on Japanese usage:

> *kokka* : 1. *kuni, hokoku* [where both Chinese characters '*hō*' and '*koku*' mean 'country' or 'nation' but the first may also refer to Japan itself, as in the word '*hō-bun*' meaning the Japanese language]. 2. (state; nation [in English]) a political community/association which has exclusive sovereignty and power [*kenryoku-soshiki*: literally 'empowered organization'] to govern/rule the inhabitants of a fixed territory. Since the beginning of modern times, the concept has normally been defined by reference to the three features of territory, people and sovereignty.[2]

The *Kojien* entry then refers the reader to the term '*kindai kokka*' (modern state), where the dictionary definition draws on the European experience (though an old-fashioned Japanese Marxist could apply the implied schema to modern Japanese history as well). The *Kojien* defines '*kindai kokka*' (modern state) as:

> The centralized centralizing [*chūō-shukenteki-na*] state, possessing territory, a people ['*kokumin*': literally the people as a nation or an *ethnie*], and sovereignty, created in the modern period, under the aegis of Absolutism, after the destruction of the feudal state at the end of the Middle Ages.[3]

Having stressed the ambiguities of Japanese usage, it is also right to observe that the Japanese term '*koku-min*' (literally nation/country-people) is difficult to render into English without disguising the way that the two Chinese characters reinforce each other, giving the compound a semantic weight and economy which is lost in translation. Conventionally rendered as 'nation' or 'people', it means both. Oddly, Napoleon's quip about the English being 'a nation of shopkeepers' ('*shōgyō-kokumin*' in Japanese) reproduces the interplay of two dimensions of nationality that the Japanese see as reinforcing. More to the point, '*kokumin*' in historic Japanese usage has carried a specific hierarchic implication, that is the 'people' as the ruled. The nuance here reflects the neglect of the peasant masses in pre-Meiji 'public policy'.

It is also important to keep in mind that the Japanese translation of 'public policy' (*kōkyō-seisaku*) retains the patina of uninhibited state power. The '*kō*' in '*kōkyō*', the conventional Japanese rendering of 'public', has never shed this meaning. Whatever hopeful resonance the word 'public' may evoke in the English ear, it must be stressed that 'government of the people, by the people, and for the people' is not a Japanese administrative tradition. At best, the Confucian bureaucratic tradition is about paternalistic benevolence, not power-sharing with the masses. The word '*kō*' conveys a specifically illiberal weight which is untrue of the English word 'public'.

The *Shorter Oxford English Dictionary* helps to bridge the gap between the definitions offered by Collins and the *Kōjien*, and to refine them in a useful way. According to *The Shorter OED*:

> nation I. 1. A distinct race or people, characterized by common descent, language or history, usually organized as a separate political state and occupying a definite territory. II. 1. a. A family or kindred clan. b. A tribe of North American Indians. [4]

The use of the term 'nation' to refer to a clan is salient here because, first, the word '*kokka*' in Japanese is a suggestive compound of two Chinese characters meaning 'country'/'nation' and 'family', and, second, in pre-war Japanese ideology, the shared blood ties were stressed as the focal point of national unity under the literal or suggestive 'fatherhood' of the Japanese emperor. Even today the idea that the Japanese nation is united by blood purity is a commonplace in journalism regardless of the ideological orientation of the author or the internationalist content of the piece of writing. Such linguistic exercises are anything but trivial. In part the question is about what it means to say that cultures differ. In the Western encounter with the non-Western world, no continent has offered more intellectual resistance than Asia. The Gulf War has offered a recent episode in the bloody politics of mutual incomprehension. There is another Asian–Western conflict that has inspired still more wonder at the cultural divide in question. In her Pulitzer-prize-winning study of the Vietnam War, Frances FitzGerald, using only French and English sources, set out the problem in this way:

> In going into Vietnam the United States was not only transposing itself into a different epoch of history; it was entering a world qualitatively different from its own. Culturally as geographically Vietnam lies half a world away from the United States. Many Americans in Vietnam learned to speak Vietnamese, but the language gave no more than a hint of the basic intellectual grammar that lay beneath. In a sense there was no more correspondence between the two worlds than that between the atmosphere of the earth and that of

the sea. There was no direct translation between them in the simple equation of *x* is *y* and *a* means *b*. To find the common ground that existed between them, both Americans and Vietnamese would have [had] to re-create the whole world of the other, the whole intellectual landscape.[5]

Japan is an infinitely more modern and complex (that is institutionally diverse) society than post-colonial Vietnam. But the Chinese inheritance that has informed Vietnamese state practice over the centuries has also influenced the governance of Japan, which has what William Theodore de Bary has called its own 'continental past'. There is no more complex or significant exercise in political scientific analysis than the precise rendering of a Japanese public policy document into English, such are the cultural densities on each side of the linguistic chasm. To seek to recreate the whole world of the Japanese policymaker, the whole of his intellectual landscape, is to risk what in information theory is termed 'total regress'. This is because the language of Japanese public policymaking encapsulates the linguistic essence of the entire Japanese heritage of collective action in the public sphere. Such facts of language must be set against the conventional scepticism of the social scientist towards cultural explanations of political phenomena. Such scepticism is not groundless. Nevertheless, to disregard the cultural and linguistic dimension of politics in the name of amiable or hopeful comparability is intellectual folly.

Translations

There is little doubt that the language of Japanese nationalism tends to set it apart from other forms of national consciousness. This makes it difficult to understand. Words are at the root of the problem. Any analysis of Japan as a nationalist polity in a language other than Japanese will almost inevitably get the nuances wrong for the good reason that Japanese maps social reality in different ways from English, to take the language at issue. But the Japanese nationalist experiment translates into some languages better than others. This is because there are some striking similarities between Japan's modernization drive and the ways that certain Continental European nations (France and Germany, for example) have shed their feudal heritage.

To make this argument is to insist on two points. The first is about how language and political reality relate. It is futile to ask which came first, the language or political reality. Languages are living things that reflect experience but also form and reinforce it. Logicians will be uncomfortable with the implied circularity of reasoning (the chicken is the egg). Such discomfort must be endured. Language and political development are mutually indispensable. How does one tell the dancer from the dance? Second, whatever the disparities between the German effort to catch up with Britain in the nineteenth century and Japan's attempt to overtake America in the late twentieth century, the British and American experience of nationalism and modernization is of a radically different character from that of Germany or Japan. Today, Britain and America, Japan and Germany, are all modern democratic societies. This encourages one to draw valid comparisons between Japan and the United States.

What must be emphasized here is the linguistic dimension of such comparisons. The concepts of '*zenshinkoku*' (not '*senshinkoku*') and '*kōshinkoku*' are Japanese loans from German. Such terminology reflects the Japanese perceptions of their national contest with Britain and the United States. English has not developed such terminology because the British and American experience of modernization has been different from that of Japan and Germany. The same may be observed of the term 'industrial policy', another import (this time from the French). Here, again, it is the weight of the Japanese experience of public policymaking that has forced an alien idea on Anglo-American economic discourse. Terms such as 'catch-up nation' or 'industrial policy' are undomesticated in English usage for good historical reasons. Policy practice reflects these linguistic borrowings. Here is one lesson that the reader who would correctly appreciate the nature of Japanese public policy must master. It defines the central negative task of this book: to prevent the native-speaker of English, who is in some sense imprisoned by the natural grain of the English language and the political experience reflected in that language, from drawing the wrong conclusions about Japanese politics merely because he or she speaks English, and not Japanese.

THINKING NATIONALISM

Nations are ancient; nationalism is modern. It is therefore always essential to keep in mind how the ethnic foundations of national identity, which are frequently pre-modern, differ from the ideological articulation of nationalist self-awareness that has coloured modern nationalism almost everywhere. Nationalism is a universal phenomenon, but in the West a comparatively recent one. Indeed many Western writers insist that modern nationalist doctrines are a Western invention and one of Europe's most consequential exports to the Third World.

In his essay 'Nationalism: Past Neglect and Present Power', Berlin calls for a careful distinction between national consciousness or identity and nationalism.[6] In such linguistic niceties there is a determination to construct a rigid barrier between patriotism and chauvinism. Berlin would have us not only erect a thick wall between the national sentiments alive in the king's battlefield speech on Agincourt in *Henry V* and the Nürnberg Rallies of the 1930s, but also between the patriotic feelings roused in the final scene in Shakespeare's *Henry IV* (*Part II*) and the disconcerting passions that Wagner pandered to in the crowd scene that brings to a close *Die Meistersinger von Nürnberg* (1868). English national consciousness, as it developed after the defeat of the Spanish Armada of 1588, and as celebrated in Shakespeare's plays, is ancient by modern European standards. By contrast, nationalist sentiment slumbered in the German, Italian and Slavic nations during the same period only to be awakened with destructive force during the past 200 years.

But nationalism, however chauvinist, is more than chauvinism. In the European context, nationalism has served as the ideological justification for the urgent mobilization of a society's energies in order to protect or enhance a country's economic and political security. In this sense, nationalism, translated into a public policy agenda, is crucially about nation-building and modernization. Viewed in this way, important events of the past may take on very different meanings. Such a standpoint may even suggest the unlikely rubric of 'thinking nationalism'.

If Napoleon is remembered by the English as a threat to their liberty, then the French emperor is also regarded by many Europeans as a necessary evil, even a hero, because he broke the back of a reactionary and debilitating feudalism in many of the continent's emerging but still 'catch-up' nations, such as Germany and Italy. Napoleon's 'continental system' transformed the European debate over national tariffs. After his defeat, nineteenth-century English trade competition, inevitably a more peaceable business than Napoleonic conquest, came to be seen in a less than peaceful light. The economic nationalist Friedrich List (1789–1846), who sought to foster a formidable German manufacturing base, was mindful of both the French and British challenges to German autonomy, but in *The National System of Political Economy* (1841), the British threat was the one he stressed. How likely were the British reflections on public policy, in the work of Mill or Bentham, to reflect this revolutionary shift in Continental perspective? Is there not a German lesson behind the failure of the campaign to protect Britain's manufacturing base that Joseph Chamberlain launched in 1903? Does not this lacuna in the British public policy experience explain *The Economist*'s slippery wrestle with the impact and values of Japanese industrial policy today?

This is not to claim that German and Japanese nationalism, and the world view (German: *Weltanschauung*) they reflect, are identical. For example, the key assumption of Japanese nationalism is the primacy of the collective. Japanese individualism tends to be rather 'soft' at best. German individualism, after Luther and Kant, is cut from stiffer cloth, inward-looking, perhaps, but a real social force. More than the German, the Japanese example demands at least a temporary bracketing of any methodological insistence, such as one finds in Hayek and Popper, that the behaviour of collectivities must be understood solely in the light of individual motivations and desires. Certainly this is essential if a non-Japanese is to gain either an objective grasp of Japanese nationalist ideology or a feel for its inner workings. In their collectivist orientation, what were individual Japanese?

Until deep into the twentieth century, the great mass of the Japanese population, as is still true of almost every East Asian polity, was composed of peasants. Farming to survive, such people had obvious economic interests. But the Confucian *Analects* provide a more accurate gloss on Asian peasants as political actors than John Locke or John Stuart Mill: 'The essence of a gentleman is that of the wind; the essence of small people is that of grass. And when a wind passes over the grass, it cannot choose but bend.'[7]

Though it is not always the case in *The Analects*, the term 'small people' here refers to the ruled. By a complex evolution of enormous consequences for East Asian government, the Confucian 'gentleman' became the mandarin official, the backbone of Chinese imperial administration. Translated into a very different idiom, the concept of 'gentleman' exerted decisive influence on the ethos of the samurai-bureaucrats who ran the Tokugawa *bakufu* and later on the administrators of the modern Meiji state and their contemporary heirs as well.

The Meiji Restoration made the subject peasant population of the Edo era into the imperial subjects of a modern authoritarian state. The post-war reforms of the American Occupation (1945–52) attempted to transform this nation of subjects into one of democratic citizens. A better approximation of the Western model of civil society resulted, but the struggle to remake the Japanese people into a nation of individuals failed. Without the historical weight of the European Renaissance, Reformation or Enlightenment behind it, such a programme of political re-education was never likely to succeed, and only the *naïveté* of the policymakers of the Occupation encouraged the attempt. Although the left-wing has staged mass demonstrations against what it saw as objectionable legislation or threats to democracy, notably under the Occupation and in 1960, it remains a fact that the Japanese as a people have never rebelled against their state in an authentic bourgeois revolution. No Japanese soldier has ever died fighting for democracy. This truth of the Japanese experience of government has major implications for the Japanese definition of 'public' and 'policy'. Western values, particularly Anglo-American ones, applied unalloyed to Asian politics, may subvert genuine understanding. With an eye to Confucian tradition and Japanese administrative practice, it might be well to begin with the assumption that Japan is a bureaucratic polity rather than a liberal one.

The Westerner who lacks Japanese but remains keen to penetrate the Japanese logic of national development could do worse, when confronted with some resistant aspect of Japanese public policy, than to recall French or German practice in a similar situation. This is correct of a number of areas of recent policymaking, but even more accurate of great nationalist transformations of the past.

The transmutation of a largely peasant population into a mobilized mass was probably the most consequential achievement of the Meiji modernizers. The word 'mobilize' is a military term, and the language of this sustained effort to get Japanese housewives to save more and consume less (to take one notable example of this crusade) both before and after the Second World War, is replete with military metaphors. This is no accident. In Western politics, war has been midwife to the cultivation of nationalism. In this sense, the Revolutionary Wars and the Napoleonic adventure turned the French into Frenchmen. In a more subtle way, it is possible to argue that the nature of American nationalism, especially among northerners, was transformed by the Civil War.

The Meiji era experiment with modern nationalism put a unique Japanese twist on this nationalist metamorphosis. Here, the Continental experience is more relevant than the Anglo-Saxon. The French Revolution transformed peasants into Frenchmen, that is nationalists of a particular sort – ones for whom, in the words of the petition of the agitators to the Legislative Assembly of 1792, 'The image of the *Patrie* is the sole divinity which it is permissible to worship'. At numerous points, this French Revolutionary demand contains an effective gloss on the rationale behind the cult of state Shinto fostered by the Meiji modernizers. But in the end it was the Germans from whom the Japanese would learn the most.

10 Japan, Germany and the alternative tradition in modern public policy

War is the mother of effective bureaucracy. It is conflict between nations that brings out the best in policymakers and therefore the best in their policies. It is bureaucratic 'red tape', not the truth, that is the first casualty of war. Floundering Leviathans in times of peace, the great state bureaucracies flourish during war. It is no surprise that one of the most perceptive students of the British bureaucracy has concluded that, 'the last person truly to reform Whitehall was that well-known expert in public administration, Adolf Hitler'.[1]

The Second World War revitalizied bureaucracies everywhere. This was in part a response to memories of the First World War for which all the great powers, with the possible exception of Germany, were wholly unprepared. It was the demands of that war that forced the abandonment of the gentlemanly pace and procedures of the British higher civil service by Lloyd George's War Cabinet after December 1916. The forced-march reforms that overtook British policymaking between 1914 and 1917 have some close parallels in the American rush to mobilize from 1940 to 1943.

Just as European military officers were posted to the USA to learn the new technologies of war that had been tested with such bloody results in the American Civil War, the greatest nineteenth-century conflict after 1815 outside China, Japanese experts in wartime supply and logistics were dispatched to France, when Japan entered the war as an ally of Britain in 1915, to observe how the more advanced nations mobilized their resources for total war. The Japanese were appalled by what they witnessed, not only the slaughter but also the scale of the undertaking which they knew was beyond Japan's capacity. Their country had fought and nearly lost a war against Russia only a decade before because Japan was poor and unsuccessful at translating her war-making potential into effective state power. This nightmare haunted Japanese strategic thinking throughout the inter-war period, and for good reason.

It was largely this failing of the Japanese machine of state that made her Pacific contest with America between 1941 and 1945 so one-sided an affair.

Wartime mobilization imposed heavy burdens on both the Allied and the Axis states. It also generated extraordinary productivity. It is thought that the reforms introduced by Churchill's first wartime cabinet in 1940 helped to double the volume of British arms production, already accelerated by Chamberlain after the Munich débâcle. In war, it is not only arms manufacture but almost everything else that must be done, as it were, at the double. Churchill maintained a brutal schedule that was notorious for the way it wore down his staff. All levels of the British bureaucracy were affected. Thus the story is told about Beryl Millicent le Poer Power, one of the legends of wartime Whitehall, who like many of her sex was accosted by men in the blacked-out streets of London. Thus importuned, Miss Power would shine her torch into her face and say, 'Over forty and very busy'.[2] No more was necessary.

In the end, of course, peace returns. It is then that there occurs the second important bureaucratic transition, and in this story of post-war Japanese public policymaking it is the shift from war to peace that has mattered even more than wartime mobilization. Peter Hennessy glumly observes that, 'The reform Hitler forced on Whitehall was undone by the peace because neither the politicians nor the senior Civil Servants tried or cared to devise its peacetime equivalent.'[3] The sense of sudden deceleration sickened many. Much of the transparent gloom of Le Carré's spy novels (and spies, too, are civil servants) reflects less the decline of empire than a professional man's disappointment at the British rush to the tea-time tranquillity of an imperfect peace, after the stimulus and achievement of a great victory. It is true that in all nations the imprint of war left permanent marks. The creation of the American President's National Security Council in 1947 is often thought, especially by British observers, to have been a direct imitation of Lloyd George's War Cabinet. In Australia, the impact of war was greater still. The trauma, real and imagined, of having been cut off from Imperial Britain and American naval power by the advance of Japanese arms encouraged a drive for self-sufficiency, a kind of manufacturing autarky, that determined the goals of Australian trade policy for the next four decades.

In Germany the catastrophe of defeat ensured a sustained peacetime emergency. But, as perhaps nowhere else, it is public policymaking in post-war Japan that has demonstrated that the busyness of war may matter more than the business of peace. Japanese policymakers sought to maintain the aroused state of wartime national emergency in peacetime. They sought not only a peacetime equivalent to war, but to reverse the outcome of the war by peaceful means. This perception brings to us the Janus-like quality of our times.

WAR AND PEACE

More than peace, it has been war that has given our century its fundamental character. Literary critics claim that it was with the Great European War of 1914–18 that military metaphors dug deep under the skin of peacetime discourse; in the mass media, in letters, in social scientific analysis. The language of Japanese politics, business and economic commentary also is replete with the language of war, although the borrowings appear to come as often from the film script of *The Seven Samurai* as from the tactician's handbook at Pearl Harbor.

Was the nineteenth century any different in Europe or Japan? Despite the long peace that prevailed almost without interruption in Western Europe between 1815 and 1914, and in Japan with few exceptions until 1894, public language grew vulnerable to the crude demands of philosophies of contesting nature, such as social Darwinism and its 'survival of the fittest' logic. George Steiner, the literary scholar, has observed of European sensibility in the decades after Waterloo that, 'In manufacture and the money market, energies barred from revolutionary action or war could find outlet and social approval. Such expressions as "Napoleons of finance" and "captains of industry" are semantic markers of this modulation.'[4]

Such a 'modulation' also appears to be at work in Japanese writings about business, politics and economics during the long post-war peace that began in 1945. Japanese energies, barred from war, have poured into the competitive struggle to win markets and break competitors, especially foreign ones. In contemporary Japan, reporting on economic competition with other nations is still often served up in the pre-war idiom of gleaming swords and uninhibited economic nationalism.

Such language should be seen as the outward expression of an inward state, one that has marked the modern public policymaker in Japan with particular force. The continuity of language points to a continuity of values. As in Hobbes' dark vision, war is presumed to be man's natural state. In the Japanese reformulation of the Hobbesian nightmare, the human condition sets man against man, not an individual against another individual, but 'us' against 'them'. The opponent may be another team, firm or nation, but, just as one of the oldest forms of human association is the hunting pack, the ubiquitous sporting metaphors of contemporary business and political analysis conceal a more ancient and less gentle truth: that collectivity inspires loyalty, and never more than in time of conflict. It is against such rooted claims for collective identity that pupils of Hayek or Popper should test their dogmatic insistence that collectivities, such as the firm or the state or the nation, do not exist. Such assertions are unpersuasive in Japan.

War and conflict is the rule. Peace, however lasting, tends to be viewed in Japan's corridors of power as an ever vulnerable, if valued, illusion that must not be allowed to obscure the reality of competitive struggle as the defining feature of man's reduced nature. Tested against the grit of post-war Japanese policymaking and corporate practice, Clausewitz's famous dictum should be read not as the Prussian strategist formulated it – 'war is nothing but the continuation of politics by other means' – but rather as: 'Politics is nothing but the continuation of war by other means'. Here politics includes the struggle for commercial superiority.

In this language, in these values, lurks an important economic insight. In his sharp 1841 critique of *laissez-faire* economics, Friedrich List drove a complex point home: 'J.B. Say openly demands that we should imagine the existence of a *universal republic* in order to comprehend the idea of general free trade.'[5] List challenged the long reasoning chain that underwrites the claim of this famous French economist: a universal republic is important to free trade because only a universal republic can prevent wars between nations. An absence of war permits the 'economic man' to maximize his wealth. International conflicts conspire against the creation of wealth. List believed that such reasoning explained why, in Smithian economics, war tended to be neglected as an organizing concept in human affairs.

Say's thought-experiment reflects the key assumption of *laissez-faire* theory that only markets and individuals exist. The nation, as idea and fact, is either marginalized or ignored. Indeed, List cites the example of one early American student of Smithian economics who pushed this kind of reasoning to what this American saw as its necessary conclusion: 'the "nation" is a grammatical invention'. Thus argued Thomas Cooper, a president of Columbia College.[6] As a convinced nationalist, List will have none of this. On this issue he remains unmoved in the face of the evident powers of free-market theory. Nations and international conflicts most emphatically exist. Outside the lecture hall, Say's universal republic is nonsense. Hence List's conclusion is that:

> If we wish to remain true to the laws of logic and of the nature of things, we must set the economy of individuals against the economy of societies, and discriminate in respect to the latter between true political and national economy (which, emanating from the idea and nature of the nation, teaches how a given *nation* in the present state of

the world and its own special national relations can maintain and improve its economical conditions) and cosmo-political economy, which originates in the assumption that all nations of the earth form but one society living in a perpetual state of peace.[7]

Such reasoned clarity about the nature of the real world, about war and peace, makes List one of Europe's leading contenders for the title of intellectual 'godfather' of the Japanese miracle. No claim of equal force may be made for any follower of Adam Smith. Japanese thinkers made their own way to List's conclusions. They fathered their own miracle. But List demonstrates the unrivalled importance of the German Historical School for any Westerner who would grasp the nature of national economics, in its German or Japanese guise. And List does not let the matter rest there. He is keen to establish the power conditions that have allowed British and American economists in the Smithian tradition to indulge in such otherwise unworldly speculation. List's answer has become a cardinal assumption of Japanese thinking on this issue. German and Japanese economic nationalists have been consistently alive to the fact that the greatest proponents of free trade have tended, during the past two centuries, also to be spokesmen of the world's dominant economic power.

One result is that the fact that Britain and America have been the victors of the great conflicts of the twentieth century is rarely lost on Japanese policy analysts. Peace has a different meaning for the defeated. List sets forth in deadpan style his assault on the logic of the *Wealth of Nations* because he knows how ironic and false its neglect of military realities in the name of universal peace will seem to his German readers:

Adam Smith concerned himself as little as Quesnay did with true political economy, i.e. that policy which each separate nation had to obey in order to make progress in its economical conditions. He entitles his work 'The Nature and Causes of the Wealth of Nations' (i.e. of all nations of the whole human race). He speaks of the various systems of political economy in a separate part of his work solely for the purpose of demonstrating their non-efficiency, and of proving that 'political or *national* economy must be replaced by 'cosmo-political or world-wide economy.' Although here and there he speaks of wars, this only occurs incidentally. The idea of a perpetual state of peace forms the foundations of all his arguments . . . Adam Smith naturally understood under the word 'peace' the 'perpetual universal peace' of the Abbé St.Pierre.[8]

The hidden and vulnerable premise (the *petito principii*) of free-marketeers is the assumed absence of military conflict from the human condition. It was one of those hopeful errors that the Enlightenment delighted in, a marvellous utopian vision. The victims and critics of Enlightenment *naïveté* about human nature agree that free market principles work best in a climate of lasting peace. But what if peace does not last? What does the proponent of the otherwise unimpeachable doctrine of 'economic man', of the rational pursuit of individual gain, a formidable intellectual weapon, have to say to the dead of Passchendaele and Stalingrad, to the victims of Nazi terror and Japanese imperialism, or to those buried in the ash hills of Hiroshima or Nagasaki? To observe that market principles operated even in Nazi concentration camps and the Gulag is an answer no nationalist would accept.

The contours of this argument over human nature and history have influenced, to cite another telling example, the debate over the significance of East Asia's oddest political community: Hong Kong. In a television series, Milton Friedman, the Nobel prize-winning economist, has celebrated Hong Kong as a pure example of a free-market economy, where government responsibility is confined to raising the Union Jack in the morning and lowering it at night. In East Asia, on the contrary, Hong Kong is an object of unblinking pity. For many East Asians, it is a painful example of the belief that without a nation there is no state, and without a state, a community has little chance of survival. True, the region is changing and Hong Kong may survive the 1997 transition in something like its present form; but no one, not even the most bullish of Hong Kong Chinese, can be certain of it. It is the Asian nationalist who has grasped the real nature of the dangers that threaten Hong Kong.

Such nationalist lucidity is important. It may explain, for example, why List articulates the fundamental assumptions of Japanese policy-making and business strategy in the twentieth century better than any other Western thinker. Lacking, as we do, a *locus classicus* setting out the principles of Japanese nationalist policymaking – what List rightly termed a 'true political economy' of national need – the Western student of modern Japan will neglect List's writings to the peril of his understanding of Japanese public policy. This is true of List in a way untrue of a comparable neglect of Marx or Friedman or even Keynes.

GERMAN LESSONS

It is no accident that List was German. Behind his *National System of Political Economy* stands the long and profound German meditation on the practical problems of turning the state into a war machine, on how to achieve bureaucratic rationality and efficiency, on the principles of national identity in an era of fierce ethnic conflicts, on the economics of national competition, and on revolutions 'from above' to achieve such policy ends. Such ends have demanded means, and bureaucratic ones in particular. Its vast reserve of state and national experience allowed Professor Herman Finer to conclude that Germany was 'the country with the longest serious study and experience of a Civil Service and its problems'.[9]

The reasons for this comparison between the philosophy of the Prussian state and that of post-Meiji Japan are two-fold. First, the German imperial example exerted direct impact on Japanese state policy and practice; in administrative law, constitutional theory, the organization of the imperial Japanese army, economic theory and the management of state finances, even the organization of the banking system. There is little doubt that many members of the famous Iwakura Mission (1871–3), sent abroad by the Meiji authorities to examine policy practice and economic organization in Europe and America, were impressed above all by the lessons that Imperial Germany had to teach the new Japan.

Second, there is the question of family resemblance. The Japanese elite brought to the business of nation-building a formidable native tradition of reflection on politics and statecraft. It was this school of experience that informed the design of the Meiji state, the modernized monarchy and the Meiji Constitution. Nevertheless, the striking parallels in national history and outlook should not be ignored. Take, for example, Bismarck's three wars of national unity. The Japanese conducted their own campaign of internal unification, provoking and then crushing the 1877 uprising led by Saigō Takamori. Japanese authority was also asserted abroad, in expeditions against Korea and Formosa. Finally there were the successes of the Sino-Japanese War (1894–5) and the Russo-Japanese War (1904–5).

But Japan was not Germany. Prussia bequeathed to Imperial Germany, via Bismarck, one of the world's strongest military machines, with a heavy industrial complex to match. By contrast, Japan was a slender reed. Germany was overwhelmed in the First and Second World Wars by an iron ring of opponents which could summon extraordinary industrial power to the task of defeating her. Japan was too poor, too disorganized and too badly led to have survived such a war. Isolated off the coast of Korea, Japan had only once in her long history before 1853 been threatened by conquest, and even then the Mongols in the thirteenth century were crushed before they landed. The East Europe of the late medieval and early modern times was a much harsher place.

One may concede all of this and still acknowledge the remarkable parallels in attitude and values that made Germany so instructive to

Japan's modernizers. A focused and deeply felt realism about the true nature of *realpolitik* united both countries. However much the wartime alliance of Germany and Japan make a comparison tempting, a more telling one is between Imperial Japan and Bismarck's Germany. Today, few thinking Japanese hold views as blimpish as even those of Max Weber (1864–1920), the father of Western sociology, but it remains true that public values and policy practice in Japan remain outside the mainstream tradition that the modern West inherits from the Renaissance, the Reformation and the Enlightenment and also from post-Holocaust liberalism. This is not just because Japan is an Oriental society, but also because its experience of the nineteenth and twentieth centuries has been, like Germany's, different from that of Britain and America.

Another feature of this analogy is the heroic role of bureaucrats in the epic task of nation-building in Japan and Germany. There is a narrative drive to the history of how state institutions were created and evolved in both countries. Modern national history is not only the story of valour on the battlefield but also of the mobilizing of state resources by bureaucratic means. Such tales of motivated bureaucracy are a crucial part of the lesson of the alternative tradition of modern public policy. It is no accident that Chalmers Johnson's classic study, *MITI and the Japanese Miracle* (1982) is in essence a bureaucratic epic. The drama of national greatness informs the melding of the military and the economic in the campaign of Japanese bureaucrats to create an 'economic general staff' (*keizai sanbō honbu*) in the 1920s and to nurture a post-war heir to the wartime Ministry of Munitions that became MITI.

As in Japan, the origins of modern German statecraft were largely medieval. But to this inherited tradition the leaders of Brandenburg (later Prussia) brought a set of military and economic problems which encouraged radical innovations and improvements. The penalty for failure in post-medieval Eastern and Central Europe was brutal. The region is a graveyard of states and religious bodies unable to meet the competitive challenges. Prussian state-building required a level of organizational performance and efficiency well beyond the powers and abilities of a medieval liege lord. Military success encouraged Brandenburg's rulers to take ever greater risks in conflicts with more formidable opponents. Such consequent demands, both to tax and to fight, 'led to an expanding and deepening cameralism, a set of territories with more or less uniform institutions (consolidation) and a very numerous specialized bureaucracy, both civil and military (differentiation of function)'.[10]

In addition to the continuity of state purpose provided by four single-minded rulers over 146 years (1640–1786), the essential ingredients of Prussian success were military organization, efficiency of tax collection and financial frugality. As seventeenth-century wars were fought with expensive and often ill-disciplined mercenaries, financing and administrative control were vital. In Brandenburg, the link between these forces and the prince was the War Commissariat. When standing armies became permanent in Brandenburg, so did the War Commissariat. In the process it began to compete with older bureaucratic structures, the central *Amtskammern* and the local *Statthaltern*. In a largely barter economy, this made the Brandenburg court, through its War Commissariat, 'recruiter, barracks and feeding agent' for its increasingly successful army.[11] Under such conditions, the War Commissariat grew continually more powerful.

With the formation of the *Generalkriegskommissariat* or GKK ('the soul of the state') in 1680, the military apparatus achieved effective influence over state policymaking. In 1712, the GKK was split from the Royal Privy Council, which probably reflects an important departure from the programme of internal specialization within the Council begun in 1657. These reforms by the Great Elector and King Frederick I of Prussia were continued by their successors and laid the foundations for Frederick the Great's military successes in the War of the Austrian Succession (1740–8) and the Seven Years War (1756–63). There was more to this success than the arts of Mars. Indeed, it may be argued that Brandenburg's central achievement, and cardinal advantage over its rivals, was financial, both in conservation of resources and in the effective harvesting and investing of tax income. This also highlights the importance of the royal domains. Thrifty state policies allowed King Frederick William I to expand his army from 38,000 to 80,000 men without a proportional increase in the burden of taxation upon his kingdom. It was the great expense of war which made taxation 'the goal of goals' for Prussia's nascent civil service.

In 1689, an Exchequer or *HofKammer* was instituted under the direction of Von Kuynhausen. Later reforms transformed this 'chamber' into the *Generalfinanzdirektorium*. One result was that, 'The national accounts were unified and clarified and a budget of income and expenditure established, financial administration over the whole country was reduced to like items, and uniform administrative principles were laid down for all parts of the state.'[12] Under the Great Elector, a long twilight struggle was fought over burgher tax duties between the House of Brandenburg and Königsberg, finally resulting in local submission in East Prussia to a show of armed force by the sovereign (former landlord) in 1663. The agents of taxation were subsequently so effective throughout the holdings of the Hohenzollern that, 'by 1772, the Tax Commissioner had practically become the guardian of the town, which lost all independence'.[13]

The Brandenburg tax collector was not only a member of the War Commissariat, but also the most active agent of state paternalism. Though the Prussian treasury remained divided until Baron von Stein's reforms after Jena (1806), its prestige in Prussian society as the main non-combat section of the bureaucracy made civil service an attractive vocation for what in the Confucian tradition would have been called 'men of talent'. Herman Finer comments that:

> The Tax Commissioner's profession was the training ground for the best Prussian officials of the eighteenth century, and they brought to their central departmental duties a fund of experience, which explains why the Prussian state, incapable constitutionally of being reformed from the outside or 'below', could at decisive times be reformed from within or 'above'.[14]

Prussia's bureaucracy was already well on its way to becoming a modern civil service via the spread of examinations, between 1700 and 1737, for judges and other senior officials. This professionalization was further accelerated by the creation of the eighteenth century's equivalent of a public sector MBA degree at the University of Halle and Frankfurt where a Professorship of Cameralism (*Staatswirtschaft*) was established in 1727. With a bureaucracy governed by the highest professional standards in Europe, what need did Prussia have for further reform?

Despite all these achievements, the Prussian bureaucracy was still at root only a supply train of the army and the footstool of the monarchy. In terms of state tasks, the Prussian state was focused so completely on the 'reduction of the opposition' (at home and abroad) that the provision of daily utilities, that is paternalism – one of bureaucracy's most natural callings – was never effectively put into practice. Similarly, centralization, exhibited in such creations as the 'General Supreme Finance War and Domain Directory', after the failed reorganizations of 1709 and 1722, was caused by an over-reliance on the ruler to animate state structures. Having a defined place where 'the buck stopped' was not enough. When Frederick the Great died in 1786 without an equal to succeed him, his top-heavy state drifted off course.

Worse was to follow. Dumouriez's victory at Valmy (1792) should have served as a sharp warning to Prussia, no longer the beneficiary of great leadership, of impending changes in the paradigm of state power. But the new lessons were not mastered, as Prussia's sputtering diplomacy from the collapse of the First Coalition to Austerlitz (1805) shows, and the House of Brandenburg's military machine, this 'army with a land', was finally smashed by Napoleon at Jena (1806). This disaster reflected the impact of a double failure: to modernize the executive and other state agencies, and to persuade the mass of the population to identify with the destiny of the Hohenzollern monarchy.

During the long and creative nineteenth-century aftermath of the crushing of the old Prussian state at Jena, the country's leadership initiated a set of four major policy revolutions that transformed Prussia into the core of the new German empire:

1 Stein's 'revolution from above';
2 the creation of a Prussian customs union;
3 Bismarck's three wars of national unification;
4 the 'Iron Chancellor's' historic compromise with the German worker classes over social insurance and other welfare programmes.

Not only do all of these policies have significant implications for the student of Japanese policy practice, but, equally important, they offer a practical demonstration of the philosophy and goals of what might be called the 'alternative tradition of modern public policy'.

This different school of public policy thinking must be borne in mind by anyone whose understanding of how public policy does and should work has been decisively coloured by the mainstream Anglo-American approach, rooted in the science and values of John Locke, the Scottish Enlightenment and the Federalist Papers. German and Japanese policy practice constitutes an anti-Enlightenment school of public admin-istration, but one upon which the charge of 'obscurantism' rests only uneasily.

Behind these four sets of policy changes stands the modern nationalist revolution in German sensibility. This momentous shift in communal and state ideology and values was set in motion by German nationalist thinkers of the late eighteenth and early nineteenth century. Two of the most famous were John Gottfried Herder (1744–1803) and John Gottlieb Fichte (1762–1814).

Herder, who when young had been a proponent of the universalistic impulse in the French Enlightenment, began to break with its cosmo-politan assumptions in such works as his *Treatise on the Origin of Language* (1772), where he developed the idea that cultures were unique social forms because individual language housed that uniqueness and gave it life. In Herder's phrase, 'language expresses the collective experience of the group'. Herder thought it was the group, animated by a shared culture or religious values, that made human beings human. But the community that counted most in his thinking was the 'nation'. Thus, for Herder, collectivities define an individual's essence; they make him what he is; they determine his potential.

First taken up by other German nationalists, Herder's ideas helped to give intellectual substance to the Slav nationalist spirit. Some European writers argue that Herder's philosophy of cultural nationalism has cast a significant spell even on Third World nationalism during the twentieth century. The parallels between Herder's ideas and the ideology of Japanese nationalism and public policy practice are remarkable. They confirm Herder's unique importance among Western writers for anyone who would understand Japan in the light of modern European thought and German experience.

But Herder was no chauvinist. He refused to concede the existence of any international hierarchy, of superior and inferior ranks among different nations. Many of his followers were less liberal in their thinking. None of these more aggressive nationalists has had greater intellectual influence than Fichte. For this German philosopher, 'the primal datum of the universe is ceaseless goal-creating, goal-pursuing activity; men's projects create the world, not the world their projects'.[15]

It would be hard to conceive of a remark by a Western thinker that better encapsulates the essence of the modern nationalist spirit of Japanese enterprise and public policymaking. Only Nietzsche's aphorism in *The Antichrist* (1888) – 'Formula of our happiness: a Yes, a No, a straight line, a *goal* . . . ' – comes close. It is no accident that several strands in Fichte's thinking bear close comparison with the ideas of such original pre-modern Japanese political philosophers as Yamazaki Ansai (1618–82) and Ogyū Sorai (1666–1728). It should also come as no surprise that Fichte has been an active presence in the writings of some of the more influential Japanese nationalist ideologues, reflecting the anti-Enlightenment patina that these intellectuals give to their widely read polemics.

The role of the state emerged only slowly in Fichte's thinking. A crucial turning point was the publication of *The Closed Commercial State* (1800) and *Characteristics of the Present Age* (1806) where Fichte called for greater national economic self-sufficiency, for the vigorous central control of trade, a closely managed public policy, and full mobilization of his country's resources for concerted collective action in the pursuit of national goals.

Shocked by the collapse of Prussian arms at Jena, Fichte issued his *Addresses to the German Nation* (1807–8), where he set forth the organic character of the nation in which the individual will find 'his own extended self'. His fierce commitment to *realpolitik* appears in later essays, but it must be stressed that the emphasis on the contest of civilization and the stark realism of his pronouncements on power are better understood not as a departure from Christian morality and human decency but rather as a submission to the realities of how the world is.

Like Machiavelli's, it is Fichte's unflinching realism that unnerves the Enlightened moralist. For the German nationalist, the world was a palpably dangerous place, where neglect of the sciences of war and administration risked the destruction of the nation as a state. A morality that pretended that the world was otherwise was dangerous nonsense. German history – certainly the Prussian struggle to survive and expand in East Central Europe – offered repeated demonstrations of this sobering truth. Why this view of the world and its politics has exerted so profound an impact on East Asian thinking in general and Japanese thought in particular is a complex story, but the fact of this influence is beyond dispute.

The key policy innovations of nineteenth-century Prussia (and, after 1871, the German empire) both reflected this new spirit and deepened its impact. First, there were the Stein reforms (the famous 'revolution from above') in the immediate wake of the Jena debacle. Serfdom was abolished, local self-government resuscitated, trade and industry restrictions eased and universal military service instituted. Wilhelm von Humboldt organized a common school system for the state. The University of Berlin was created. All these reforms have precise equivalents in the Meiji programme of nation-building. Only in the field of local government did Japan's centralizers pursue another course.

In reforming the civil service, Stein emphasized the need for decentralization, popular consultation and the reorganization of the government's central structures. Before Napoleon forced his dismissal in November 1808, Stein had outlined a proposal for replacing the King's cabinet by a council of department heads to formulate general policy. Stein also advocated a single Treasury. But many of these reforms were stillborn or quickly reversed (just as compulsory military service was abandoned). Thirty years later, Stein's complaints about the inefficiency of old bureaucratic structures would be echoed by Bismarck in his 1839 *Referendar*. Nevertheless, Stein's ideas had impact. In the hands of Frederick William III, Stein's proposals for cabinet reform contributed to the rise of a new and formidable concentration of policymaking initiative and power: the modern German chancellorship.

The second policy landmark of the post-Jena German mind was the creation of the Prussian customs union. This is how Professor Tsuruta Toshimasa of Senshu University sets out Prussia's problem after the overthrow of Napoleon in *Sengo Nihon no Sangyō Seisaku* (Industrial Policy in Post-war Japan):

> The customs union inaugurated by Germany in the 1830s was designed to encourage the development of domestic manufacturing so as to enable Germany as a late developer to resist the more advanced British. The issue of a national tariff had become the central question of trade policy from the time of Napoleon's embargo on British goods through his 'Continental system' (1806). The adoption of protectionist policies, via a customs union, was crucial to building a national economy. This was particularly true because German industrialization had to be carried out in the face of Britain's overwhelming competitive advantage in manufacturing.[16]

In seeking new policies, the disunited states that composed the residue of the Holy Roman Empire (minus Austria) were motivated by their country's unfavourable trade position. By adopting protectionist policies the larger states of Continental Europe had shut out competitive German imports. At the same time, the disunited Germans, lacking a common trade policy, were exposed to the full competitive weight of their neighbours. The German market was, in modern parlance, entirely 'open' or 'liberalized'. Without protectionist policies, German industrialists knew that they would never be able to overtake their foreign competitors, particularly the British. On the other hand, the German commercial sector benefited strongly from the freedom to import.

The conflict between protection-minded industrialists and liberal commercial interests defined the battle over trade policy in Germany during the early and mid-nineteenth century. In reviewing this battle of interests, Tsuruta compares it with what he sees as an analogous struggle in post-war Japan between domestic car makers, who benefited from trade protectionism, and distributors of foreign-made automobiles, who called for open markets.

The lack of a parallel case in the post-war commercial history of the United States is striking. It is the American commercial sector that has benefited from open markets for imports into the US, and it is American manufacturers, particularly auto makers, who have suffered. What is striking about the US car industry is how half-hearted and ineffective their campaign for protectionist policies (informal import quotas and the like) has been. Protectionist-minded manufacturers in nineteenth-century Germany and Japan from the 1930s used import barriers to build and maintain competitive industries capable of capturing foreign markets. In this crusade, German manufacturers never took their eyes off the British; the Japanese have always kept Detroit in their sights.

By contrast, the American car industry has been relatively indifferent to foreign competition, and has abandoned markets both at home and abroad largely without a fight. German and Japanese manufacturers welcome this lack of competitive drive, but find it incomprehensible. No economic nationalist would dream of surrendering so easily to foreign competition. This is how Tsuruta summarizes the key lesson his country's policymakers and industrialists would draw from the experience of nineteenth-century Germany:

> Drawing on the experience of the 1818 Prussian tariff law, the German Customs Union was brought into effect in 1834. The impact of this legislation was promptly felt, and from the latter half of the 1830s German industrialization proceeded at a rapid pace. By the early 1860s, the customs union covered a wide territory (all of Germany outside the old free towns of the Hansa). The result was that by the beginning of the 1870s Germany had managed to transform herself from a net importer of heavy manufactures to a net exporter, and this revolution was achieved despite the continuing domination by the British of the international division of economic labour that prevailed in the middle of the nineteenth century.[17]

Reviewing this success, liberal market economists would be keen to point out the 'costs' of this policy achievement. The question of costs and other criticisms of industrial policy are addressed in Chapter Seven. But what such economists could not contest is the victory of this protectionist-minded drive to industrialize Germany. Such success stands at the heart of the Listian vision of national economics.

International peace was the defining condition of nineteenth-century Europe after Napoleon and of nineteenth-century Japan before its late Meiji adventures abroad, but war has dominated the landscape of the 'blood-dimmed tide' of global politics in the twentieth century. Bismarck's three wars of national unification – against Denmark in 1864, against Austria in 1866, and against France in 1870–1 – formed an essential part of the Prussian and German drives towards international greatness.

The military-bureaucratic traditions of the Hohenzollern monarchy before Jena, the Stein reforms afterwards, the growth and conscious fostering of a German nationalist spirit (drawing on Herder and Fichte), the creation of a Prussian and then a German customs union, which in turn resulted in the creation of Europe's most formidable heavy industrial complex, all contributed to the growth of German imperial power. This complex web of foreign and domestic policies makes it implausible to define the meaning of the term 'public policy' too tightly.

Indeed, it was Bismarck who taught the modern policymaker, in Japan and elsewhere, that welfare policy is not an innocuous domestic concern. This is how Kent Calder summarizes nineteenth-century German social policy in *Crisis and Compensation: Public Policy and Political Stability in Japan, 1949–1986:*

> For Bismarck, preemptive conservative reform was an explicit "carrot and the stick" policy, conceived largely in material terms. It involved systematically adopting popular elements of the opposition socialist program in an attempt to undercut the socialist political movement itself and to generate popular support for political measures aimed ultimately at repressing the socialists themselves. After attempting to severely circumscribe the Social Democrats in 1875 and 1878, Bismarck suddenly proposed a comprehensive state welfare program, the first of its kind in the world. In April 1881 he proposed establishing an Imperial Insurance Office to insure against accidents all workers in mines and factories with incomes under 2,000 marks a year. The Sickness Insurance Law of 1883, the Accident Insurance Law of 1884, and the Old Age and Invalidity Law of 1887 were all enacted during Bismarck's chancellorship. Later, in 1911, these acts were unified into a great social insurance code which set a standard for the world.[18]

It is not surprising that when Meiji Japan sent missions to the West to seek answers to the pressing questions raised by the threat of colonialization and the policy conundrums generated by modernization on Western principles, leaders such as Itō Hirobumi chose Germany. The choice says as much about the national ethos and ideology of Meiji Japan as it does about Bismarck's Germany, but this nationalist dimension must be taken to heart by anyone who would grasp the spirit and dynamic at work in Japan's drive to economic greatness both before and after 1945.

11   Making history

Japan's grand narrative and the policymaker

HISTORY AS MYTH

History is more than a chronology. It is the story that gives historical dates meaning. After decades of dismissive abuse by professional historians anxious to promote drier, more scientific genres, narrative has today regained some of its old appeal. With the educated reader, including bureaucrats, narration has never been out of favour. Postmodern theorists such as Jean-François Lyotard have scrutinized the influence of great stories or narratives. They call these grand narratives '*récits*', and believe that they serve society as legitimating myths. The epic struggle for human liberation and equality, from the Enlightenment's critique of the *ancien régime* to contemporary feminism, is, in their view, one such narrative. Frederic Jameson, the American Marxist, argues that two grand *récits* are 'disengaged' by Lyotard in *The Postmodern Condition: A Report on Knowledge*, and both have served as justifications for 'institutional scientific research' down to the present.[1]

> The first – political, militant, activist – is of course the tradition of the French eighteenth century and the French Revolution, a tradition for which philosophy is already politics and in which Lyotard must himself clearly be ranged. The second is of course the Germanic and Hegelian tradition – a contemplative one, organized around the value of totality rather than that of commitment, and a tradition to which Lyotard's philosophical adversary, Habermas, still – however distantly – remains affiliated.[2]

Another *récit* is active in the celebration of modern technology, a transforming myth in which the scientific quest to subdue nature is laced with utopian promise. The engaged ecologist is moved by the counter-myth. Such grand narratives may fool society about its origins and disguise flaws, but they also allow it to get on with the business of being human. This is what myth means.

The grand narrative of modern Japanese nationalism is out of step with all these essentially Western *récits*. This condition may help to explain Japan's curious orphan status in modern global sensibility. The exclusive nationalist thrust of Japan's heroic struggle to achieve economic ascendancy provides higher bureaucrats with one of their principal motivations, and one that the Western *récit* of liberation has yet to overthrow. The provocative nationalist gloss that Japanese commentators and intellectuals give the vision of a technological utopia may be the exception that proves the rule.

The epic of bureaucratic-driven and corporate-sustained national ambition, as a narrative archetype, serves as one of the psychological sources of official resistance to Western campaigns to normalize or liberalize Japan. Such foreign pressure, or *gaiatsu*, would undermine this *récit*, this way of looking at one's past and feeling honourable, while offering nothing satisfyingly Japanese in its place. One can imagine the response of Americans if some foreign power demanded that they collectively abandon 'the pursuit of happiness'.

This *récit* is a significant feature of the public memory which informs Japanese policymaking, especially in the economic sphere. There are other, amythical, strata which influence this grand narrative and in turn are coloured by it. Thus, with a broad brush, it is possible to paint a picture of the major changes in the Japanese economy since the Meiji Restoration in a manner that even a non-Japanese will find convincing and objective. But the *récit* is always there. Myth nibbles at the margins of the driest documents, even the official and scientific. This is what distinguishes much native analysis of Japan's economy from that of Westerners.

THE BROAD BRUSH OF ECONOMIC CHANGE

Between 1868 and 1941 the Japanese economy experienced three important phases. First, there was a period of consolidation and structural modernization, with agriculture paying for the foundation of a modern transport system, the main costs of creating the Meiji state when the foundations of Japanese manufacturing, including heavy industry, were laid. This period lasted roughly from the Meiji Restoration to the Russo-Japanese War (1904–5). The second phase was one of disturbed progress. The strains of modern capitalism began to show in Japanese society as it moved through the boom and bust generated by the First World War, in which Japan was an important supplier of goods to the Allies as well as a minor participant. Textiles emerged as a key Japanese export, but persistent problems beset Japanese agriculture during the 1920s.

The third phase, from the invasion of Manchuria (1931) to Pearl Harbor (1941), is in many ways the most important for the student of Japanese public policy. Japan was hit hard by the Great Depression, and again agriculture suffered the greatest dislocations. This was an era when the tragedy of the rural poor impressed itself yet again on national consciousness. Even now the period is recalled as one of poverty so desperate that Tōhoku farmers sold their daughters into service and rural discontent fuelled a violent radicalism that destroyed the liberal hopes of 'Taishō democracy'. But this was not the whole story. Even during this early period of difficulty, the grand narrative of modern Japanese history was taking shape. The foundations for an economic miracle were being laid.

In the 1930s Japan began to undertake one of the most important twentieth-century experiments in state-driven change. The Japanese economy grew at 5 per cent per annum. Japan was engaged in an expansionist struggle on the Asian mainland as well as the indust-rialization of Manchuria. The nation underwent a significant shift in economic structure, with industry steadily gaining ground from the still large agricultural sector. By the time Japan went to war with the United States and Britain, factory output stood at 30 per cent of gross domestic product, the farm labour force had shrunk to around 40 per cent, and capital formation had reached 20 per cent of GNP. This suggests a need to rethink Karl Popper's classic contrast between 'open' and 'closed' societies. Japan in the 1930s witnessed simultaneously ever tighter constraints on civil liberties while benefiting from the economic vitality of an open society. But the larger story was that of national success.

True, the war was a catastrophe for Japan, but not a total one. Japan's grand narrative showed remarkable resilience. Historians writing about the war have tended to overstate the importance of the destruction of perhaps 25 per cent of Japan's capital stock. Much survived, but far more important the huge pre-war investment in human capital – skills and training – was there to be exploited in rebuilding the nation. Policy tools, including Keynesian demand-led growth, had been tried and found effective. From the ashes of war rose a nation hungry and anxious to rebuild and an elite united by an unprecedented consensus on Japan's future course. From this hunger and this consensus, an economic miracle would be born. Japan's post-war expansion unfolded in five stages: post-war reconstruction, economic take-off, high-speed growth, the two oil shocks, and economic ascendancy.

Post-war reconstruction, 1945–53

The period of post-war reconstruction lasted from the end of World War Two until the end of the Korean conflict. The dislocations of the war had been severe. Japan was bankrupt and under foreign occupation. Some planning for post-war recovery had begun during the war and the potential of the nation remained great, but the burdens on the economy were daunting. American aid and loans helped to keep Japan from starvation, but shortages of capital and resources forced the introduction of 'priority production', sometimes called 'graded production', policies which consciously favoured basic industries, such as coal, a temporary measure which encouraged the translation of wartime policies into peacetime practice. The 'Dodge line', named for Joseph Dodge, the American economic 'adviser' to the Japan government, enforced a sharp bout of deflation, which helped to discipline expenditure and stimulate investment.

The Dodge line is one of the first examples of post-war policymaking which could be misconstrued by the free-marketeer trained in Anglo-American economic principles. On the face of it, the Dodge line was a straightforward application of liberal economic orthodoxy. But its impact on particularly Japanese ways of doing business and making policy (Japanese attitudes towards corporate rationalization, for example) was subtle and not consistent with free-market principles. The Dodge line was an early example of an extended list of economic phenomena and state measures that have made Japan appear to be more Western, more economically liberal, than it is. At the same time, this list has obscured much that departs sharply from orthodox Anglo-American practice. Many of the key features of Japanese post-war economic policy constitute an intellectual conundrum. This is not true of the other great reforms of the American Occupation, including land reform and the break-up of the zaibatsu; nor, for that matter, the stimulating effect of heavy American procurements during the war in nearby Korea.

Economic take-off, 1954–61

It is a convention of economic writing about this period to see it as the initial phase of the era of high-speed growth (*kōdo seichō*) that followed. This is wisdom after the event. It was an anxious period, especially in the minds of policymakers. The worst of post-war exigencies had been overcome, and indeed, by 1952 consumption had returned to pre-war levels, but there were residual problems, especially after the ending of the

Occupation and the Korean war. Balance-of-payments difficulties ensued. A major realignment of political parties occurred in 1955, including the launching of the Liberal Democratic Party (LDP) which has governed ever since. Party politics were more turbulent during this period than at any time during the post-war era. It was an age of uncertainty, and it was not until 1956 that the Economic Planning Agency acknowledged that the post-war era was over. It was only in retrospect that the period between 1952 and 1960 acquired its character as a time of crucial transition.

High-speed growth, 1962–72

Two decade-long plans are remembered with special attention by the policymakers who experienced the 1960s. One is President John Kennedy's pledge to land an American on the moon by the end of the decade. This bold target was achieved, and represented a remarkable success for a nation that prides itself on its ideological resistance to state enterprise and to state planning. Yet the NASA project was a triumph for both.

The other is the plan of Japanese Prime Minister Ikeda Hayato to double the income of the average Japanese before the 1960s were over. This, too, was achieved. This epoch in Japanese economic growth is recalled by many Japanese as an undreamt golden age, and it was an astonishing national success. Under the aegis of the 'Ten Year Income-Doubling Plan of 1961–70', the ratio of investment to national income and the share of this investment poured into private industry climbed to levels previously unseen in Japan. Indeed, growth accelerated so forcefully that not even the 'Nixon shock' – the Nixon administration's decision in 1971 simultaneously to sever the dollar's link with gold, to devalue the US currency and to impose a surprise 10 per cent surcharge on Japanese exports to this largest of all Japanese overseas markets – could halt it. Only the great oil shock of 1973 brought this extraordinary period of rapid Japanese growth to a close.

Some day America's lunar conquest may reduce that country's current financial problems, like those of Queen Isabella I, Columbus's patron, to a footnote of history, but a quarter of a century after two very different nations achieved two very different objectives, it is the Japanese success which today appears to be the more consequential.

The two oil shocks, 1973–81

The Yom Kippur War (1973) signalled the revival of the Middle East's claim to the title of the world's most troublesome region. The oil embargo and the rise of the Organization of Oil-Exporting Countries (OPEC) that it helped to engender brought to an end the long post-war era of cheap energy and easy growth which had underwritten the expansion of mass consumer democracies in Japan, Western Europe and North America.

Japan was shaken by this oil shock, and the term itself is a translation from the Japanese. Between 1974 and 1979, Japan's growth rate was barely half that achieved during her dash for growth between 1967 and 1972. The index of industrial production actually fell in 1973 after years of astonishing advance. The 1972 figure was not matched until 1978. Manufacturing ceased to be the cutting edge of Japanese growth.

However bad things were in Japan, everywhere else in the advanced capitalist world they were much worse. The massive expansion of the Japanese economy up to 1973–4, and the relatively high rates of growth (vis-à-vis its competitors) that Japan sustained throughout the 1970s helped to ensure that the LDP, which had a become a high-spending welfare-minded political party during the 1970s, did not suffer the decline that affected so many Western social democractic parties, including the Labour Party in Britain and the Democratic Party in the USA. The LDP's redistributive bias survived even the second oil shock (1978–81) that broke for a decade the claim of left-wing parties, however moderate, to be the natural parties of government. It was from this period that Japan began to emerge as the world's most successful economy. But much of Japan's new reputation was the result of comparison with faltering economies elsewhere.

Economic ascendancy, 1982–93

This decade saw Japan achieve a long-desired ambition. It was the decade when Western economic and business commentators with no particular interest in Asia began to acknowledge the fact that Japan was the world's premier manufacturing, financial and commercial power. The decade was characterized by a whole set of important economic developments – liberalization, internationalization, 'big bang' and sky-rocketing boom and bust – but Japan's emergence to the first rank of economic powers was a historic achievement. No fact of the 1980s merits greater emphasis.

The huge capital flows that the liberalizing of world bourses encouraged was perhaps the economic development with the greatest short-term global impact during this period. But Japan's relationship with the international community offered a foretaste of her new influence. The achievements of the 1980s, in high technology, in the acquisition of major capital assets abroad, in direct capital investment, in the rise of a yen bloc in East Asia, in Japan's new status at the centres of international decision-making, marked the return of Asia to the forefront of economic progress for the first time since Europe burst onto the global scene during the Age of Exploration. The 1980s saw Japan accepting the kind of social changes, in declining work hours and greater expenditure on leisure, which had transformed social life in other advanced industrial countries decades before, but with one important difference: Japan could now afford them. The lessons for the student of public policymaking could scarcely be plainer. As the millenium draws to its close – and the year 2000 is the one year in the Christian calendar which obsesses the Japanese policymaker – the advent of the 'Japanese century' may be upon us.[3] The Japanese have learned how to make history.

PROUSTIAN POLITICS

Grand narratives unite the elite and the mass of a country's population. More often it is the next milestone that defines the arrival of the future in the life of the ordinary man or woman, while the long-term planner sees years, decades and even centuries ahead. What is true of the future is even more so of the past. Public opinion surveys of advanced industrial democracies – North America, Western Europe, Japan, and Australia – demonstrate that the average voter has an extremely short memory of 'headline' events. The American 'spin manager' and his counterpart elsewhere recognize this when they plan election campaigns and policy statements. But a nation's *récit*, like the grand narratives of ecological pessimism or human liberation, uniquely mediates reality and identity, and this makes *récits* a crucial form of public consciousness.

The elites themselves are often prisoners of historical awareness. Old buildings and ancient rituals tend to reinforce this past that is a present. When senior ministers of the Japanese government, for example, meet in the cabinet room at the prime minister's residence they sit around a table in an arrangement that reflects pre-war precedent among Japanese ministries. Even the seating plan and the order in which they speak is directly influenced by the former status of the once formidable Home Ministry (*Naimushō*), Japan's version of the powerful interior ministries of Continental Europe. This arm of the Japanese bureaucracy was abolished in 1947. In contrast with the amnesia of current schooling practice and modern sensibility, the professional political animal, in Japan or elsewhere, is a firm historicist. But grand narratives overcome this gap. They ensure that almost everyone, not just policymakers, feels part of a great shared drama acting out in time. Like Proust, the public mind is dominated by the remembrance of things past.

What do Japanese policymakers remember? The longest memories in Japanese government are no doubt found at the Imperial Household Agency (*Kunaichō*) where officials see themselves as responsible for the dignity of an ancient imperial house and its millennial past. But for the policymaker, particularly the nationalist, at the genuine centres of power, there is one continuing period that overshadows the mundane ambitions and concerns of workaday planning and policy execution, especially in any branch of the Japanese civil service with a responsibility for the internationally traded sector of the Japanese economy.

This chronological line begins with the arrival of the US fleet under Admiral Perry in 1853, which forced the end of Japan's self-imposed isolation from the rest of the world, and it stretches unbroken towards the day when Japan will be able to boast the largest GNP in the world. Along this line certain years are circled to indicate when old rivals were overtaken: Canada (1960), France and Britain (the mid-1960s), West Germany (1968), the Soviet Union (officially 1991, in fact much earlier). Only the gap with the United States remains to be closed. True, if the populations of the two nations were the same, Japan would have already won the prize because its per capita output has been higher since the late 1980s.

But to overtake America will be a tremendous undertaking. It means achieving a Japanese per capita output more than double that of the US whose population is more than twice that of Japan and growing rapidly. This achievement, in twenty years or fifty, will cancel, in the minds of those with long memories, the humiliation of 1853 and Perry's black ships. More important still, it will affect another key year in the nationalist's chronology of the past: 1945, the year of national defeat and shame at the hands of the Americans. Such is the stamina of institutional memory that this goal, the object of diminishing excitement among the Japanese electorate and perhaps even the workforce, remains evergreen among the old guard of Japanese civil servants and opinion leaders. Why else would the editors of *Tōyō Keizai*, the influential economic weekly, commemorate the publication of the magazine's 5,000th issue on 8 June 1991 with a cover story: 'The Day [our] GNP becomes the world's largest'? The year 2010 was the suggested date. How could Japanese perceptions be otherwise when catching up with the West has been a Japanese national goal for so long? One needs only to recall that the Japanese cry 'Overtake Europe and America!' (*Ōbei ni oikose*) is a slogan of the Meiji era (1868–1912).

The beginning of the Meiji era, the year 1868 in the Western calendar (traditional Japan had its own chronologies based on imperial reigns), is the key year of early modern history in the memory of all Japanese, including their politicians and officials. It was the year, Japanese Marxists and nationalists agree, when the old feudal order, and the last Tokugawa shogun who presided over it, were overthrown. That year marks the official launch of Japan's modernization drive and the beginning of Japan's active return to world politics. But the nature of the Meiji regime, its goals and ambitions, is a matter of dispute, and in ways that affect the chronology of the policymaker. Was the Meiji objective truly to catch up with or to overtake the West? Given the backward state of Meiji Japan by the most advanced standards of contemporary Europe, '*Ōbei ni oikose*' was for many Japanese little more than a bit of idle phrase-making, consistent with the Confucian tradition throughout East Asia of rousing calls and stern admonishments.

The question of 'overtake' or 'catch up with' has recently become an issue of importance in Western writing about Japan. It is of particular consequence in the debate over whether Japan should surrender to Anglo-American economic 'normality'. In *Japan's Unequal Trade*, Edward J. Lincoln of the Brookings Institution insists that the main goal of Japanese public policy in the traded sector has been to catch up with the West rather than to overtake it.[4] If he has misread Japanese intentions, then all his policy recommendations suffer because they are based on a false premise.

If Japan's goal was only to match the best Western practice, then Japanese policymakers have achieved this objective and it is time for them (in the view of Lincoln and many other Anglo-American economists) to dismantle the institutions and to dilute the nationalist values that were indispensable to this crusade. The term 'economic maturity' applied to Japan carries this message. Having caught up, it is safe for Japan to 'normalize', or be normalized under foreign pressure, particularly from the United States. That it is taking foreign pressure to make Japan change has been a consistent theme of her interaction with the Western world for the past century and a half. This condition has ensured that *gaiatsu* is less a concept than a kind of shorthand for characterizing the unfriendly and uncompromising nature of the real world. This phenomenon, as reflected in this cliché of Japanese reporting and commentary, has left its scars on contemporary sensibility, and nowhere more strongly than on the policymaker.

Thus, in the popular Japanese mind, memories of previous episodes of *gaiatsu* are imprecise because routine: they are a recurring feature of their country's interaction with the global community. In contrast, memories of past examples of foreign pressure in the bureaucratic world are precise, but the elite response is more ambiguous than that of the public because foreign pressure occasionally has its domestic uses. The Bush administration's demands for 'opening Japanese markets' and EC calls for its own version of the American Structural Impediments Initiative (SII), both policies designed to alleviate the trade imbalance between Japan and its main Western trading partners, remind the Japanese of Perry's 1853 intrusion and the whole painful era of imperialist bullying before and after the Meiji Restoration.

But more important, if the goal of Japanese national ambitions remains unrivalled economic supremacy, then foreign demands for liberalization and the dismantling of Japan's growth machine take on a very different meaning. In this sense, foreign insistence that Japan has now caught up with the West and therefore must change misses the point. Western critics would dismantle Japan's GNP machine before the goal has been reached.

Which chronology defines Japanese ambition? In 1889, Takahashi Korekiyo, one of the great figures of pre-war Japanese politics and author of the country's Keynesian-style 1930s recovery, delivered a farewell address to the students of Tokyo Agricultural College. In his speech he called on the students to rise to the challenge that history had presented them:

> Gentlemen, it is your duty to advance the status of Japan, bring her to a position of equality with the civilized powers and then carry on to build a foundation from which we shall surpass them all.[5]

This is not a Keynesian sentiment. The century-long rise of Japanese power that links Takahashi's pregnant vision with the present suggests a marvellous continuity of national purpose. The mind of a nation, it appears, is what it remembers.

Theories and controversies

12 The revolutionary 1980s and the rise of Japanese public policy studies

We are now at a watershed in the Western understanding of the Japanese political system. If twenty years ago an American Marxist could warn of a 'coming crisis' in Western sociology, now the study of Japanese government and politics by scholars working in Europe, North America and Australia may be on the verge of a critical transition. To adopt a complex notion from two masters of modern thought – Freud and Althusser – this intellectual crisis is 'overdetermined'. It is the consequence of so many powerful factors as to be almost irresistible. Ivory towerism may define other branches of political science, but today the whole world seems to be knocking at the door of the Japan specialist. Quite simply, Japan's new place in the world is not only pressing on the concerns but also altering the status of the expert on this Oriental society. Nowhere is this more true than in the political science of Japan.

TWO SCHOOLS

The resulting *engagement* (a choice but also a response to an unwilled situation) with the outer community has left its mark. During the 1980s, it fuelled a set of creative divisions that in turn have profoundly influenced the character of the Western study of Japanese politics, particularly in the United States. This process has transformed the discipline's most rooted assumptions and approaches: a paradigm (in the Kuhnian sense)[1] has been metamorphosed.

Looking back now, it appears that the struggles of the 1980s were nothing less than the birth pangs of a new academic field: Japanese public policy studies. A decade of substantial growth in the secondary literature on public policy in Japan has made this subject, together with party politics, one of the two pillars of the political science of Japan as practised in the West. This intellectual restructuring of the discipline has in turn redefined the special niche that has been traditionally reserved for the study of Japanese foreign policy.

This is, however, a retrospective assessment. To understand this creative epoch in the light only of its chief consequence would be to impose a false teleology on this episode of development and change. This would not only be specious history, but it would be seriously to misinterpret what happened in the 1980s. Two propositions must be stated clearly from the outset. One is that the second oil crisis (1979–80) marked a turning point in the Western study of this Oriental polity. The second, certainly an unintended outcome, is that the process which gave birth to Japanese public policy studies during the 1980s has not only bestowed on this field its creative edge, its unusually controversial patina and zest, but also helped to recast the discipline of the political science of Japan as a whole.

One result is that, from the late 1970s, Western researchers have increasingly divided into two camps: the scholars who have studied Japan 'because it is there' (the 'Everest-ites') and those who work on Japan because it is important (the 'miracle men'). The harvest of evidence, the sifting of fact, the construction of the hard-won generalization, are cardinal moves in the labour of love that is involved in discovering merely 'what is there'. Having sampled the achievements of a generation of scholars who have made Japan their Everest, only a hidebound behaviouralist would continue to insist that the description and analysis of political institutions, both their past evolution and contemporary function, are either secondary or simple.

To this dance of fact the student of national miracles would marry the adventure of ideas. The meteoric rise of Japan to the rank of economic superpower constitutes one of the most extraordinary developments in the history of modern Asia. As a political phenomenon, it challenges some of the best established assumptions of the Western mind. Explaining Japan's post-war miracle, a phenomenon at once political and economic, is now one of the key problems of the age.

This distinction between Everest-ites and miracle men can be restated in another way. Although perfectly aware of Japan's success in the economic sphere, Everest-ites felt no need to alter in any significant way the kind of questions that they asked about the workings of Japanese government in response to this era of high-speed growth or its powerful aftermath. Japan's growing importance in world economic affairs meant more readers for the scholarship of Everest-ites, but it did not force any revolution in how such scholars characterized the regime as a polity. For miracle men, on the other hand, explaining Japan's success became the question of the hour. It opened up a vast new vista of research, although this perception appears to have dawned only later, and subtly challenged the then ruling concern with party politics and Cold War diplomacy. A schism, at once intellectually bracing and divisive, was at hand.

A conflicting pair of strongly held views within the same household is, however, an unlikely recipe for domestic harmony. But, like the creative tension that exists between Stanford and Berkeley, located as they are within shouting distance of one another, this divide between political scientists has been fruitful. One may go further and argue that both camps were and remain essential, indeed finally complementary. Political scientists working before 1980 will be criticized from time to time for their apparent neglect of the political dimension of the Japanese miracle; but what is also clear is that, since 1980, the discipline has reordered its priorities and entered one of the most fruitful periods in its history.

It may also be recognized that the schism between Everest-ites and miracle men has been anything but neat. A productive ambivalence has resulted, sometimes in the mind of the same scholar. Princeton Professor Kent E. Calder is an excellent example. Having written *The Eastasia Edge*, a provocative miracle man tract in 1981, he went on to tackle some of the most central Everest-ite themes seven years later in *Crisis and Compensation: Public Policy and Political Stability in Japan, 1949–1986* (1988).[2]

In spite of this example, despite the fact that the thoughtful scholar's sympathies will be engaged by both camps, and indeed notwithstanding the notion – sensible in theory – that these two approaches should make perfect bedfellows, the truth of the matter appears to be otherwise. It now seems safe to conclude that the decision to opt decisively for one perspective or the other has in turn generated some of the most incisive work in the contemporary study of Japanese government.

The choice has been sharp. To paraphrase the Greek poet Archilochus, the fox (the Everest-ite) wants to know many things, but the hedgehog (the miracle man) wants to know just one big thing: How has Japan succeeded? Nowhere are the consequences of this choice more evident than in the key question: Where does power lie within the Japanese polity? Ever mindful of the big picture, Everest-ites tend to see Japan as pluralist and not subject to decisive influence from the country's elite alliance of the central bureaucracy, the ruling party and the largest of established firms. Defined in this way, Japanese politics provides a large and ever-altering field for political research. This points up a significant contrast with the miracle man's more narrow, and sometimes static, concentration on Japan's ruling establishment.

To such open-ended empiricism, the Everest-ite will often apply a democratic twist. In the tradition of James Madison, the Everest-ite will tend to see the vitality of grass-root or interest-group politics as a barometer of the health of the entire political system. This in turn leads to another perennial Everest-ite question: Just how sturdy is Japanese democracy? Miracle men have tended to view the phenomenon of interest politics in a different light. Given that 'all politics are local', the miracle school has sought to learn how the Japanese elite has managed to insulate the strategic sectors of public policy from the ravages of pork-barrel politics and politicians. Differing objectives have meant different objects of research. Miracle men tend to study the Japanese bureaucracy; Everest-ites, Japan's Diet or parliament.

The best known work of the miracle school is Ezra Vogel's *Japan as Number One*.[3] In *MITI and the Japanese Miracle*, Chalmers Johnson provided this school's most consequential meditation on why the Japanese example is important *politically* by explaining the bureaucratic sources of its economic success.[4] The most sober formulation of the Everest-ite or pluralist perspective is almost certainly Arthur Stockwin's *Japan: Divided Politics in a Growth Economy*, a textbook soon to appear in its third edition.[5] More recently, the Oxford–Australia school, of which Stockwin is the leader, has updated its pluralist interpretation and broadened it to include policy issues in *Dynamic and Immobilist Politics in Japan*.[6]

To repeat: the nub of the problem is the resultant 'creative ambivalence'. Both words matter. Once Japan had ceased to be a military threat after the last war, then the study of that nation could proceed as if it were any other middling power. There could be retrospective analyses of 'what went wrong', but by and large the formal study of Japan could proceed according to its own lights, and academically evolved paradigms, despite the often intense ideological contentiousness of the era. The result was 'normal science' in a rather stronger sense than Thomas Kuhn argued in *The Structures of Scientific Revolutions*.[7]

Two series of events outside the academy changed this. First, Japan moved from strength to strength in the economic field. Second, the Western world entered into a period of relative decline and internal tension. The fact that Japanese economic competition exacerbated the Western problem made the question still more vexed. The process was further complicated by a series of extraordinary academic defections. Robert Bellah, the distinguished student of Edo society, turned from Japan to the religious sources of America's social crisis. Ronald Dore refocused his attention on the causes of British economic feebleness. Ezra Vogel began to diagnose US industrial weakness in the light of Japanese success.

Initially the new orientation was dismissed as trendy journalism or worse. But a set of influential monographs – in some cases, classics – including Johnson's *MITI and the Japanese Miracle* (1982), T. J. Pempel's *Policy and Politics in Japan* (1982),[8] Vogel's *Comeback* (1985),[9] Dore's *Flexible Rigidities* (1986)[10] and *Taking Japan Seriously* (1987)[11] – transformed the debate in Japanese political science from within and from without. Just as explaining British economic decline was the central pre-Thatcherite theme in British studies, the dissection of Japan's economic advance, including the full range of its consequences, for better or worse, emerged during the 1980s as the focal concern of Japanese studies. This shift was complicated by a trade-off, often unwelcome, between interested and disinterested scholarship, or in the view of some critics of academe, between interesting scholarship and pedantry.

It also put strong pressure on the existing distribution of labour among Japanese specialists. Increasingly, the boundary between political science and economics began to resemble the porous and often contentious divide that distinguishes scholars in business studies from economists. The example of Peter Drucker's treatment of Japan in his extensive writings and the vigorous dissent from economists against his views comes to mind.

The new influence of the miracle or industrial policy or statist school was resisted in some circles. Kent Calder's *Crisis and Compensation* was the most ambitious attempt to combat what he believes is the new miracle-school bias in recent studies of Japanese politics. His counter-critique was provocative in its insistence that Japan's economic weakness, an old Everest-ite theme, as well as its political instability, a more ticklish notion, be made the chief themes of Western research on that country. But Calder's complaints about the miracle-school bias aside, his own massive study further accelerated the rapid growth of interest in public policy studies among Western students of Japanese government.

One result should be obvious. In Japanese government and politics, public policy issues, under a variety of guises, have been the flavour of the month for a decade now. No topic in the field has generated more expert comment or intellectual excitement in recent times than industrial policy, particularly the role of the Ministry of International Trade and Industry, or MITI, probably the most studied bureaucratic agency in the world. In 1988, Karl Boger's *Postwar Industrial Policy in Japan: An Annotated Bibliography* of English-language studies of the subject, very broadly defined, listed 520 publications.[12] Many more could be added to his list now.

At the end of the 1980s, four fine studies – Daniel Okimoto's *Between MITI and the Market: Japanese Industrial Policy for High Technology*, Richard J. Samuels' *The Business of the Japanese State: Energy Markets in Comparative and Historical Perspective*, Frances McCall Rosenbluth's *Financial Politics in Contemporary Japan* and *Politics and Productivity*, edited by Chalmers Johnson, Laura D'Andrea Tyson and John Zysman – helped to bring to ripe conclusion a decade of often brilliant Western analysis of the role played by public policy in Japan's rise to the status of economic superpower.[13] These books confirmed public policy, as a branch of learning, as one of the two central pillars of Japanese political science in the West. Only electoral politics can now sustain a claim to equal importance, and it is being increasingly recast in favour of public policy issues.

In turn, public policy research and the industrial policy question have fuelled sharp growth in the literature of the field. Okimoto's book, for example, should be seen as a vigorous attempt to bring intellectual order to a field increasingly buffeted by interpretational near-chaos and a flood-tide of fresh commentary and research. But even when a political scientist had doubts about the interpretations being argued, the energy and scope of the new studies were a source of scholarly pride. It all suggested that the political scientific study of Japan was at the door of an unprecedentedly golden age.

It must be observed, however, that the researcher's triumph had the makings of a pedagogic nightmare. When a student reads Chalmers Johnson, and then turns to Kent Calder, these two authorities appear to be talking about two different planets. Reconciling two unlikely stereotypes – Japan as either an omni-efficient economic superpower or a banana republic regularly tottering on the edge of political crisis – is of course impossible. It therefore appears to be the remarkable achievement of this battle of the monographs that it has made an academically sound, as well as parsimonious, description of contemporary Japanese political economy much more difficult, if not impossible.

Towards a synthesis

This premised impossibility stands at the heart of the contemporary intellectual crisis that now colours the Western science of Japanese government. If the finest fruits of the 'revolutionary 1980s' are to be harvested, then the central job confronting the political scientist of Japan today is one of synthesis, of putting our theoretical and empirical mansion, with its many chambers, in order.

Such a project should be rooted in the conviction that students, inside and outside the classroom, have the right to ask for a framework of ideas and interpretations upon which to build a sound understanding of how the Japanese polity works and how Japan has fostered the growth of its formidable powers as a nation. If the requisite economies of learning are to be ensured, then the academic paradigm – the set of values, assumptions, and privileged facts that provide researchers with their rubrics for study – must be made explicit, and capable of plain statement.

This is the 'crisis' that now threatens the teaching of Japanese political science. The only way forward lies in synthesis. Even an unhappy marriage of the Everest-ites and the miracle men would be preferable to an intellectual double-bind in the lecture hall. But between these two extreme views rests an ample *cordon sanitaire* from which a proper synthesis may be shaped.

It is central to the argument of this book that nationalism provides a framework for intellectual synthesis. This task demands that scholars reject the old Japan hand's love of paradox in describing this country's social make-up. Paradox in Japanese studies should be recognized for what it is: an admission of failure to think hard enough about the question.

The scholarly response to this condition has been varied and creative. Calder's recent study makes an imperative of theoretical parsimony. His premise is that muscular theorizing can curb empirical excess. In 'Japanese Interest Group Behaviour: an Institutional Approach', on the other hand, the Australian scholar Aurelia George would tame the dangers of theoretical protestantism ('every man a theoretician') with catholic empiricism: all solid empirical research programmes, even those with broad implications, are to be encouraged as long as they do not engage in heretical grand theory.[14]

But a synthesis between the Everest-ite and miracle schools will involve more than methodology. Scholars will need to recognize the importance of the central bureaucracy while remaining sensitive to the new vitalities of the periphery of Japanese political life, including local government. The importance of the Diet and the 1947 Constitution in public policymaking and elsewhere may be stressed without repeating the nineteenth-century legal scholar's mistake of confusing con-stitutional appearances for the substance of power and policymaking. Attention to the rise of the activist minister and the *zoku* phenomenon, two important topics, must not invite soft-peddling of the endemic corruption of the ruling party. Similarly, hopes for a more liberal Japan must not obscure the pernicious impact of 'peasant politics' (*hyakushō seiji*) that still scars national elections and state spending policies. Finally, miracle men must not demand that their special concern define all study of Japanese government, nor Everest-ites pretend that the Japanese miracle did not happen.

THE 'POLITICAL ECONOMY' QUESTION

All this reflects an attempt to solve the field's problems from within. But the new energies behind liberal market doctrine since the 1970s points to a different and, some would claim, far more powerful guarantee of theoretical parsimony and research success in recent studies of Japanese politics. For its proponents, the doctrine of economic individualism is contemporary social science's answer to 'Occam's razor'. There is no doubt that economic individualism reformulated into the dogma of market efficiency has had an impressive impact on other branches of political science, particularly in the English-speaking world; but the influence of this approach on the thinking of Western political scientists studying Japan has hitherto been limited.

The most eye-catching exception has been the growth of interest in research and reflection on 'the political economy of Japan'. In 1987 and 1988, a monumental two-volume collection of scholarly articles was published under the title *The Political Economy of Japan, Volume 1: The Domestic Transformation* (edited by Kozo Yamamura and Yasukichi Yasuba), and *Volume 2: The Changing International Context* (edited by Takashi Inoguchi and Daniel I. Okimoto).[15] Their findings were complemented by a wide-ranging set of academic articles compiled by Daniel I. Okimoto and Thomas P. Rohlen, *Inside the Japanese System: Readings on Contemporary Society and Political Economy*, which appeared in 1988.[16]

Even here, however, and this appears to be the case in the occasional cross-fence dialogues between students of Japanese government and economists who write about Japan, there has been, in effect, an agreement to disagree. How could it be otherwise when the over-whelming majority of economists studying Japan subscribed to the Smithian or Anglo-American school of '*kindai keizaigaku*' (modern or non-Marxist economics)? The differences in approach are profound, and probably unbridgeable.

Nevertheless, the liberal concepts of economic individualism and market efficiency claim to be theoretically strong. The influence of liberal market doctrine on political scientific discussion of public policy outside Japan has been so large as to force treatment of this perspective, despite the relative indifference with which it has been received among many experts on Japanese government proper. There is another view. Some mainstream economists insist that *The Political Economy of Japan* represents not a break with the 1970s research paradigm but merely a significant updating of the findings and approaches in *Asia's New Giant: How the Japanese Economy Works*, edited by Hugh Patrick and Henry Rosovsky, published in 1976.[17]

This conclusion is not convincing. Political science proper casts a small shadow on *Asia's New Giant*. Only one of the book's thirteen chapter titles includes the word 'politics', and this is in an article by Philip Trezise and Yukio Suzuki which contains the pregnant, because programmatic, remark that, 'To suppose, however, that politicians and officials in league with businessmen were able to plan and guide Japan's explosive growth in detail is neither credible in the abstract nor supported by the realities.'[18]

The use of the phrase 'in detail' is unctuous, some would say obscurant. More important, if Western political scientists had accepted the implied strictures (the whole page of argument in which this quotation is embedded must be read in full to grasp the import of the ideology that Trezise is defending), then the explosive growth in Japanese public policy studies during the 1980s would never have taken place.

Fortunately, political scientists took little or no notice of such economic dogma. One result is obvious. In contrast with *Asia's New Giant*, orthodox political science, in the Western sense, plays a prominent role in the analysis offered in the first two volumes of *The Political Economy of Japan*.

Another major difference between *Asia's New Giant* and *The Political Economy of Japan* is the conspicuous place occupied in the newer book by specifically Japanese-style assumptions and arguments about the workings of not only the modern Japanese state and economy but also its culture and society. In *Asia's New Giant*, the empirical data may be wholly Japanese but the analytic framework was almost entirely Anglo-American and narrowly positivist.

Rigorously probed, in the full light of the very different academic *Weltanschauung* or ideologically tinged worldviews at work in contemporary economics and political science, as practised in the West, the expression 'political economy' is fraught with difficulty. In the nineteenth century, the term referred to mainline post-Smithian economic positivism with a window-dressing of political concern. Take, for example, John Stuart Mill's *Principles of Political Economy* of 1848. After Alfred Marshall, strictly political scientific concerns were forced out of the political economic curriculum in Britain and America. The result is that a book such as *Modern Political Economy* by Richard B. McKenzie and Gordon Tullock is not about economics or politics but rather an introduction to one school of economic thought (positivism) parading as the whole, while seeking to poach, in an intellectually illegitimate way, on the territory of the student of government.[19]

Today, the term 'political economy', in its latest reincarnation, more frequently reflects a high-minded and well-meaning academic ecumenism, an agreement by political scientists and economists to speak politely of the opposing camp. But the fact remains that mainstream economics is a positive, mathematically-based science, and political science is an empirically word-based science. True, there exists a variety of middle positions which permit some useful dialogue, and it must be admitted that the editors of *The Political Economy of Japan* exploit this middle ground to the full, but the argument between Anglo-American economists and Euro-American political scientists must end in an agreement to disagree.

Fail to recognize this profound gap in scientific approach, remain deaf to the ideological implications at work on both sides, and the result will be intellectual confusion, often stimulating and suggestive, but confusion just the same. Courses about Japan jointly taught by economists and political scientists must be recognized for what they are: bold in the extreme.

This question underscores the importance of Okimoto's 1989 study, *Between MITI and the Market: Industrial Policy for High Technology.*[20] He uses classic liberal market theory to deflect errant views which intrude on his model-building. There is little question that Okimoto has turned to market theory because of its evident power. Nevertheless, and this is crucial, Okimoto rejects the notion that market theory provides the only respectable framework for explaining how public policy works.

Three issues are involved here. First, there is the considerable scepticism or lack of interest among experts on Japanese government concerning the claims of liberal market theory and therefore about the influence of the advocates of such theory on other branches of political science. Second, there is a pervasive sense that market theory represents a cross-boundary intrusion by economists into political science; in other words, an intuitive protectiveness about the field's integrity as an independent discipline is at work. Third, there are residual Japanese doubts, even among economic experts on Japan, about the powers of market theory to explain human behaviour in the political or any other aspect of Japanese society.

Such criticism should encourage political scientists to be less deferential to the economic assertion grounded in positivist reasoning.

Positivism cannot do justice to all economic phenomena, including public policymaking.

CONCLUSION

In retrospect, it is possible to argue that the impact of the miracle man, or Japan-as-model school, has helped to open the door to what might be called the 'tyranny of the economic' in the study of Japanese politics. But it is also important to stress just how keen these miracle men have been to ground such national success, economic or otherwise, in the workings of the Japanese political system. The miracle school's fascination with the question of whether or not Japanese government policies caused the Japanese economic miracle was one consequence. Its insistence on the primacy of bureaucratic policymaking over party politics within the Japanese polity was another. The focus on the strategic traded sector of the Japanese economy at the expense of minor interest groups or other expressions of pluralism within the Japanese system was a third consequence.

This political concern with economic policy and the relationship of government with big business has, in turn, made the growth of the importance of public policy a predictable phenomenon within the field. Public policy studies, broadly defined, has arrived in Japanese studies borne on powerful shoulders, those of the Japanese miracle itself.

The achievement does not end there. During an era when other branches of political science have remained net importers of ideas and approaches from other disciplines, the political science of Japan has demonstrated its unquestioned potential to become a powerful exporter of concepts and theories to other academic fields. One result should be clear. Properly pursued, the intellectual breakthroughs achieved during the 1980s may permit political scientists working on Japan to achieve something undreamt even by the ambitious generation of scholars who sustained the productive largesse of the 'Modernization School' during the 1960s: the opportunity for the political science of Japan to become a discipline of consequence within Western political science as a whole.

Public discourse outside the academy already points the way. How else is one to explain the impact of the Japanese miracle and the decade-long debate in the United States over industrial policy, of the parallel struggle to learn from the example of MITI by the reformist wing of the British Labour Party, of the celebration of the Japanese model in Singapore, of its forthright imitation by the government of Malaysia? Indeed, *pace* their amateurish and chauvinist excesses, how else are we to interpret the popularity of Japan's so-called revisionist critics in

America and Europe, where Chalmers Johnson is proclaimed 'the father of revisionism'?

These are just first fruits of political science's role in the larger public discourse about the influence of Japan on the world, and indeed about the whole nature of post-industrial society as the twenty-first century approaches. For scholars, the miracle school has been the harbinger of still another decisive shift of perception. At the beginning of the 1980s what was termed Japanese economic 'success' was by the end of the 1980s called Japanese 'power'. Power is a political concept. Market economists have little time for it. But the revolution of Japan's place in the hierarchy of international power relationships may now transform the paradigm of the study of Japanese government and politics by once again linking Japan to the very core of political concern and thought: power itself. Static, single-minded in their pursuit, the hedgehogs of Japanese studies have, after all, made their point. A new dramatic chapter in the history of our discipline has been written; the political science of Japan will never again be the same.

13   Yellow Athena

The Japanese model and 'The End of History'

THE ARGUMENT

The chief task facing the post-communist regimes of Eastern and East-Central Europe today is how to create a civil society 'from above'. No major European thinker has been more discerning about the complex interplay between the state and civil society than Hegel; no society has better demonstrated how such an interplay can be made to succeed than post-war Japan. Eastern Europeans have torn down the old Stalinist edifice, but must now attempt to create the institutions and values essential to the successful working of a civil society. This is the point where the argument must begin. The American or British free-market model has been proposed as the solution to Eastern European ills. This chapter asks: Might the post-war Japanese model suggest a 'third way'?

The question may be put in a still more provocative way. In a controversial 1989 essay titled 'The End of History?', Francis Fukuyama attempted to give Western capitalism's victory over communism a Hegelian gloss.[1] He argued that the end of history has eliminated all but one intellectual option for the future evolution of the planet. The 'American way of life' was canonized as the sole coherent system of values and practices; everything else was obscurant barbarism that would inevitably be scattered by the force of this new Enlightenment.

This argument, if correct, would put the political and philosophical problems of Eastern Europe in a complex and arresting light. First, the challenge of creating a civil society from above demands clarity about both the theory being applied and the practical results being pursued. This, Fukuyama believes he has achieved by updating Hegel. Fukuyama rightly insists that thought and action must not be viewed as contrary modes of human behaviour, and the 'end of history', as Hegel first used the term, would meld thought and action in a powerful, directed way. Second, Fukuyama's thesis appears to give the nod to economic forces at the expense of political choice. If the end of history has truly arrived, then the political is henceforth condemned to an ontological status inferior (politics no longer counts as a first-class piece of reality) to that of the economic, where the reference is to neo-classical economic liberalism alone. Third, Fukuyama's thesis must be seen to reject as irrelevant or obscurant all the values and memories that history has hitherto grafted on to the mind of Eastern and East-Central Europe. As life there has never been governed by the principles at work in the neo-conservative interpretation of the 'American way of life', most of the heritage of Eastern European culture is either irrelevant to its future needs or a hindrance to be discarded.

Japan's modern experience rejects all of these assumptions except the first. The Japanese model offers a subtle and complex design for fostering a civil society, but one that is capable of clear statement. The Japanese example demonstrates the importance of politics as a means to achieve economic ends. The Japanese model is no calm surrender to the arbitrary outcomes generated by market forces. It is about making things happen: setting national goals and achieving them. Political ends are given preference over economic interests. In practical terms, the Meiji reformers built their plans around the Japanese realities inherited from the Tokugawa, just as the future of Central and Eastern Europe must be built on what history and regional values have made those Europeans.

This is not to deny the attractiveness of any vision of post-communist society, as proclaimed by the neo-liberal monetarist, that would promise a fresh institutional beginning and an 'epistemological break' (to borrow a term from Bachelard) with the perceived failures of communism. In fact, however, such monetarist visionaries aim to free Eastern Europe, particularly Russia and Poland, not just from the pernicious effects of communist rule but from any aspect of the national character of these peoples or their past that conspires against remaking Russians or Poles in conformity with the doctrine of 'economic man'. The suggestion would be that Poland, for example, has suffered from a 'captive mind' (in Czeslaw Milosz's phrase) throughout its history, rather than just during the 1940s and 1950s. Monetarism will now bring to a close the 'dark ages' that have dominated the whole of the Polish past. More radical still, monetarists demand that Russians break with their past. Given the horrors of Russian history, this is a tempting dream, but how likely is it to be realized in practice?

This, no doubt, constitutes a bold example of economic theory-spinning. But it is also an impracticable programme that goes against the grain of Eastern European social reality. In contrast, the view is taken here that Eastern Europe must begin from what it is and has been. The pre-war statist tradition, the nightmare of the Second World War, and communist industrial foundations (*jūkōgyō-ka* is the Japanese term) laid between 1945 and 1989 are the defining facts of Eastern European reality today. The task of rebuilding the nation would be far easier if the mere evocation of market forces, as monetarists conceive them, could erase a thousand years of East European experience, as distinct peoples, nations, and states.

Is such a philosophy in any sense persuasive? It may yet succeed; the free-market model is, after all, a formidable body of theory and experience, although it sometimes appears necessary to speak English to make it work. But if modern Japan is a model that is more consistent with Eastern European realities, and can offer a reform programme more likely to succeed in today's fiercely competitive economy, then detailed examination of the Japanese model as a guide for a capitalist Eastern Europe becomes not only desirable, but essential. If the Anglo-American neo-conservative model, which presently occupies pole position, begins to falter, then it will be time for hard questions, many of them with Japanese answers.

Footnotes to Hegel

To raise such objections is to break with the ruling assumptions, one is tempted to say dogmas, of the Anglo-American neo-liberals, those who in America are often called 'neo-conservatives', who dominate the current debate over where Eastern Europe is to go now that its anti-communist revolution has been achieved. In contrast to the Thatcherite or Friedmanite approach, it is argued here that the contemporary crisis of the Central and East European state and society is better interpreted in the strong light of Hegel's meditations, set out in his *Philosophy of Right*.[2] The experience of post-war Japan will be used to give concrete meaning to Hegel's abstract schema.

If List may be regarded as the European godfather of the Japanese economic miracle, then perhaps Hegel may be one of Europe's most fruitful thinkers, *avant la lettre*, about the late-nineteenth- and twentieth-century experience of the Japanese state. Certainly no political philosopher working in the Anglo-American tradition has matched the insights of Germans such as Hegel into the Japanese model. This Hegelian gesture to an Oriental polity has found a contemporary echo in the Continental European tradition. It may be no accident that the most famous, because most intriguing, footnote in all European writing about Japan is by an Hegelian. It occurs in *The Introduction to the Reading of Hegel*, the collection of Alexandre Kojève's celebrated lectures on Hegel's *Phenomenology of Spirit* (1807), delivered at the Ecole Pratique des Hautes Etudes in Paris between 1933 and 1939. In the second edition of these lectures, the author observes:

> Now, several voyages of comparison made (between 1948 and 1958) to the United State and the U.S.S.R. gave me the impression that if the Americans give the appearance of being rich Sino-Soviets, it is because the Russians and Chinese are only Americans who are still poor but are rapidly proceeding to get richer. I was able to conclude from this that the 'American way of life' was the type of life specific to the post-historical period, the actual presence of the United States in the World prefiguring the 'eternal present' future of all humanity. . . .
> It was following a recent voyage to Japan (1959) that I had a radical change of opinion on this point. There I was able to observe a Society that is one of a kind, because it alone has for almost three centuries experienced life at the 'end of History'. . . . This seems to allow one to believe that the recently begun interaction between Japan and the Western world will finally lead not to a rebarbarization of the Japanese but to a 'Japanization' of the Westerners (including the Russians).[3]

Kojève's peripatetic meditations are pregnant with insight. In the light of the Revolution of 1989–90 in East-Central Europe, the crushing of the student protest in Tiananmen Square in June 1989, and the tumultuous wave of change that has overwhelmed the Soviet Union, the question of whether Sino-Soviet man is merely an impoverished version of American man looms large. Is it true that only the slightest adjustment of the Chinese and Russian mentality, combined with the freeing of market forces, will transform these societies into vibrant capitalist nations? On the other hand, if Japan is the key exception to 'the American way of life' then this, too, is an issue of some moment in the reformation of economic and social life as it is lived in Eastern and East-Central Europe.

It has been dogmatically asserted that the neo-liberal model of Hayek, Friedman and Thatcher is the only way of addressing the problems of Eastern Europe. But this model is not consistent with the region's history or with the religious and ideological evolution of these European peoples or with their varied national characters. It is being insisted upon because there is no other viable course for them to follow if they are to make their way in world markets.

From Kojève to Fukuyama

Reflecting on the opportunities, or lack of them, that face Eastern Europeans today, one could conclude, upon reading Hegel's *Phenomenology of Spirit*, that they have reached 'the end of history'. In a remarkable turnabout in recent thought, it is neo-liberal economists who now entertain this possibility. The phrase 'the end of history', which has been brooded on by European students of Hegel since the early nineteenth century, has been brought to the attention of a wider readership by Fukuyama. In his article, he observed that:

> In watching the flow of events over the past decade or so, it is hard to avoid the feeling that something very fundamental has happened in world history . . . the century that began full of self-confidence in the ultimate triumph of Western liberal democracy seems at its close to be returning full circle to where it started: not to an 'end of ideology' or a convergence between capitalism and socialism, as earlier predicted, but to an unabashed victory of economic and political liberalism.[4]

By stating it in this manner, Fukuyama helped to give a widely held view a sharper edge. Had he stopped there, he would have been echoing a commonplace about the ending of the Cold War. But he went further, and by doing so he provoked often abusive rebuttal from uncomprehending critics:

> The Triumph of the West, of the Western *idea*, is evident first of all in the total exhaustion of viable systematic alternatives to Western liberalism. . . . What we may be witnessing is not just the end of the Cold War, or the passing of a particular period of postwar history, but the end of history as such: that is, the end point of mankind's evolution and the universalization of Western liberal democracy as the final form of human government.[5]

In his advocacy of the 'end of history', Fukuyama is, of course, reaching back to Kojève and to Hegel. Because Fukuyama's use of the term 'the end of history' has been perversely misunderstood, his own words on the issue deserve careful reading, especially by the school of 'common-sense' commentators:

> Kojève sought to resurrect the Hegel of the *Phenomenology of Spirit*, the Hegel who proclaimed history to be at an end in 1806. For as early as this Hegel saw in Napoleon's defeat of the Prussian monarchy at the Battle of Jena the victory of the ideals of the French Revolution, and the imminent universalization of the state incorporating the principles of liberty and equality. . . . To say that history ended in 1806

meant that mankind's ideological evolution ended in the ideals of the French and American Revolutions; while particular regimes in the real world might not implement these ideals fully, their theoretical truth is absolute and could not be improved upon. . . . We might summarize the content of the universal homogenous state as liberal democracy in the political sphere combined with easy access to VCRs and stereos in the economic.[6]

This suggests that Hegel, whatever his early nineteenth-century blinkers, has not only proved to be a seminal generator of provocative and stylish texts, but is also a bookish 'real presence' of some intellectual weight in the contemporary discussion of world affairs. It will be argued here that the status of Hegelian thought as 'a past that is a present' (to borrow a phrase from Hegel's great critic, Kierkegaard) extends to the claim that Hegel may also prove to be something of an honorary Orientalist.

A beginning can be made by noting what has been artfully elided in Fukuyama's neo-liberal reading of Kojève. First, there is the uncomfortable, if understandable, way he imposes a near-uniformity of meaning and ideological character on the French and American Revolutions. It is obvious, or should be, that when the 'Petition of the Agitators to the Legislative Assembly' on 20 June 1792 proclaimed that 'The image of the *Patrie* is the sole divinity which it is permissible to worship', the French Revolution broke with both American and East European sensibility. Abbé Sieyès insisted in 'What is the Third Estate?' (1789) that 'The nation exists before all, it is the origin of everything. Its will is always legal, it is the law itself.' He veered sharply away from the weak theory of state and nation, which has characterized almost all Anglo-American political reflection since Locke, towards traditional Continental theory.

Whatever the personal shock of Hegel's encounter with history at the Battle of Jena – he was a witness to Napoleon's victorious campaign – the German philosopher was, in his youth, a student of the Scottish Enlightenment, and recognized early the epochal importance of Locke's revolutionary doctrine and of England's industrial revolution. Nevertheless, to concede the importance of something is not necessarily to embrace it. In a way untrue of either Kojève or Hegel, Fukuyama's celebration of the 'American way of life', his recipe of 'economic and political liberalism', smells more like *réchauffé* Manchester School economics than the Hegel of even Georg Lukács' Marxist, therefore economic-minded, biography.[7]

There is a further twist in Fukuyama's borrowing of the notion of an 'end of history'. Hegel's strict concept of 'absolute knowledge' has had little impact on public philosophic discourse in the English-speaking world, but the conviction of finality that Fukuyama, and most neo-liberals, ascribe to the doctrine of free markets can be seen to embody a conviction-politics version of absolute knowledge, although one finally more political than philosophical in content. Hegel would not have approved. This may say something damning about the nature of the debate over how best to revitalize the economies of Eastern Europe. All too often neo-conservative wisdom has painted in absolutist tones.

The Japanese model, as imitated across the face of East and Southeast Asia, suggests that Fukuyama is wrong. There may be another path for a nation to take, and one that is more consistent with European identity and history, and its Ontology, its meditated sense of self.[8]

One lacuna in Fukuyama's definition of Hegel's 'universal state' as political liberalism plus 'easy access to VCRs and stereos' hints at a vulnerability in his reasoning. Fukuyama unctuously refers to 'access to', not to the manufacture of, VCRs and stereos. In the wake of the collapse of America's domestic electronics industry before the advance of East Asian and even West European competition, what else could he say? Such contentious issues point to the larger question of whether the American way of life does provide the sole comprehensive definition of the universe of the future. They underscore the significance of the Japanese model and raise questions about the wisdom of the campaign to persuade Eastern Europeans to embrace a monetarist-driven revolution.

Japan and Hegel

Drawing on Hegel's political philosophy, a different picture of Eastern Europe's predicament can be drawn. In his *Philosophy of Right*, he defines civil society as the community of producers and consumers. He sees civil society as but a single, if crucial, dimension of society as a whole, which also includes the state, the family and related kinship groupings. In the most radical of monetarist readings, on the other hand, the sole obligation and duty of the present states in Eastern Europe is for them to fall on their swords. This may be perfectly consistent with neo-liberal ideology, but such a hope is incompatible with European political tradition or the likely future of the eastern half of the continent.

Hegel's approach to thinking about civil society allows us to 'bracket' (in Husserl's sense) some of the more dogmatic or foundational assumptions (*die Grundprobleme*) of neo-conservative proponents of Hegelian doctrine, such as Fukuyama's. Hegel's vision encourages us to see that civil societies are made, not born; made, in some cases, by the state. It can be insisted that all late-capitalist states, from nineteenth-century Germany and Japan to contemporary Poland and Korea (the South today, the North tomorrow) have been obliged to fashion, animate, and direct their own versions of 'civil society'. This contradicts the economic liberalism that is being urged on East and Central European societies. This contradiction does not apply to the Japanese 'development state' model. The Meiji State first created itself from the ruins of the Tokugawa regime, and then tried to discipline and guide Japan's answer to 'civil society', an approach much closer to Hegel's idea than, for example, to Locke's in *An Essay Concerning the True Original, Extent, and End of Civil Government* (1690) or Adam Ferguson's in *An Essay on the History of Civil Society* (1767).

True, the idea of 'civil society' translates only poorly into the Japanese language. The expression '*shimin-shakai*' rings no ontological bells for the Japanese. In fact, it is sometimes difficult to distinguish precisely between the terms 'state' and 'nation' in the Japanese language. Just what did Prime Minister Nakasone Yasuhiro mean when he insisted that Japan must become a '*kokusai-kokka*'? An international 'state' or 'nation', is the most prosaic of renderings. 'A nation among nations' comes closer.

Such Japanese incomprehension of European concepts has another dimension. Consider, for example, the sustained effort of the Bush administration to liberalize Japan's markets. This acrimonious American campaign, four decades after SCAP's radical reforms, may be seen as an attempt to strengthen the economic foundations of Japan's civil society. But how is it possible, at this late stage of Japan's economic ascent, that American policymakers are still trying to turn Japan into the kind of civil society that would win the approval of Smith or Hume or Bentham? This interminable American crusade to transform the economic and bureaucratic *essence* of the Japanese polity must thus far be judged to have failed. Post-war Germany has also become a capitalist democracy in its own way. The examples of Japan and Germany suggest that a fundamental pluralism may be at work in the world's encounter with modernity. Eastern European reformers should not ignore such pluralism.

YELLOW ATHENA

The Japanese achievement should not be seen as an inevitable conse-quence of human nature, as eighteenth-century empiricists interpreted this term, or philosophical essence or scientific monism, but rather as the product of pragmatic thought and experiment, invigorated by the force of political imagination and theory. Just as a great novelist, such as

Proust, may literally extend the reach of our sensibility, the Japanese experience should enlarge the Western sense of the possible in any definition of dynamic social order and human governance. Perhaps it takes an Hegelian like Kojève to see that Japan's heroic drive to modernize is part of an extraordinary *intellectual* conquest. Whatever Japan's failings, and they are many, it is this achievement of mind that makes the teachings and philosophical foundations of her miracle into Japan's supreme gift to contemporary European thought. It can be seen to make post-war Japan into a 'Yellow Athena'.

Japan's post-war miracle, as a model of competitive success, confirms the *'pluralité des mondes'* (to adopt Fontenelle's phrase) of the social world of man. The Japanese model illuminates, with unique force, the idea of 'pluralism' as it is used, for example, by Sir Isaiah Berlin in his essay 'The Pursuit of the Ideal'.[9] At work in monetarist economics, as in all positive economic theory, is a kind of dogmatic monism. This is Berlin's summary of this tendency:

> At some point I realised that what all these views [of the eighteenth-century empiricists and their predecessors] had in common was a Platonic ideal: in the first place that, as in the sciences, all genuine questions must have one true answer and one only, all the rest being necessarily errors; in the second place, that there must be a dependable path towards the discovery of such truths; in the third place, that the true answers, when found, must necessarily be compatible with one another and form a single whole, for one truth cannot be incomparable with another – that we knew *a priori*.[10]

Later, upon reading Machiavelli, Vico and Herder, Berlin confesses the need he felt to revise this view. The discovery of the true meaning of pluralism, he admits, came as a shock, but it encouraged him to rethink the conventional definition of political pluralism:

> 'I prefer coffee, you prefer champagne. We have different tastes. There is no more to be said.' That is relativism. But Herder's view, and Vico's, is not that: it is what I should describe as pluralism – that is, the conception that there are many different ends that men may seek and still be fully rational, fully men, fully capable of understanding each other, as we derive it from reading Plato or the novels of medieval Japan – worlds, outlooks, very remote from our own.[11]

In their rational pursuit of ends that differ from those posited by the Anglo-American economic model, the modern Japanese has demonstrated, with unique force, the importance of Berlin's doctrine of pluralism. Pluralism, thus defined, should encourage us to resist economic Procrusteanism both when interpreting Japan and applying the lessons of its experience elsewhere. The Japanese experience is theirs; the lessons are ours to draw.

In *Black Athena: The Afroasiatic Roots of Classical Civilization*, Martin Bernal has argued that the classic Greeks were 'black' in a flat racial sense and that the chief intellectual fruits that have tradition-ally been viewed as the products of European Greece were in fact derived from the Levant and ancient Egypt.[12] The racial matrix of thought may be of interest, but thought is vastly more important than race. To describe Japan as a 'yellow Athena' is to reject Bernal's racist approach.

In Hegel's essay on tragedy as dramatic art, he used Athena, the goddess, to stand for the life of classical Athens, imagined in its essential unity. To call Japan 'a yellow Athena' is to raise three issues. First, it is to stress that, in a way analogous to the modern Japanese polity, the ancient Greeks rarely drew the distinction between public and private spheres, and when they did primacy was constantly accorded to what the modern European would call the public sphere. The ancient Greeks were not individualistic in the modern European sense; they lacked what Hegel called the subjective moral sense. It is import-ant to recall that *civilis societas* is a Latin doctrine; not a Greek one.

In this attitude to society, if in no other, Japanese tradition stands closer to that of classical Athens. Hegel saw the modern subjective moral sense as setting post-Renaissance Europeans above the ancient Greeks, but it is this emphasis on an inner moral sense, articulated by Kant, that contributes to the unrealism of modern moralistic doctrines. One example is Rawls' *A Theory of Justice*. The Japanese example should encourage us to assay the impact of such moral doctrines on the West's economic life.

Second, modern Japanese practice may be seen also to concur with the Continental statist interpretation of Socrates' final gesture of sub-mission not only to the law but to the polis, to the state. The doctrine is set out in the *Crito*; the gesture in the *Apology*. Third, to treat Japan as a 'yellow Athena' is an attempt to domesticate an alien political tradition to Western circumstance, to make reflection on this Ori-ental polity into a cardinal intellectual move *within* our tradition. This is something the West has not attempted since medieval times and not even contemplated in over three centuries. To give such concerns a skin-deep gloss is also to acknowledge the racial hurt that stands behind the bitter anti-Europeanism of nationalist intellectuals, including *Nihonjin-ron-sha*.

To plead for a 'yellow Athena' is to urge the recognition that, after more than twenty-five centuries, the Western dialogue on the nature of government and the meaning of politics should embrace a continuum that will reach from ancient Athens to modern Japan. Our encounter with the Japanese model should shake us, as Berlin's reading of Machiavelli shook him. Such an encounter has methodological implications for the Western or – if American scholars are uncomfortable, under the press of 'political correctness', with the term 'Western' – the European political theorist. The present predicament of the post-communist countries of Europe points to the need to develop a political version of *la nouvelle critique*, one that is concerned with the applications of the lessons and language of classic political texts *to the present*. This approach will stand opposed to *la critique universitaire*, again to borrow from the debate in French literary circles over classic texts in the 1960s, which for academic reasons defines the job of the textual interpretation in narrower, period-bound terms, a method dominated by textual positivism. Applying Hegelian thought to the present demands a fresh approach.

Civil society in Hegelian perspective

In the 'Theory' section of List's *The National System of Political Economy*, he analyses some of the implications of classical political economy. He takes issue with the claim of economists in the Smithian tradition to have evolved a universal science; that political economy, in the words of J.B. Say, 'lastly, relates to the interests of all nations, to human society in general'.[13] Again, the issue here turns on a defence of pluralism. In pursuing the worthy goal of a universal science, classical political economists, in List's view, wilfully neglect the importance of the nation in the name of the profit-maximizing individual. The root of the limitation may be traced to the ontology of classical political economists which acknowledges the existence only of individuals: the nation is, as it were, a fiction. As List notes, 'The first of the North American advocates of free trade, as understood by Adam Smith – Thomas Cooper, President of Columbia College – denies even the existence of nationality; he calls the nation "a grammatical invention", created only to save periphrases, a nonentity, which has no actual existence save in the heads of politicians'.[14] And, one might add, in the heads of the peoples of East Asia and Eastern Europe.

Margaret Thatcher's attack on the idea of 'society', her insistence that only individuals exist, not collectivities, may be seen to repeat the same error. But Mrs Thatcher's argument is part of a long tradition among

English-speaking theorists. The main intellectual consequence of such methodological individualism, the philosophical conceit that only individuals exist, is that in nearly every Anglo-American meditation on the nature of civil society, the state, like Lewis Carroll's Cheshire Cat, is at best a spectral presence, and all too often disappears.

The anti-statist propensity within Anglo-American reasoning has, by tradition, aroused considerable suspicion among those educated outside this tradition. The counter-orthodoxy, Continental European or East Asian, has proven unbearable to English-speaking neo-liberals. Indeed, this ideological intolerance may be seen to have fomented a kind of conceptual imperialism in recent English-language thinking on the 'problematic' (as the term is used by Bachelard) posed by the relationship of state and market.

Thus, in the name of the Anglo-Saxon ontology (the rationally disciplined self-understanding of a society), not only is the East European or Japanese Ontology (its meditated sense of collective identity) perversely misunderstood, but its right to further existence is denied. The claims of a European or Japanese ontology to validity are dismissed in the name of universal science. The final cut is contained in the discovery that this universal science is in practice, if not in theory, the congealed essence of English or American common sense. In other words, East Europe and Japan are to be redesigned to suit the insights and the whims of what is nothing more than the ruling Ontology of American and British society.

The limits of English thought

The problem is well illustrated in one of the most generous and open-minded readings of Hegel's *Philosophy of Right* in the English language: John Plamenatz's treatment of Hegel's theory of civil society in his two-volume study, *Man and Society*.[15] According to Plamenatz, 'civil society', as Hegel conceives of it, may be roughly defined as 'a community of producers of the kind described by the classical economists together with the public services needed to maintain order inside it'.[16] This definition is similar to the Victorian notion of the 'night-watchman state'. This also highlights the shift of interest in English-language theorizing from 'producers' to 'consumers'.

But Hegel insists that society is more than just a collection of individuals, more than just civil society. It includes, notably, both the family and the state. Plamenatz concedes:

> If Hegel had studied Hume's or Bentham's theory of the State, he would doubtless have said that it falls far short of the truth, taking no

account of what the State essentially is. What Bentham or Hume called the State would have seemed to him merely an aspect of civil society.[17]

If civil society is, in Plamenatz's reformulated definition, merely 'the whole system of economic and political relations considered as satisfying individual needs and serving private ends' alone, then Hegel would reject such a notion as providing an inadequate concept of the state, the nation, the family or society as a whole.[18]

Beyond this Plamenatz will not go. Like Moses, he is allowed to see the conceptual promised land, but is not permitted to enter it because of the intellectual tradition with which he identifies and which he thinks valid. Hegel did not suffer from this limitation: 'The State is actual only when its members have a feeling of their own self-hood, and it is stable only when public and private ends are identical'.[19]

The most important part of Hegel's observation is the first four words: 'The State is actual'. This, Plamenatz, despite his open-mindedness, cannot accept. It is not therefore only Hume and Bentham who can be seen to have 'an inadequate theory of the state', but Plamenatz himself. He comes very close to the boundary of disciplined English-language understanding of the state when he draws this line on his Hegelian peregrinations, a line he will not cross. If Plamenatz cannot cross it, even as a thought experiment, then what monetarist would even attempt to transgress it. What else are we to make of the ontological timidity of his observation that:

> Society or the community or the State, except where we use these words elliptically to mean those who govern or exert the greatest influence on others, is not active; it is merely a sphere of activity, a living together of men.[20]

'The State is not active.' Is there a nineteenth-century or twentieth-century European nationalist or post-war East Asian state-builder who would accept this view? The political philosophy reflected in the Japanese model rejects this position out of hand. The argument can be put more strongly. If, for example, MITI officials *think* the Anglo-American view of the state is untrue, *act* as if this view were untrue, and *achieve* results which demonstrate that this view is untrue, then at some point neo-liberal political philosophers will need to rethink their position. In the meantime, it is not obvious that East European thinkers and politicians should be made to jump hoops to suit the expectations of their monetarist critics. It is conceivable that Hegel was right, and that history did end at Jena in 1806. Fukuyama would wrap the triumphs of

Americanism in 1945 and 1989 in this Hegelian cloak. But Kojève points to a different contest, and it is not obvious that the Yellow Athena has lost it.

14 Japanese public policy as foreign policy

A post-war revolution?

SAMSON IN THE TEMPLE

Did Japan cause the Gulf War? On the face of it the question is absurd. Article 9 of Japan's constitution bars it from making war on its neighbours and places key constraints on sending its 'self-defence forces' abroad. True, Japan helped to finance the Allied cause in the Gulf with a contribution of $13 billion, paid mostly to the United States. This offering was, however, made with the greatest reluctance. But for American pressure it might not have been paid at all.

The state of Japanese opinion on the cause of the United Nations in the Gulf reinforces the view that Japan is the world's supreme military wallflower. It is in the world, but emphatically not of it. More of the Japanese electorate is pacifist than that of any other major country. Involvement in what appeared to many in Japan as an entirely unnecessary war was the last thing thoughtful Japanese wanted for their country. How could it be then that Japan might be responsible, in any sense, for the Gulf War?·

The very constitutional restraints which govern Japanese military conduct point to a troubling phenomenon. Japan voluntarily refused to take part in the frenzy of arms exports to Iraq that involved almost every other industrial power. Evidence is murky, but it appears that the Soviet Union exported MiG-23s in huge quantities as well as advanced air-to-air combat missiles, tanks and artillery. Germany has been accused of supplying combat helicopters, via an Indonesian company, as well as the raw ingredients for nerve gas. France reportedly delivered hundreds of military aircraft, including the latest version of the Mirage fighter-bomber. Military training was also provided on a grand scale by the French. Austria, perhaps through Jordan, shipped some 200 of the longest-range pieces of artillery in current manufacture. China may have sent a billion dollars' worth of tanks. The Iraqi war machine benefited from massive imports of a wide variety of war-related goods from Brazil,

South Africa and Britain. The United States was not left out of this Iraqi arms bazaar, and was, in any case, arming many of Iraq's neighbours and potential foes. Only the Japanese abstained. Or, to put the issue precisely, only the Japanese could afford to abstain. Their national export prowess in manufacturing ensures that Japan does not need to export weapons to pay its huge import bills. That was not true of any of the main exporters of arms to Iraq. The United States and most European countries have to pay for their oil imports as best they can. The question therefore arises: Has Japanese export competition forced many Western and Third World nations to compete in the only major market for manufactures that is immune from Japanese competition: the market in arms?

The same logic may be applied to the European Revolution of 1989–91. Did Japanese competition, and the competition in manufacturing that its example encouraged in other countries – South Korea, Taiwan, Brazil – help to bankrupt the communist regimes of Eastern Europe by squeezing them out of world markets for heavy manufactured goods? Shipbuilding was vital to communist Poland; Hungary specialized in rolling stock; and the Soviet Union was, until its collapse, an exporter of automobiles and the world's largest manufacturer of machine tools.

What better means was there for European communist regimes to try to attract the support of the urban working class (the pillar of the communist workers' state), or failing that, to neutralize its discontent, than by building and subsidizing a vast enterprise in heavy manufacturing? Despite Lenin's hopeful censure in his 1916 essay 'Imperialism', the leaders of post-war communist states in Europe understood all too clearly the fatal consequences of excess international competition for overseas markets. As Europeans losing their share of the market, they were merely retracing the footsteps of their capitalist predecessors. Britain is thought to have built 80 per cent of the world's ships in 1880. Today that figure has shrunk to 2 per cent. What European would have better understood this decline than a shipbuilder in communist Poland? But one does not have to be British or Polish to know where, over the past century, this 'lost' production has gone.

There is a larger question. What constitutes the real foundation of foreign policy in a world where Japanese industrial success might have helped to cause the Gulf War or the Gorbachev Revolution? Economic and military power are of course linked. But the traditional view, sanctified by the classics (Livy's loving meditation on the Punic Wars hardly mentions the decisive Roman economic advantages over Carthage), has nearly always obscured the penny-pinching economic realities in mists of military valour and glory.[1] This preference for the military dimension over the economic defines the modern view of war and the relationship between economic power and military strength. The Gulf War illustrates the point. The morality of the Allied cause, the mobilization of the United Nations Security Council, the dispatch of huge stocks of conventional arms to the Gulf, and the importance of geography all made that brief conflict a satisfying reprise of the Second World War. Oil supplies and democracy were being defended; Kuwait, a victim of aggression comparable to Belgium in 1914 and Poland in 1939, was liberated from brutal tyranny. Even the ground over which the struggle was waged – the territory of the old imperialist powers in what we now call the Third World – underscores the perception that there was hardly an institution or value formed in Western foreign policymakers' minds before 1945 that was not engaged in the 1991 struggle. In the Western, particularly the American and British, view, it was a near-Churchillian triumph capped by previously unimagined scenes of Kuwaitis, jubilant in liberation from their oppressors, waving the Stars and Stripes and the Union Jack. Nasser would have been appalled by this spectacle. Many analysts now argue that total success should have been sought, in Second World War fashion, by occupying Iraq and liberating it from Saddam Hussein. Is that not the way that democracy was bestowed on the Axis powers, Germany, Italy and Japan? Have not all three countries prospered after the Allied victory of 1945?

Viewed from East Asia, the Gulf War took on a very different hue. In geo-political terms, Japan stumbled badly. Early in the crisis, both her politicians and public opinion were caught in a pacifist fog which blinded them to the kind of moral distinctions at the heart of the United Nations' enterprise. The suffering of the Kuwaitis or the Kurds moved the Japanese people hardly at all – certainly not to action. But this emotional patina was a part of the problem. In the Japanese policy response, a distinct realism was at work.

First, the Iraqis, however tyrannical, were going to have to sell their oil to somebody. This would remain true even if Iraq overran all the oil fields of Saudi Arabia, a fear that, more than any other, galvanized Western determination to resist Iraqi expansionism. Second, and more alarming, to engage Iraq, especially when Saddam Hussein's forces were believed to be far more formidable than they were, involved risking the destruction of such oil facilities. Such damage would have threatened Japan, which remains dependent on the Gulf for over half her oil supplies, with economic catastrophe. Why risk this for the Kuwaitis? This Japanese fear, which evoked no flicker of concern in American calculations, was the one that counted for the foreign policymaker in Tokyo with realist credentials. Finally, while the United States, indeed even Britain and France, reasserted their roles as great powers, none of them could afford to meet the total cost of the Desert Storm campaign.[2] Thus the central question that the Japanese policymaker would ask: How ample is one's purse? Indeed the same question could be asked of American, British and French foreign policy design during every decade of the post-war era.

If such conflicts matter so much, if the injustices that the Kuwaitis and the Kurds suffered at the hands of the Iraqis weigh so heavily on the world's conscience, then surely an industrial policy that ensures a nation's capacity to act in such crises matters as much, perhaps even more, than a foreign policy dominated by such expensive and unproductive doctrines as 'mutual assured destruction', 'nuclear umbrellas' and 'collective security' – the doctrines of NATO, the Warsaw Pact and the like. Further, if a nation's inability to compete in overseas markets encourages it to pad its trade figures with massive weapons sales to Third World Hitlers, then here, too, an industrial policy that obviates this need may be a higher priority than the tired counter-logic of free-market neo-classicism would have us believe. If geo-politics matters that much, then a nation must learn to compete in the economic sphere. Public policy failure will impair a nation's ability to act in almost every arena of international life. Japan did not cause the Gulf War. But can the same be said of public policymakers in other countries who neglected national competitiveness? In the answer may lie the Japanese lesson of the Gulf War.

WHO IS MARGINAL NOW?

One of the great values of the post-war evolution of Japanese economic policy, particularly in the area of trade, is the way that it forces the Westerner to question his assumptions about what is fundamental in international relations. Is it true, for example, that Japan has played a marginal role in world affairs since 1945, and is only now emerging as a great power? If one accepts that the geo-military sphere is central, and that the economic realm, including commerce, is inherently secondary or marginal, then Japan has been a bystander in post-war international relations.

But how is it possible that Japan has become a pivotal power by pursuing marginal policies? To stress the often unexamined primacy of the geo-military sphere is to confuse cause and effect, or worse, to assume that some effects, such as military power, have no causes; that they are not rooted in economic strength.

Let us take an example that closely parallels the Japanese case. It is plausible to argue that the United States became a great power by spilling half a million lives in the carnage of the First World War, rather than by the extraordinary husbanding of economic power that reshaped the nation after the Civil War. President Woodrow Wilson's unprecedented role, as an American statesman, at the Versailles Treaty negotiations in 1919 was the direct consequence of the heavy expenditure of national blood and treasure between 1917 and 1918. But behind the US intervention in the First World War stood a half-century of prodigious economic advance. It would be blinkered to claim that the success of America's expeditionary force did not rest on such economic foundations, and unpersuasive to insist that the pursuit of national economic wealth was somehow marginal to the dynamic of twentieth-century power. Both the American and Japanese examples argue the contrary view.

At a ragged moment in the now forgotten domestic debate over the would-be 'greening of America', John Kenneth Galbraith asked with damning force: 'Who is minding the store?' The Japanese example forces one to ask the same question of the entire global diplomatic show since 1945. Looking back from the commanding heights of the technological and economic revolution of our past half century, it is obvious, or should be, that decolonization, as a nationalist crusade, was misconceived; and that in far more cases than not the nationalist struggle did little or nothing to prepare the Third World for the challenges of the twenty-first century. Indian economic policy since 1947 has been the great test case. China, Brazil and Mexico are also vulnerable on this count, and these countries are put forward as economic successes. It is not Nigeria but South Africa that constitutes the great economic machine without which Africa will not make its way into the future. Analogous critiques can be pressed against Egypt, Yugoslavia and Cuba. It is the leaders of these non-aligned powers that have cut the greater figures in global politics since 1945, but it is Japan, South Korea, Taiwan and Singapore that have discovered the secret of sustained economic growth. Who is marginal now?

There is another painful parable of the dangers of misplaced concreteness in post-war thinking about global realities: the long destructive war in Indochina between 1945 and 1991. With Vietnam's 1991 campaign to win membership in ASEAN, the dawning realization must be that nothing could have served the cause of the future prosperity and development of Vietnam less well than the bloody manner in which its communist rulers pursued the struggle for national unity. Millions of lives have been wasted and untold human suffering endured in Indochina so that Vietnam would not be prepared for the tasks of the twenty-first century. Only the Khmer Rouge, in its unforgivable slaughter of one in every five Cambodians, including almost all of that country's economic elite, has done a more thorough job in killing twenty-first-century hopes in Southeast Asia. Reality has been fundamentally misread, and not only in Hanoi.

In Vietnam, America spent 65,000 lives, endured hundreds of thousands of casualties, and wasted precious national resources it could ill afford on a battle against communism, a movement that would, less than fifteen years after the fall of Saigon, collapse under its own weight. The entire episode was a grand illusion that ensured America lost its pole position in the economic contest to invent the twenty-first century, and that Indochina, now the permanent backwater of the world's most dynamic economic region, would have no role to play. Thailand, Malaysia, and Indonesia – the old and wholly misunderstood dominoes that so stimulated the Manichaeist fantasies of the Eisenhower and Kennedy administrations – are now being carried along by the jet-stream of East Asian dynamism.

Such perceptions have a place in any critical assessment of current demands for the liberalization of Japanese markets in geo-political terms. In *Japan's Unequal Trade*, Edward J. Lincoln contends that, 'Japan has the resources to be a principal actor in world affairs, moving to center stage from its peripheral roles of seller and trader'.[3] Few Japanese leaders have been impressed by the implied two-stage evolutionary schema which assumes that a great power's cautious youth of steady nation-building and wealth accumulation must necessarily end in a misspent adulthood of 'imperial overstretch' (Paul Kennedy's phrase).

The Japanese know that the burdens put on the American economy by the ambitious foreign policies of the Truman, Eisenhower and Kennedy administrations have been transformed into an intolerable excess by every American president since 1963. Economic decline is a complex, almost organic, process, but if three individuals contributed more than any others to the process of American decline, then they were Lyndon Johnson, Richard Nixon and Ronald Reagan. By their military and foreign adventures that squandered vast stocks of national wealth, by their refusal, in Galbraith's phrase, 'to mind the store', these three men, and by implication every American who voted for them, have dealt a mortal blow to the American century. No wonder the Japanese are reluctant to abandon the so-called 'margins' of world politics.

One conclusion seems unavoidable. The game of global influence, as pursued by Washington, Moscow, Beijing, London and Paris, and almost every other world capital since 1945, has been a folly. It is not something a nation ever becomes wealthy enough to play. *Pace* Lincoln, such politics have nothing constructive to say about Japanese trade policy because, since 1945, Japan has stood at the secret centre of international affairs.

MERCANTILISM AND NEO-MERCANTILISM

The other Tōdai

In 1941, at the insistence of the Japanese Army and the bureaucratic managers of Japan's war effort in China, a second engineering faculty was created at the University of Tokyo, the country's most prestigious academic institution, known in Japanese as *Tōkyō Teikoku Daigaku*, or *Tōdai*. The purpose of this new faculty was to meet a desperate shortfall in the wartime specialisms, such as aeronautical engineering. It was part of the flawed Japanese effort to mobilize for total war, a campaign that peaked in 1943 when, among other changes, the Ministry of Commerce and Industry was renamed as the Ministry of Munitions, an important MITI pre-incarnation. Under the Occupation, the Tokyo Imperial University 'Number Two Engineering Faculty, Tokyo' (*Tōkyō Teikoku Daigaku Dai-ni Kōgaku-bu*) was closed down, but its legacy would live on in Japan's post-war economic miracle. This engineering faculty turned out to be a hotbed of managerial excellence. One reason may be its advantageous location in rural Chiba, away from the bombing that repeatedly threatened the Hongo district of Tokyo, home to Tōdai's first engineering faculty. But regardless of the reason, the Chiba faculty's graduates included literally hundreds of future senior executives who subsequently helped to make post-war Japan a success.

In its impact on the Japanese economy, this other *Tōdai* can stand comparison with the best of America's business schools, even that powerhouse on the Charles River in Cambridge, Massachusetts. In the conditions of its founding, and its specifically nationalist orientation as a vehicle of war-making, this Japanese wartime creation differs radically in intent from the business schools of Harvard or Stanford. Nationalist institutions such as Tokyo University's 'phantom faculty', as it is known in Japanese, form an important piece of the complex mosaic of business nationalism. This phenomenon, so often neglected in Western discussion of the relationship between the state and the firm in post-war Japan, has contributed in a vital way to the fostering of elite consensus and to the success of Japanese-style mercantilism.

Nationalism forms the backbone of Japanese business culture, an orientation which may explain why even now hardly a month passes without a Japanese wartime hero being celebrated on the cover of

Japanese executive magazines such as *President*. The contrast with the editorial line at *Fortune* or *The Economist* is arresting. It is another reminder of how the wartime emergency in Japan continues to bloom half a century after peace returned to the Pacific.

Neo-mercantilism: An idea

At the end of John Maynard Keynes' *The General Theory of Employment, Interest and Money*, the greatest English economist of the century attached a set of notes on 'mercantilism, the usury laws, stamped money and theories of under-consumption'.[4] The piece has been something of an embarrassment to Keynes' followers because of the suggestion that he held 'a primitive and indefensible *monetary* theory of interest'.[5] Such unease is not confined to the monetary question, but embraces a grosser insight that the master, so incisive elsewhere, is here toying with ideas. Alvin H. Hansen's summary in *A Guide to Keynes* is redolent of the suggestion that 'even Homer sometimes nods'.

This harks back to an older problem. For the modern positivist economist, Keynesian or monetarist, mercantilism is a dead doctrine. The real question is whether Japanese public policy has effected its resurrection. If the old mercantilists were cleverer than the modern neo-classicist is prepared to admit, then the neo-mercantilist is cleverer still.

In analysing Japan, the principal burden inflicted by modern economists is the ban on the open discussion of the virtues of mercantilism. The collection of otherwise excellent articles in *Japan's Economic Structure: Should It Change?*, edited by Kozo Yamamura, is marred by the doctrinal defence of free-market theory.[6] This ignores the essence of Japanese industrial policy which is rooted in economic nationalism, a subtle mix of mercantilist goals and structural means. Such economic nationalism, tightly disciplined by mercantilist theory, tells a nation where it wants to go; policies of structural change, and the implied tools, provide the means for getting there. Jacob Viner, no mercantilist, set out what he believed to be the main tenets of the mercantilist school, ancient or modern:

> I believe that practically all mercantilists, whatever the period, country, or status of the particular individual, would have subscribed to all of the following propositions: (1) wealth is an absolutely essential means to power, whether for security or for aggression; (2) power is essential or valuable as a means to the acquisition and retention of wealth; (3) wealth and power are each proper ultimate ends of national policy; (4) there is long-run harmony between these

ends, although in particular circumstances it may be necessary for a time to make economic sacrifices in the interest of military security and therefore of long-run prosperity.[7]

The Japanese post-war miracle offers two powerful correctives to this famous formulation. First, it has abandoned the military dimension in favour of economic growth and prosperity, in both the short and the long term. It has been free-market America that has been the Sparta, the policeman of the post-war world, not Japan. Second, and intellectually as important, Japanese-style neo-mercantilism (and Japanese practice defines modern mercantilism) offers evidence that a nationalist economic programme, structural in its tools and mercantilist in its ends, can significantly improve economic performance. The Japanese economy has outstripped all its free-market rivals since the end of the Pacific War. In other words, 'Japan's economic structure enables Japanese firms to outcompete American firms in many industries'.[8]

Such assertions tempt one to conclude that the most important intellectual consequence of the Japanese miracle is the overthrow of some of the foundations of neoclassical economic theory. Even if this prospect is denied, it is essential that mercantilism be granted a legitimate place at the table where the nature and impact of Japanese public policy is dissected. The sceptic might reason, from ample evidence, that the oil of positivism and the water of empiricism will never mix. In this resistance to compromise, there is a Voltairean impulse at work in positivist economics. Economists would crush the infamous thing (*écrasez l'infâme*), even if sometimes that thing is the truth itself. In the study of Japan, this position must be recognized for what it is: obscurant. Since 1945 the world has been at least as much in the age of Friedrich List as that of Adam Smith.

Intellectual tolerance is indispensable if Western science is to grasp the complex processes that have allowed public policy, during the course of the last half of the twentieth century, to determine foreign policy, and to understand the role of Japanese nationalism in this revolution.

15   Unblinking politics

McCarthyism, grand theory and wild empiricism

The argument that Japan is a nationalist polity that is becoming a liberal one, even if on Japanese terms, forms the core thesis of this book. There are, of course, other points of view. Three different modes of analysis provide useful counter-arguments to the position set out here, and, in this concluding section, these dissenting perspectives will be scrutinized.

First, there is what might be called the 'McCarthyite question' or the challenge that truth-telling poses to the student of Japanese politics. After assessing the nature of this challenge, the issue will be examined in the light of the critique of Japan-hand expertise made by the legal and economic advisers and administrators who animated US policymaking during the initial phase of the Allied Occupation of Japan. Second, there is the issue of grand theory and classicism, the problem of large truths that last. The claims of political classicism will be explored in connection with Francis Fukuyama's *The End of History and the Last Man*, which raises a distinct set of issues about the Japanese model untouched by his famous 1989 essay, 'The End of History?' Third, under the heading of 'Significant others', this book's principal thesis has been contrasted with alternative empirical approaches, journalistic or scholarly, which are necessarily at odds with the position taken here. Finally, the chapter concludes with a plea for 'an unblinking politics'.

TRUTH-TELLING

The goal of this book is to grasp the nature of the Japanese political system *as a whole*. Its thesis is rooted in an implicit defence of a middle level of analysis, which falls short of grand theory but rises above micro empiricism. To this end, a view of Japanese political reality has been offered, but this offering turns on an argument about how to look at the particular slice of political reality in question.

This is also the work of a Westerner observing an Asian society. It is an analysis in English of a political system whose language is not

English. It employs large terms such as 'public policy', 'nationalism' and 'models of growth', all of which are imported ideas in Japanese. Despite an obvious overlap of data and conceptual tools, there is little doubt that a Japanese attempting a similar task for a Japanese audience would approach the problem in a different way. In this sense, this book is by a Westerner for a non-Japanese reader who, in trying to grasp the nature of Japan as a regime, seeks a vantage point above the flood-tide of facts and analysis pouring daily from the mass media and the universities. This is an ambitious task, and it has its dangers.

These dangers can be illustrated. Observed in a certain light, they suggest that the problem with McCarthyism is that it did not go on long enough. This spasm of anti-communist hysteria in America during the early 1950s shook the Asian scholar as no event before or since. In the climate of fear generated by this witch-hunt, academic and intellectual careers were broken and reputations destroyed. Even suicide had its place in this tragedy. In a century that has often been brutal to intellectuals who sought the truth, this episode of American red-baiting taught cloistered scholars that truth-telling could be a dangerous profession even in a liberal democracy. What other conclusion is to be drawn from 40,000 pages that filled the FBI file on Owen Lattimore, the Central Asian expert and Nationalist China adviser who McCarthy blamed for 'losing China' to the communist revolution?

But did the scholars in question know the truth in order to tell it? Such has been the influence of the scholar-diplomat on Western relations with the non-Western world that it becomes useful to ask, citing some important American examples of the scholar-diplomat, whether Owen Lattimore's grasp of China was sounder than John Vincent's (another target of McCarthy); or whether the Chinese knowledge of either matched George Kennan's understanding of Russia; or whether Joseph Grew's penetration of Japanese politics was richer or poorer than Edwin Reischauer's.

The retrospective view is often painful and not confined to diplomats. How would Edgar Snow rewrite his 1937 classic *Red Star Over China* now? What does Frances FitzGerald now make of the resigned welcome she extended to a North Vietnamese victory in her Pulitzer-winning *Fire in the Lake* (1972)? Would E.H. Norman's *Japan's Emergence as a Modern State* (1940), with its armour of Marxist interpretation, remain unaltered after half a century? One tends to assume that such revisionism is necessitated by intervening changes, but the question that haunts us is a different one: If we had thought harder at the time, might we have understood more clearly the true character of the Asian regime in question? The Orientalist or area expert sits with a society, learns its languages, meets its leaders, walks its streets in an infinitely nuanced but also resistant enterprise of cross-cultural understanding. But what is sought from this complex attempt at apprehending the genuine nature of society from without?

The real provocation that McCarthyism posed to the Asian expert was not the warning it contained about tactless honesty – China's communists were set to win their struggle with the nationalists, but the journalist or scholar would be damned as disloyal if he said so – but rather the way it called into doubt a scholar's gifts for objectivity and penetration. At its ontologically most serious, McCarthyism, this otherwise shoddy and obscurant phenomenon, bears on but one topic: What is the essential character of this or that Asian regime? Is it a friend or foe, an open society or a closed one, a nationalist polity or a liberal one, an apple or an orange?

American scholars know the price of getting it wrong. They count their dead. This has been the painful legacy of two generations of geo-political confrontation with Asia, a period punctuated by three American wars: first against Japan, then against North Korea and communist China, and finally against North Vietnam. The price for misreading Asia, and each of these conflicts was rooted in a misreading of the regimes in question, has been heavy. America alone can claim perhaps 250,000 battle deaths; the figure for America's Asian opponents and allies runs to millions.

When one passes through the cemeteries where these honoured dead are remembered, the questions that consumed their lives seem strangely academic. Was wartime Japan fascist? In what sense has any government of Laos been legitimate? Would South Vietnam ever have been viable as an independent state? How is it conceivable, in the light of the failures of Gorbachev, Ulbricht and Tito, that any communist movement should have created states as seemingly resilient as North Vietnam or communist China or even North Korea? To a remarkable degree, America's crusades against the communist threat, for example, were founded in a cultivated blindness towards the role of revolutionary socialism as midwife to the birth of post-colonial Asia.

McCarthy played on this blindness when he was not actually inflicting it. The impact on Asian studies in America can scarcely be exaggerated. It encouraged the unlikely belief that the pre-1949 nationalist regime on the Chinese mainland was a viable enterprise that merited generous American support, and that all those who argued otherwise were victims of treachery. After the flight of the nationalists to their redoubt on Taiwan in 1949, thus 'losing China' for America, the knives came out. The question 'Who lost China?' would echo sharply in the halls of academe, and no doubt encouraged two decades of spurious claims, especially among American economists, that Taiwan was an enlightened liberal regime that adhered to American-style free enterprise principles. Yet misreading or misrepresenting the nature of Taiwanese economic nationalism was of a piece with the consistent refusal of American economists to dwell on the overt mercantilism of post-war Japan.[1] US–Japan relations today bear the bruises caused by this blinking at the truth.

McCarthyism may have helped to smother any radical tendencies within the Modernization School of the late 1950s and 1960s even when addressing post-war Japan. It made the American defence and diplomatic experts dangerously uncritical towards rash and facile dissections of the 'communist threat' in Asia from the late 1940s. The 'know-nothing' attitudes towards Asian complexities fanned by McCarthyism would in the end exact a terrible price.

Under such political pressure, the scholar or journalist will turn on himself and ask: Have I grasped the true nature of Japanese politics or Chinese society? The knowledge that the lives of thousands of their fellow countrymen may to some degree hang on their answers should give scholars and journalists pause for thought. More frequently, the area expert's views are but one factor in the complex weave of international relations and policymaking. But McCarthyism as a spectre in Asian studies will not be exorcised unless scholars and journalists are willing to bring what Henry James called 'the deep breathing fixities of total regard' to bear on the job of assessing the nature of Japanese politics, its regime characteristics, *as a whole*.[2]

What do we know?

The insistence on the need to comprehend Japan as a political system, as a complete polity, is a cogent and defendable position. But it can be further refined by asking whether the knowledge that might underwrite our understanding of Japan, as a whole, should be pure or applied. This issue took on fresh force during the debate over anti-Japanese revisionism in the Bush administration and the American mass media at the end of the 1980s and the beginning of the 1990s. It was particularly germane to the design and execution of Bush administration policy as reflected in the Structural Impediments Initiative (SII). During the course of those contentious talks, US negotiators issued demands for changes in Japanese public policy the detailed and comprehensive character of which surprised Japanese bureaucrats and journalists alike. Much of the evidence, to cite one controversial example, about the practice of Japanese computer firms of making 'zero' bids (that is offering the product in question at no charge) to supply educational equipment to state-funded schools, appears to have been the work of the applied researcher.[3] It was, in turn, more often than not a professional lawyer or economist who orchestrated America's case in international forums. Where did such mountains of applied knowledge of Japan, about the operation of large-scale retail stores or public works expenditures, leave the established political scientist who regarded himself as a Japan expert?

For scholars with long memories, the intrusion of the legal and economic professions, of experts in applied knowledge, into the Japan-hand's bailiwick recalled the defeat of Ambassador Joseph Grew and his State Department Japan experts at the end of the Second World War. As the stakes in the defeat of these Japan hands in the Truman administration were even higher than in the SII struggle, the earlier example will be examined in some detail.

The prospect of a Pacific War had, of course, stimulated the centres of Japan research in all the Western powers with exposed Pacific interests. During the course of the struggle, the foundations for the expansion of post-war studies in the social sciences were laid, despite the lingering influence of the classical textualist approach of the Orientalist. But an ambush was waiting for these well-cultivated Japan hands just as the moment of victory arrived.

Until 1944, the US Department of State exercised what Theodore Cohen in *Remaking Japan: The American Occupation as New Deal* describes as 'a cozy monopoly of Japanese post-war policy'.[4] The State Department's 'old Japan hands' hoped for little more from the Occupation of Japan than the restoration of what Cohen dismisses as the 'old liberal, civilian elements of bygone times'.[5] The fact that this restoration was partly achieved is not the main point. The real question is: What kind of knowledge did State Department Japan experts bring to the task of 'remaking Japan'?

The question of expertise proved decisive to the rout of State Department diplomats as players in the American Occupation of Japan. When Major General John H. Hilldring sought to prepare the groundwork for the post-war administration of Japan for President Roosevelt, he naturally turned to the State Department. According to Cohen, he drew up a long list of pragmatic questions that would have to be addressed by any post-war occupying authority in the Far East, twenty-three of which focused on Japan. These questions included:

> Would the occupation of Japan be divided into zones or be unified?
> How long would it last? Would it be punitive, mild or concerned only

with safeguarding reparations? What obnoxious laws should be nullified, and what political parties prohibited? What should be done about the Emperor, Shinto, freedom of worship, labor unions, public works, social insurance – even what proclamations should be issued.[6]

State's answers were imprecise and took five months to prepare. Few of Hilldring's questions were answered in any useful way. Cohen's gloss is deadly: 'The fact was that State, steeped in its traditional view of diplomacy and foreign policy, shunned anything that smacked of operations, even to the point of disdaining its own nonregional specialized offices.'[7] In its failure to meet the expectations of Hilldring's twenty-three questions, the limits of State Department influence were written. There is little to suggest that the centres of Japanese studies in America's universities, at least to the degree that such institutions shared the Department of State's gentile ethos, would have filled the breach any better.

Roosevelt had well-nurtured suspicions about the political colours of one obvious candidate to substitute for the floundering diplomats: the Military Government Division of the Provost Marshall's Section, which had overseen the military policing of French and Belgian towns occupied during the First World War. So Hilldring, in creating the Civil Affairs Divisions to design post-war policy, increasingly turned to the civilian war agencies which had assiduously drafted talent and Japan-related expertise from America's universities during the early years of the war.

Cohen concludes that by the end of 1942 'Washington had a greater concentration of foreign area and professional expertise available to work on foreign country problems than ever before or since'.[8] But this claim is undermined by Cohen's assertion that under Hilldring Occupation planning 'moved out of the cocoon of specialized Japan "experts" and into the world of broader realities'.[9]

Some might argue that the Bush administration's adoption of a tough line with Japan offered a challenge to the Japan expert to return to the rough-and-tumble glory of the Truman era. But the term that raises doubts in Cohen's summary is 'broader realities'. What can these two words mean when pre-war Japanese studies so obviously aspired to the ideal of general knowledge? Cohen is not clear on this point. According to him, in the early stages of Hilldring's effort, the Civil Affairs Division was confined to civilian experts in law, banking and finance who could boast little or no knowledge or experience of Japan. Later, there was a leavening of Japanese-language specialists from the Office of Strategic Services (OSS). This blend was quickly diluted in practice by a flood of new experts in a diverse set of specialisms who found roles in the unfolding Occupation. 'Those people in the new war agencies did not buy the mystique of Japan assiduously promoted by the 'old Japan hands'. Japan was, to them, a country like any other.'[10]

But is Japan a country like any other? Cohen is right to insist that as America's 'Japan problem' captured more of the post-war limelight, domestic political pressures and philosophies came to dominate the Occupation's agenda. This is the point of his subtitle, *The American Occupation of Japan as New Deal*, and it appears to be a valid one. But did the bold assumption of the US Occupiers, that the American way of life was the best, preclude the necessity to master the unique features of the Japanese political and social landscape?

On this issue the contemporary heirs of Joseph Grew, America's ambassador to Tokyo between 1932 and 1942, have every right to challenge the cultural hubris and blindness housed in Cohen's sweeping dismissal of culturally sensitive knowledge of Japanese realities. Did the Occupation really 'remake Japan' or did it fail (Japan was not turned into a compact version of America) precisely because so many Occupation administrators knew all too much about statistics and labour law but all too little about Japan and the Japanese? The suggestion would be that at some profound level they had no idea what they were doing. Is this the conclusion that Cohen would unwittingly have had us draw?

In his spirited defence of practical knowledge and of 'broader realities', Cohen appears to assume that what a scholar knows about Japan is not worth knowing. Between the lines of his commentary there lurks a philistine's contempt for learning. Like McCarthy, Cohen also encourages doubts about an academic's gift for objectivity and penetration. Who therefore better grasped the essence of Japanese political reality: the Occupation farm experts who reformed Japanese agriculture or the old Japan hands in the State Department who gambled their reputations when they insisted that the emperor not be put on trial for war crimes? The answer lies in how one answers the McCarthyite question: What is the nature of the Japanese regime? Is it friend or foe, an apple or an orange?

THE CHALLENGE OF GRAND THEORY

Japan is nothing. This was the bitter conclusion that Takeuchi Yoshimi (1910–77), the Japanese intellectual and student of Chinese literature, drew in the wake of Japan's defeat in 1945. Takeuchi's assertion housed a curt dismissal of Kyoto School philosophers, such as Kōsaka Masaaki and Kōyama Iwao, who endorsed Japan's war against China and believed that Japanese battlefield success during 1941–2 against America and Britain demonstrated that Japan had, in Hegelian fashion, overcome the challenge of modernity (*kindai no chōkoku*) and the provocation of Westernization.

It is an ironic twist that, like Kōsaka and Kōyama, Francis Fukuyama has turned in *The End of History and the Last Man* to the German philosopher Hegel in elaborating his often elegant and stimulating case for the view that, with the collapse of communism in Europe, history has now reached an end.[11] But unlike those militant Hegelians of the pre-war Kyoto School, Fukuyama has made his own way, via Hegel, to Takeuchi's conclusion: Japan is nothing.

Is Fukuyama's thesis in any sense correct about Japan's relationship to the ultimate nature of the world? In answering this philosophic question, one must observe at the outset that the article that made Fukuyama's name, 'The End of History?', in the US neo-conservative journal *The National Interest* (Summer 1989), bears small resemblance to his 1992 book.[12] The article's treatment of Japan is discussed in some detail in Chapter 13.

Writing before the destruction of the Berlin Wall, Fukuyama argued with prophetic force that the disintegration of Stalin's empire signalled the final victory of the Western liberal ideals that had first swept into Central Europe on the tips of Napoleon's bayonets. Hegel, having watched the French emperor's troops march off to crush the Prussian state at the Battle of Jena in 1806, declared in his 1807 masterpiece, *Phenomenology of Spirit*, that history had reached its conclusion.

As the meaning of the term 'history' in Fukuyama's discourse is the object of repeated misunderstanding, both in Japan and the English-speaking world, it cannot be emphasized too strongly that by 'the end of history' Hegel meant neither that armies would cease to fight nor that the minutiae of daily life would evaporate. What he did mean was that a central contest of ideas, between premodern and modern modes of political, social and economic life, had been fought, and that the moderns had won. Feudalism was dead never to return.

Drawing on the writings of his mentor, Alexandre Kojève, the great Russian-born French Hegelian who died in 1968, Fukuyama declared in his 1989 essay that with the Gorbachev revolution the long twilight resistance of authoritarianism to liberal ideas in Eastern Europe was now broken. This was a triumph for the American way of life, that is, liberal democracy plus capitalist consumerism (what Fukuyama jauntily termed 'access to VCRs').[13] Note the word 'access'. Fukuyama could not say 'the design and production' of VCRs because this is beyond the capacity of the US electronics industry. This blindness to a singular triumph of Japanese technology hinted at the weakness in his argument: the failure to take Japan seriously. As was argued in Chapter 13, Fukuyama's article 'The End of History?', stumbled on the issue of the Japanese challenge.

In *The End of History and the Last Man*, Fukuyama the philosopher triumphs over Fukuyama the political scientist and journalist. His book is not an exercise in errant empiricism, but a meditation on first principles. This 'philosophic turn' makes the book a much more powerful statement, and one that has considerable bearing on the work of the student of Japanese politics. This is because Fukuyama's resort to grand theory allows him to sustain a critique of the Japanese model on a level of abstraction – abstractions being ideas and truths that do not change – rarely attempted by the journalist or political scientist.

Fukuyama has not tried to make a master-statement about Western philosophy, but the philosophic nature of the book must not be ignored. Political philosophers such as Princeton's Alan Ryan or Cambridge's John Dunn have been critical, even dismissive, of Fukuyama's handling of philosophic argument, either because he appears to be a poor student of Leo Strauss, the legendary German-born American political philosopher who has an extraordinary following among American neo-conservatives, or because Fukuyama has sought in an ill-informed way to smooth out the resistant ambiguities at work in Hegel's *Phenomenology of Spirit*.[14] Such scepticism is important, but Fukuyama's philosophical inadequacies do not thereby transform his book into sociology or empirical political science. *The End of History and the Last Man* remains grounded in an argument from first principles, and this means that Fukuyama's thesis cannot be overturned by citing the troubles of Alberto Fujimori in Peru or US–Japan trade tensions, which Fukuyama's framework would reduce to mere epiphenomena.

Granted, he has invited empirical criticism by his celebration of the rising liberal tide in Europe, Africa and Latin America, but this is finally neither here nor there. One can damage his argument by contrary evidence, but mortally wounding it demands a counter set of first principles about the nature of political and social reality.

The core of Fukuyama's thesis is an updating of Hegel's classic distinction, drawn in the *Phenomenology*, between 'the master' and 'the slave'. A master is an aristocrat who will risk death in combat; anyone who will not take such a risk becomes his slave. The master is content in his recognized superiority; the slave grows rebellious and creative from his lack of recognition. The master is the 'first man'. He is driven by what Socrates called '*thymos*' or self-esteem. More disciplined, the slave, like Marx's proletariat, slowly augments his self-esteem through work. But the danger, as Plato and Hobbes feared, lurks in the master's irrational urge for warlike superiority; what Fukuyama terms *megalothymia*.

Fukuyama argues that the mainstream of English political philosophy since Hobbes has aimed at curbing this dangerous passion for power and undiluted recognition by others. The main restrictions built into the US Constitution are, according to Fukuyama, rooted in the fear of *megalothymia*, which he insists has also been the motivating passion in modern Japanese nationalism. The Anglo-American cure for *megalothymia* is peaceful economic competition governed by free trade principles. East Asians may be better at business than Westerners, but philosophically, and therefore politically, the result is the same: *megalothymia* is curbed. East Asia, and Japan with it, is thereby marginalized in the overall scheme of world history. For Fukuyama, there is no Asian century.

This perception is crucial. For Fukuyama, history has travelled on a set of rails, defined by technological progress, desire for material well-being, and the demand for varying levels of inter-human recognition (*thymos*, *megalothymia*, and *isothymia*, the last being the demand for absolute equality between men, an impulse that animates, for example, the contemporary advocacy of 'political correctness'). Fukuyama's belief that history has a direction and that it is driven by the interplay of these three forces has important implications for the student of Japanese nationalism, public policy and the Japanese-miracle-as-model debate. Not only, therefore, should the post-war rise of Japan be explained by reference to history's rails, but furthermore the Japanese miracle does not alter the fundamental character of history as Fukuyama understands it.

Quite the contrary, the end of history demands the demise of the Japanese nationalist state as invented in the Meiji era. Besieged from below by Japanese feminists, pop decadence and minority self-assertion, and from without by free-trade pressures, the Japanese racial state is condemned by Hegelian universal necessity to slouch towards the day when a blue-eyed European or an ambitious Chinese will be able freely to win Japanese citizenship. Only when the Japanese state has abandoned blood purity (uniqueness) will it, in Fukuyama's view, cease to be irrational.

This is consistent with the entire thrust of Western philosophy since Plato, because only the universally valid merits the term 'rational'. Japanese particularism, the insistence both on the uniqueness of Japanese political institutions, for example, and that accidents of blood or genetic inheritance determine who is and who is not a Japanese, condemns the Japanese model out of hand. The suggestion is that

Japanese ethnic particularism should wilt under the strong light of universal reason as the Western tradition conceives it.

In what sense does Fukuyama's argument challenge or confirm the view that Japanese public policy embodies a 'thinking nationalism'? There seems little doubt that the Japanese drive to overtake Europe and America in the economic sphere has been motivated by the politics of national ambition, the desire for recognition by the 'other', in this case the West. In this drive, *thymos* and *megalothymia* have contended for domination in the Japanese approach. Japan's success in its competition with the West also encourages the view that the Anglo-American cure for the *megalothymic* nationalist economic ambition would weaken Japan's competitive spirit by taming what Keynes called 'animal spirits'. But such animal spirits drive economic growth. The Japanese bureaucracy has thus far rebuffed attempts, be they the Bush administration's SII offensive or its insistence that US anti-trust law should apply in Japan, to sap Japan's competitive drive.

But the decisive blow against the Japanese model of public policy or nationalist particularism is contained in Fukuyama's sources. His heroes are all 'dead white European males': Plato, Aristotle, Machiavelli, Hobbes, Locke, Kant, Marx, Nietzsche, Max Weber, and above all Hegel. Even the honoured views of America's founding fathers are mediated by a Frenchman: Alexis de Tocqueville. There are no Japanese names in this list. For Fukuyama, the Western tradition of political philosophy is a meditation about the world that has made the world. Japan is nothing in Fukuyama's discourse because it has never produced a first-rank thinker about politics.

Fukuyama may have yellow skin, a Japanese surname, and an American passport, but he is a Eurocentrist because European thinkers embody a matchless tradition of excellence. Four kinds of intellectuals will be appalled by this book: Japanese nationalists (*Nihonjin-ron-sha*) because they view European excellence as white excellence; postmodernists because they hoped postmodernism showed that Japan had transcended the mere modern; post-structuralists because they believe Eurocentrism is racist and anti-Third World; and advocates of American-style political correctness because they dread the authority of the Western canon of thought.

He is right about modern Japanese political philosophy (the premodern tradition is another matter): Japan has produced no Hegel or Plato or even a Max Weber. But Fukuyama's implicit verdict can be overturned. Post-war Japan is one of the great political experiments of history, fully comparable to Plato's Athens, Machiavelli's Florence or

James Madison's America. Now should be the hour for a classical achievement in Japanese political thought.

But to achieve what Nietzsche called the 'dancing star' of genuine excellence demands rejecting the deadening hand of mediocrity as reflected in these four schools of anti-thought. It is they, not Western genius, that keep Japan marginalized in global consciousness. It is an engaged classicism, that is textual excellence, that remains a culture's best defence against oblivion, that is nothingness.

A JAPAN-SHAPED HOLE

This interpretation, that the Japanese have achieved something extra-ordinary in the public sphere with their version of 'thinking nationalism', turns on the view that the post-war Japanese miracle offers a significant intellectual challenge to some of the more rooted assumptions of the Western mind. To neglect Japanese political and economic success is to create a 'Japan-shaped hole' in the discourse of modern Western social science and political analysis. Though the point may be lost on Europeans and Americans ensconced in the heartland of Western civilization, this incipient 'hole' is the object of bitter feelings in Japan and the Third World.

In his essay, *Kindai to wa Nani ka* (What is Modernity?), Takeuchi Yoshimi concluded that 'Modernity is the self-recognition of Europe'.[15] Fukuyama's stress on the importance of 'the struggle for recognition' may be seen to add weight to the force of Takeuchi's observation. In Fukuyama's surrender to the superiority of European thought, at the expense of Japanese political achievement, he confirms Takeuchi's doubts about the ontological nothingness of post-war Japan. *Pace* the American bias of the Modernization School of Japanese studies of the 1950s and 1960s, Fukuyama locates the centre of gravity in the Western tradition in European classicism, not in the American way of life. But this does nothing to ease attacks on Fukuyama by ideologues of Japanese nationalism or Third World critics and their Western allies. This is how the philosopher Sakai Naoki sets out the problem in the spiky idiom of post-structural analysis:

> [The West] is a name for a subject which gathers itself in discourse but is also an object constituted discursively; it is, evidently, a name always associating itself with those regions, communities and peoples that appear politically or economically superior to other regions, communities and peoples. Basically, it is just like the name 'Japan', which reputedly designates a geographic area, a tradition, a national

identity, a culture, an ethnos, a market, and so on, yet unlike all the other names associated with geographic particularities, [the West] also implies the refusal of its self-delimitation; it claims that it is capable of sustaining, if not actually transcending, an impulse to transcend all the particularizations.[16]

To recognise this impulse within the Western tradition is to penetrate the very core of the cult of Orientalism that Third World critics such as Edward Said find so offensive.[17] This apparently unique Western gift for subsuming the myriad particulars of empirical reality under its own guise of philosophic and scientific universalism stands at the heart of the Hegelian enterprise and of the struggles of Max Weber and Jurgen Habermas, since the death of Heidegger perhaps Germany's greatest thinker, to render the nature of modernity intelligible, and, in Sakai's view, to bolster the putative unity of the West in the face of particularist challenge from the Third World. Western universalism also motivates the Modernization School's schema of American-led global progress as well as Fukuyama's speculations on the 'end of history'. Sakai concludes with evident distaste that 'the West thinks itself to be ubiquitous'.[18]

For those outside the Western ambit, this ubiquity has important consequences. 'For the non-West, modernity means above all, the state of being deprived of one's own subjectivity', but Sakai's assumption of Third World passivity is unpersuasive.[19] Nevertheless, the problem of 'universalism vs. particularism' highlights a conspicuous failing: the apparent inability of Japanese thinkers on politics and culture to transcend the mental barriers posed by Japanese particularism. In recoil against this undisguised failure, the keepers of the flame of Japanese national identity have fallen back on the doctrine of uniqueness, which is in effect an admission of defeat. What Japanese intellectuals such as Umehara Takashi or Eto Jun have sought in place of Japanese universalism is universal recognition of the superiority of Japanese particularism, as manifested in Japan's post-war economic miracle and competitive success in world markets.

The business press of the West has largely recognized the fact of Japanese economic success. It is not obvious that the editors of *The Financial Times* or *The Economist* have convinced themselves that this success can be explained solely in terms of the universal paradigm of positivist Anglo-American economic thought, the creation of Adam Smith, Alfred Marshall and their contemporary heirs. Contrary to Sakai's bitter broodings, power can create facts. Whatever Japan's origins in the Third World of nineteenth-century underdevelopment and despite the fact that the Japanese are neither white nor the cultural children of the Renaissance, Reformation and Enlightenment, the representatives of Japan today occupy places of responsibility and considerable prestige in the councils of Western capitalism.

But intellectuals such as Fukuyama, formed by the European philosophy tradition, will confront such Japanese success with three objections. First, modernity is a Western invention, not a Japanese one. Second, the Japanese tradition has failed to generate a set of classic, universal insights into the nature of modern politics and society, and this precludes the necessity to view the modern condition through Japanese eyes; and, even if one wanted to do so, the textual means do not yet exist. Third, the end of history means that the main issues of humanity's future have been resolved. Japanese society may benefit from this resolution, but has contributed little or nothing to this process.

In attempting to understand the Japanese political system as a whole, there has been no effort here to contest the claims of grand theory outside the counter-critique offered here or in Chapter 13 of Fukuyama's understanding of the Hegelian concept of the state. In place of grand theory, a macro-meso mix of theory and analysis has been offered. In contending that the Japanese approach to public policy reflects a thinking nationalism, the implicit view assumed here is that history has not ended and therefore the door on a Japanese classicism is still open. This is to insist that the Japanese miracle is not an epiphenomenon. On the contrary, it is to assert the view that the current Western effort to 're-centre' itself, which appears also to be Fukuyama's supreme goal, will of necessity involve a Japanese dimension.

One is nevertheless struck by the consistent instinct among Western thinkers and scholars to marginalize Japan, in Sakai's phrase, to render it 'innocuous in the discursive formation' of the modern world's understanding of itself. Sakai has the right to demand that the Western reader now turn a sceptical eye on the racial or ethnic assumptions that appear to animate Weber or Habermas or the Modernization School or Fukuyama's own musings. But it is not only grand theory that would marginalize Japan to world consciousness, but some of the findings of recent Western political science research as well. To this issue we shall now turn.

SIGNIFICANT OTHERS

'Only writing can give meaning to the insignificant'.[20] Roland Barthes' telling observation strikes at the heart of the problems of the modern study of Japanese government by Western political scientists. The American Occupation and the SII affair both illustrated how scholarship may be marginalized. The enormous readership won by Reischauer's

The Japanese or Vogel's *Japan as Number One* is a rare phenomenon. Scholar-diplomats exercise what influence they have as diplomats, not scholars. On the question of influence, the serious journalist is often better placed to make his views felt in public discourse than his scholarly contemporary. The reasons why this should be so are complex, but one factor is the issue of the levels of analysis, that persistent struggle between the claims of the big picture (significance) and the demands of the facts, however obscure (scientific respectability). Much of the argument in *The Economist* and *The Wall Street Journal* depends on the branch of grand theory worked out by Adam Smith and his successors. In blanket concepts such as 'the market' or 'free enterprise' or 'free trade', a complex and difficult set of theoretical assumptions and a huge body of factual evidence are reduced to a shorthand. This allows writers and their readers to exploit the powers of grand theory without having continually to revise their thoughts about the fundamental nature of the economy and politics.

Macro political theory, that is ideas and interpretations about an individual nation taken as a unit, depends crucially on assumptions about grand theory. Thus the words 'America' or 'Britain' frequently stand in *The Economist* article for embodiments of more 'free-market' or 'free-trade' assumptions and values, while the struggle to fit 'Japan' into the Anglo-American model of grand theory has exercised *Economist* writers as almost no other problem. In dealing with the lower, more detailed levels of analysis, down to the sectoral (meso) and the firm or individual governmental agency (micro), it is the editor looking over the shoulder of the journalist who keeps the writer from becoming an academic. To this degree, even the serious journalist will view the demands of scientific respectability with discomfort.

The different levels can be summarized in this way:

Grand theory
Macro theory
Analysis of the meso or middle range
Micro research

Grand theory attempts to state large truths about the fundamental nature of social reality. As such it reflects an intersection of philosophical truth and political needs. For purposes of illustration, Francis Fukuyama's *The End of History and the Last Man* shows how the grand theory of classical Western political philosophy might be applied to the task of understanding contemporary Japan, of placing it in the larger scheme of things. Grand theory, by its very nature, has an enormous capacity to absorb, order and neglect vast stretches of empirical reality. This is its strength and its weakness.

Japan: Beyond the End of History is an exercise in macro theory which aims to understand Japan at the national level. The thesis that Japan is a nationalist polity becoming a liberal one is a kind of macro theory, but one which relies both on meso and micro analysis to sustain its claims. But what about those more refined and more detailed levels of analysis? Is the magazine or newspaper reader missing out by not perusing even occasionally, what the scholar who is a Japan expert has to say about modern Japanese government and politics? In Chapter 12, an attempt was made to demonstrate that Western scholars have contributed to the depth of our understanding of post-war Japan in a way untrue of Western journalism. In this chapter a controversial piece of British academic revisionism about Japan will be examined to see whether claims for the unique strengths of Western scholarly writings about Japan can be sustained. The word 'Western' here requires qualification. The study of Japanese public policy outside Japan is almost entirely the work of American political scientists and, at one remove, economists. *Dynamic and Immobilist Politics in Japan* (1988), edited by Arthur Stockwin, may be viewed as an attempt by the Oxford–Australia school to put Britain and Australia on the map in Japanese policy studies and to give the American scholars who dominate Western research some competition.[21] Given the dearth of influential European research on the subject, this was a pioneering departure.

The Promotion and Regulation of Industry in Japan (1991), edited by Stephen Wilks and Maurice Wright, is part of an even more ambitious research initiative on government–industry relations in major industrial democracies commissioned in 1984 by the British Economic and Social Research Council.[22] This multi-volume research project would make Britain a power in Japanese policy studies.

Perhaps inevitably, it is US research that provides this British effort with its indispensable point of departure: Chalmers Johnson's *MITI and the Japanese Miracle* (1982), the only seminal Western text on Japanese politics to emerge since the decline of the Modernization School in the 1970s.[23] Johnson insists that capitalist countries differ significantly, and that public policy in the US and Japan reflects radically contrasting priorities: Japan since 1868 has been a 'development state' which sought to manipulate capitalism to secure national autonomy and bureaucratic goals; America has been a 'regulatory state' which surrendered to market forces to enhance consumption.

Building on the anti-Johnson revisionism of American scholars such as David Friedman, Kent Calder, Daniel Okimoto and Richard Samuels, the Wilks–Wright study seeks to end the 'Johnson era' in Japanese political science. Or at least this is the goal that the editors would impose on the thirteen articles in this book which wrestle with the institutional nexus of Japanese industrial policy, the promotion of new industries, the management of decline and the Japanese and American public policy fracas over telecommunications.[24]

It is the Japanese example that made industrial policy a debating point in the British general election and the American presidential contest of 1992. This is partly because Thatcherism and Reaganism held that free-market principles provide the only sound formula for national prosperity. If the Japanese experience overturns this assumption, those principles are threatened.

The abandonment of such high ground in this British volume appears to condemn it to intellectual insignificance, a status implicit in most definitions of academic respectability. Why did the authors risk it? Primarily because the Western contributors (the Japanese authors are more cautious about dismissing the influence of the Japanese state) suspect that Johnson is wrong and that micro analysis, which in the Wilks–Wright study refers to the policy community or policymaking network of a sector of Japanese industry, is the only serious endeavour for a scholar. What then is micro analysis?

The editors of this volume endorse the tripartite division between macro (the nation), meso (the sector, as in shipbuilding), and micro (the policy community or network) levels of analysis already described. The distinction between meso and micro might be made clearer by observing that the Japanese workers who build ships do not normally qualify as members of the shipbuilding-policy community, but the elite managers who oversee them do.

Thus the best articles in the Wilks–Wright study encourage the belief that one is wading knee-deep in the very stuff of empirical reality at the micro level. Not even a very long piece of reporting can begin to match the detail offered. Scientific respectability has its virtues.

But there is also an ideological ambush waiting for any micro researcher who rejects the macro approach, as we find in Johnson; or grand theory, the highest level of analysis, as reflected in the work of Hayek or Marx. An article in *The Economist* (April 4, 1992) illustrates the danger.[25] In a piece titled 'Japanese Business Methods', a study on the machine tool industry is cited to blast Japanese industrial policy as 'ineffective' and 'counter productive'. The unnamed study in question is almost certainly David Friedman's *The Misunderstood Miracle*.[26] Friedman is anti-statist, but he is also an uncompromising critic of the free-market and convergence theory (the belief that Americanization is the only industrial model that counts). Nevertheless, *The Economist* winks at Friedman's conclusions and borrows from his research to bolster its free-market attack on Japanese industrial policy. A similar fate may await this British study. Johnson's macro conclusions about the effectiveness of Japanese industry policy have been swept aside and nothing offered in their place but an insistence that government–industry networking is the key phenomenon in Japanese public policy. A Reaganite advocate of 'public choice' theory will know what to do with this conclusion: exploit the attack on Johnson but ignore the rest as academic minutiae. The Wilks–Wright study may be seen to hand ammunition to those economists who call for the abolition of political science. On this issue Johnson towers above his critics.

But Friedman's critique is not idle. His remark that, 'most studies simply assert that a given [Japanese] policy led to desired economic outcomes, assuming the promulgation of a regulation or a law is the same as proof of its effectiveness', captures the cardinal impulse in this British assault on Johnson.[27] Detailed empirical research remains vulnerable if not translated into grand and macro theory. The abuse of Friedman's research shows that scholarship is not for the ideologically naive. Big questions unaddressed leave a vacuum.

The editors believe that they have overthrown Johnson's theory with detailed empirical research or 'unpacking'. Micro findings can shake meso theory; meso findings can rattle macro theory. The problem is that micro research can also be unpacked. On this point the editors resemble a nuclear physicist who doubts the existence of subatomic particles. In the *Critique of Pure Reason*, Kant defined the problem of hyper-factualization (an ugly word for an unhappy phenomenon) as the central danger of empiricism.[28] Both political scientists and natural scientists believe, indeed at some level of ontological intent must believe, in the final unity of the genus or reality. But the empiricist, with his embrace of factual knowledge, is confronted with millions of facts, relatively few of which he will be able to study. Perhaps more seriously, *true* understanding of even a small slice of reality may well be impossible. The making of Japanese public policy in the shipbuilding sector involves thousands, even hundreds of thousands, of facts. The implied learning curve is almost infinitely long. Reality does not end when one grows tired of looking at it.

In this British study, the Boyd–Nagamori article, for example, is not micro research, but a kind of sub-micro research that unpacks Young's article which is also about Japanese shipbuilding.[29] In the Boyd–Nagamori attempt to 'deconstruct' the 1978 Depressed Industries Law (*Tokutei Fukyōsangyō Antei Rinji-Sochitō*), the authors flirt with the danger of total regress. Much of the evidence presented turns on the intentions of the various members of the policy network concerned at different stages of the public and corporate response to the rolling crisis in the shipping industry. To speak with Cartesian confidence about what only the key policy players thought they were doing at any or every point in the drama would require the kind of access to individual mental processes that James Joyce provided of Molly Bloom in *Ulysses*.

This is not to overstate the scientific problem here. If Tokyo press corps rumour is accurate, a key moment in the Tōyō Shinkin scandal came and went when the IBJ's loans at issue were challenged at a board meeting of the bank. A single board member raised his voice, and declared that he would take responsibility for the matter. Consistent with Japanese corporate culture at this level, the probing of the matter at board level ended there. But what journalist or scholar is ever to know *with certainty* what was going on in the heads of the members of the IBJ board on the day in question?

It is the quest for certainty, which may in some cases turn out to be an arbitrary certainty, that motivates what Wilks and Wright uneasily call 'wild empiricism'. It is the disciplining effect of grand and macro theory on such 'wild empiricism' that makes theory important. So we are left with Pontius Pilate's question: What is truth? By way of an answer, our schema of levels of research now looks like this:

Grand theory
Macro theory
Analysis of the meso or middle range
Micro research
Sub-micro 'unpacking'
Sub-sub-micro hyperfactualization

The Wilks–Wright volume, whatever its methodological vulnerabilities, may be right about Japan. In its fundamental conclusion that Japan public policy has been an abject failure, the British-sponsored research provides an empirical grounding for Fukuyama's sovereign dismissal of Japan as nothing. On this issue, *The Promotion and Regulation of Industry in Japan* offers a provocative challenge to the pervasive Japanese pride and nationalist assertiveness that colours parts of *The Political Economy of Japan, Volume 1: The Domestic Transformation*, edited by Kozo Yamamura and Yasukichi Yasuba.[30]

The proof of the pudding will of course be found in the quality of the findings of such micro research. If micro research alone qualifies as sound scholarship, if all large questions are spurious, then not only does most journalism stand condemned but so, too, does all significant scholarship, all theory and analysis concerned with the big picture. Should this implicit rejection of significance in favour of academic respectability be embraced? Is such bourgeois scholarship, with its respectable airs, invulnerable to counter-critique?

On methodological grounds, the micro approach risks hyper-factualization. Kant's warning about empiricism unrestrained by positivism or grand theory is not to be ignored. But an even more serious danger is posed by the insistence of these authors that almost all previous research, be it Japanese or Western, journalistic or scholarly, is fundamentally flawed because earlier researchers have not looked deep enough. If so much is at stake in scholarly findings in the Wilks–Wright volume, then their research must be replicated. Yet it would be a very bold empiricist who would insist that such replication will yield results identical with the findings in the Wilks–Wright volume or any other volume of scientifically respectable research that is not positivist. More damaging, this forced reworking of the same ore would conspire against the hopes, such as Samuels has recently expressed, for scholarly cumulation in the political science of Japan.[31]

Thinking reeds

Where does this leave the journalist who writes about Japanese government or the reader who relies on journalism for his picture of the world? First, it must be acknowledged that no reputable newspaper editor would tolerate the quality of writing in some of the scholarly publications that have been discussed in this book. On this point, Barthes' observation about the necessary link between meaning and writing breaks down. Opaque prose defeats understanding. But scholarship exhibits certain powers that the thinking journalist will envy. The crossfire of perspectives at work in the four articles on telecommunications in the Wilks–Wright volume, the sheer length of the essays in question, is beyond the reach of any branch of the mass media. While journalism can demonstrate the tensions between micro and macro levels of analysis, it offers no forum for their systematic discussion.

The ideological struggles of the 1980s illustrate the problem. The revival of classical economic theory which gave an incisive edge to the policy criticism contained in *The Economist, The Wall Street Journal* or *The Financial Times* was discussed at length in all these newspapers. Thatcherism and Reaganism were assaults on the economic ideas of Keynesian social democracy. But the disinterested assessment of the truth claims, scientific and philosophical, of Keynesianism and monetarism was, with rare exception, beyond the scope of even the quality press.

More crucial still, journalism is, by nature, unable to generate a body of thought such as Keynesianism or monetarism. This is the task of the thinker. In addressing the fundamental problems of mankind – the nature of the great depression, for example – Keynes in his bath was more important than an army of journalists. No serious news commentator ever forgets this. No academic should.

All this highlights the vital importance of the Asian scholar. Did Western reporters, at any time, grasp the true nature of wartime Japan, revolutionary China or regimes as varied as Taiwan, South Vietnam or North Korea? Was such intellectual penetration likely if even Keynesianism and monetarism conspired against understanding such Asian polities? In the answers to these questions will be found the importance of the Japan scholar as 'thinking reed'. Here, too, lies the potential cure for the excesses of wild empiricism.

CODA

16 The receding roar

Last thoughts on the Japanese miracle

In his famous essay on Lord Althorp, Walter Bagehot addressed the vexed subject of national greatness. There he observed that, 'The characteristic danger of great nations, like the Romans, or the English, which have a long history of continuous creation, is that they may at last fail from not comprehending the great institutions they have created'.

Are the Japanese a 'great nation' in this sense? Have they sustained 'a long history of continuous creation' in political ideas and institutions? Are they ceasing to understand the structures and organizations that have sustained their extraordinary advance since 1945? Does failure threaten them? Such questions acquired a perturbing pertinence, sometimes spurious, in the wake of the bursting of Japan's speculative bubble at the beginning of the 1990s. This recessionary collapse appears to have provoked a crisis of confidence among some members of Japan's elite.

In 1992, when Japanese newspapers were full of scandalous revelations and the Tokyo stock exchange had lost over half of its 1990 peak value, Tachi Ryūichirō, Professor Emeritus of Tokyo University and a member of the Japanese Academy, boldly called for the abandonment of the 'Japanese model' of public policy. In its place, he urged his countrymen to embrace the 'Anglo-American' alternative.[1]

Such advocacy brings the argument developed in this book full circle. In Chapter 2, it was insisted that a sound understanding of the Japanese approach to public policy had to be grounded, not in Anglo-American ideas and values, but in the lessons of the Japanese political experiment since Meiji. As an economist trained in the Anglo-American school, Tachi might be expected to take such a position regardless of the changes of the 1990s. The recession that so worried him inflicted far greater pain on America and Britain than Japan. Indeed, his proposal appeared as the organizers of the reconstruction of Los Angeles, after that city's 1992 race riots, were appealing for Japanese financial assistance, and when

Britain had just experienced a general election in which investment-led growth, and at one step removed the Japanese miracle itself, had formed an important subtext to national debate. The timing of Tachi's defence of the Anglo-American free-market model, was, in Western perspective, oddly flattering, even unlikely.

Ironically, this distinguished economist borrowed heavily from the thesis elaborated in Johnson's *MITI and the Japanese Miracle* when he described the 'Japanese model'. This was a clever tactic. In essence he conceded the past to Johnson, but at the price of claiming the future. Because Japan, even more than America, embodies the qualities of what Hegel called 'the land of tomorrow', Tachi could be confident which frontier his future-obsessed countrymen would prefer to dwell on.

In the name of a foreign idea, Japanese free-marketeers would deny greatness to Japan. In its unsettling brilliance, the achievement of Japan's modern century represents a kind of glory unique to its millennial past. *Pace* thinkers such as Tachi and Francis Fukuyama, the extraordinary character of the Meiji and Showa developmental models make Japan one of the twentieth-century's very few candidates for a place in the Pantheon of classical political systems. Post-Meiji Japan has, therefore, in its own way, been one of the monuments of world history. An unblinking politics demands that we recognize this achievement.

Less sympathetic and intellectually of another school, economists would lay this history of continuous creation, with its roots in the pre-Meiji era, to one side. Amid the wreckage of corporate reputations and the economic unease of the early 1990s, there is an understandable temptation to neglect the great institutions that have sustained modern Japan and to seek the healing balm of free-market 'perfection'. Reformers such as Tachi, Morita Akio and Shindō Muneyuki no doubt spoke to the Japanese feeling that it was time for a change.[2] They would insist that contemporary Japan lacks the will and the ability to resist the arrival of the 'end of history'. They would announce the final triumph of Western thought and experience over Japanese particularism and invention.

The Anglo-American model, however battered, may point the way forward for the Japanese. Daniel Okimoto has criticized, and rightly, the false coherence sometimes assumed of MITI's public policy.[3] But the free-market model, as a theory, may be an even less helpful form of false coherence. The laissez-faire ideal, consistently applied, sits uncomfortably with the suggestion that Japan has become an economic superpower by following the unforgiving wisdom of positive economic laws. Indeed, so strong has the impression of the nationalist model been on post-war Japan that many who admire Tachi's free-market thesis still suspect that the new Japan will better resemble Germany and France, than Britain or America. Japan's administrative inheritance has been so different from that of the Anglo Saxons.

No liberal attack on post-Meiji centralization and modernization, not even Tachi's, can be sustained unless it overturns the foundations of Japanese nationalism by solving what Maruyama Masao calls the 'dilemmas of modernization': (1) How can national identity be maintained while embracing necessary change? (2) Should changes of values precede or follow institutional reform? (3) Should priority be given to Japan's effectiveness as an actor on the international stage or to the maintenance of domestic consensus? (4) Uncoordinated pluralism or reform from above?

The first dilemma is at work in the sensitive issues of guest-workers, Japanese citizenship for foreigners and the foreign ownership of Japanese firms. The second is alive in the debate over electoral reform, the cartel stranglehold (*dangō taishitsu*) and educational change. The third reflects the divisive questions of Japan's status as a great power, the burdens of peace-keeping operations and Tokyo's desire for a permanent seat on the UN Security Council. The fourth turns on the conundrum that decentralization and market liberalization require state leadership, but both would dilute state powers.

Japan's liberal reformers have only begun to address these dilemmas. Perhaps the Hosokawa phenomenon should be judged as an inspired complement to the Meiji paradigm, rather than as a radical transformation of regime. Indeed, there are important reasons why such a transformation should not be rushed. In Tokyo for the 1993 G-7 economic summit, the economist Anatole Kaletsky, commenting for *The Times*, sagely observed that the Japanese have thus far defeated the scourge of mass unemployment, one of the most serious 'political and economic questions of our time'. This is yet another one of those singular triumphs that explains the global appeal of Japan's encounter with modernity.

The burdens of tomorrow, what Bagehot calls 'continuous creation', may be great. But Japan will not fail so long as she understands the nature of her post-war institutions. These are grounded in Japanese ambition, and that remains strong. Ambition will guarantee that despite the pressures of a nascent liberalism, the Japanese model of nationalist economics, of *kokumin keizai*, will echo powerfully in the new century. Its long withdrawing roar is even now changing the world.

Notes and references

IN PLACE OF A FOREWORD

1 Ōtsuka Hisao, *Dai-roku-kan: Kokumin Keizai, Ōtsuka Hisao Chosaku-shu* (Volume Six: National Economics, The Collected Works of Ōtsuka Hisao) Tokyo, Iwanami-shoten, 1969.
2 In this sense, *Beyond the End of History* benefits from a long tradition of writing and thinking which extends from the Continental and English mercantilists who influenced Americans such as Alexander Hamilton, then from Hamilton to List and the other proponents of the German Historical School, including Wilhelm Roscher and Gustav Schmoller, and then finally to such Japanese writers as Fukuda Tokuzo and Ōtsuka Hisao.
3 R. Rorty, *Philosophy and the Mirror of Nature*, Princeton, NJ, Princeton University Press, 1979; and R. Rorty (ed.), *The Linguistic Turn*, Chicago, University of Chicago Press, 1967.
4 Charles Taylor, 'Inwardness and the Culture of Modernity' in Axel Honneth *et al.* (eds), *Philosophical Interventions in the Unfinished Project of Enlightenment*, Cambridge, Mass., The MIT Press, 1992, p. 88. Italics added.
5 Ibid., p. 93.
6 Ibid.

1 POLICYMAKING IN AN ECONOMIC SUPERPOWER

1 Isaiah Berlin, 'The Pursuit of the Ideal', *The Crooked Timber of Humanity: Chapters in the History of Ideas*, London, John Murray, 1990, pp. 1–19.
2 Ibid., p. 1.
3 Peter F. Drucker, *The New Realities: in Government and Politics, in Economics and Business, in Society and World View*, New York, Harper & Row, 1989, p. 4.
4 Berlin, op.cit., pp.1–19.
5 Carol Gluck, *Japan's Modern Myths: Ideology in the Late Meiji Period*, Princeton, NJ, Princeton University Press, 1985, p. 147.
6 Drucker, op. cit., p. 4.

2 UNDERSTANDING THE NEW JAPAN: SOME IDEOLOGICAL POINTERS

1 Clifford Longley, 'Religious Schools Must Uphold Common Values', *The Times*, 11 January 1992, p. 10.

3 WHY THE CENTRE HOLDS

1 J.A.A. Stockwin, *Japan: Divided Politics in a Growth Economy*, London and New York, W.W. Norton, 1982, second edition, p. 20.
2 'Central Banks: America v Japan – The Rewards of Independence', *The Economist*, 25–31 January 1992, p. 19.
3 Stanford's Peter Duus is illuminating on this issue in his short book *Feudalism in Japan*, New York, Alfred A. Knopf, 1976, second edition.
4 James Madison, *Federalist Paper No. 10*, New York, 1787.
5 Tetsuo Najita, *Japan: The Intellectual Foundations of Modern Japanese Politics*, Chicago, University of Chicago Press, 1980, p. 2.
6 Ibid., p. 6.
7 Ibid.
8 Confucius, *The Analects*, translated by D.C. Lau, Middlesex, England, Penguin, 1979, p. 60.
9 Najita, op. cit., p. 6.
10 Ibid., p. 7.
11 See David Williams, 'Reporting the Death of the Emperor Shōwa', Oxford, Nissan Occasional Paper Series, No. 14, 1990. For another corrective view of the sound and fury of Western reporting on the imperial question, see Stephen S. Large, *Emperor Hirohito and Shōwa Japan*, London, Routledge, 1992.

4 GENTLEMEN AND PLAYERS IN THE POLICY CONTEST

1 Roy Hofheinz, Jr. and Kent E. Calder, *The Eastasia Edge*, New York, Basic Books, 1982, p. 44.
2 Peter Hennessy, *Whitehall*, London, Secker and Warburg, 1989.
3 Namiki Nobuyoshi, *Tsūsanshō no Shūen: Shakai Kōzō no Henkaku wa Kanō ka* (The End of MITI: Is the Structural Change of Society still Possible?), Tokyo, Daiyamondo-sha, 1989; Yamaguchi Jirō, *Ōkura Kanryō no Shihai no Shūen* (The End of MOF Domination), Tokyo, Iwanami-Shoten, 1987.
4 Sataka Makoto, *Nihon Kanryō Hakusho* (White Paper on the Japanese Bureaucracy), Tokyo, Kōdan-sha, 1989, p. 4.
5 Ibid., pp. 330–6. This extract taken from the end-piece written by another author (here, Uchibashi Katsuhito) that often concludes Japanese books, both hard and soft cover, which rarely have prefaces by other writers in the Western manner.
6 T. J. Pempel, *Policy and Politics in Japan: Creative Conservativism*, Philadelphia, Temple University Press, 1982, p. 21.
7 Sheldon Garon, *The State and Labor in Modern Japan*, Berkeley and Los Angeles, University of California Press, 1987, p. 4.

8 Chalmers Johnson, *MITI and the Japanese Miracle: The Growth of Industrial Policy, 1925–1975*, Stanford, Calif., Stanford University Press, 1982, p. 31.
9 Kent E. Calder, *Crisis and Compensation: Public Policy and Political Stability in Japan, 1949–1986*, Princeton, NJ, Princeton University Press, 1988.
10 Ibid., p. 274. I claculate the figure to be about $117 per person.
11 Ibid., p. 275.
12 Ibid.
13 It must also be acknowledged that parliamentary tribes or '*zoku*' also influence the policymaking process. The degree of influence resists easy summary because of the difficulties that academics and journalists have had in reaching a consensus about what a *zoku giin* (*zoku* Dietman) is or what constitutes effective membership of a *zoku*.

In a lecture given at Oxford's Nissan Institute (Michaelmas 1990), Professor Lee W. Farnsworth, perhaps America's leading authority on the '*zoku*', was highly critical of the definitional confusion that divides writers on the *zoku*. He also argued that mere membership in any particular *zoku* by a Diet politician does not translate into automatic impact on policymaking. Quite the contrary, *zoku* leaders tend to be established players in the factions and party hierarchy whose influence is confirmed by their place on the *zoku* seniority ladder. It is these power-brokers who have on occasion mediated disputes between conflicting ministries. But it remains to be demonstrated that such politicians, when wearing their *zoku* hats or otherwise, are consistent promoters of the national interest, as opposed to vested, sectional, party, factional or private interests, when they address broad questions of policymaking. The power of the *zoku* must not be exaggerated. Miyazawa Kiichi has dubbed the policy tribes as mere 'cheering sections' for the key ministries. But such scepticism has to be carefully stated because it is also clear that the most powerful *zoku* players do perform a key function, particularly during periods of MOF-imposed austerity, in protecting the budget share of the ministries with which the *zoku* identify. Nevertheless, the *zoku* are in the main tools of pressure-group politics and the redistributive bribery of rural constituencies that deface Japanese parliamentary democracy. Farnsworth concludes that, 'the greatest *zoku giin* was Mr. [Kakuei] Tanaka and his Niigata 3rd District was the top beneficiary' (Lee W. Farnsworth, 'Japan's Changing Policy-making Structure', *The World Economy*, vol. 12, No. 2, June 1989, p. 165).

5 FOUR POLICY LESSONS FROM THE 1980s

1 C. Fred Bergsten, 'What to Do About the US–Japan Economic Conflict', *Foreign Affairs*, vol. 60, no. 5, Summer 1982, pp. 1054–75.
2 C. Fred Bergsten, 'The United States Trade Deficit and the Dollar', Statement before the Senate Committee on Banking, Housing and Urban Affairs, Subcommittee on International Finance and Monetary Policy, Washington, 6 June 1984, p. 4, cited in Jeffrey A. Frankel, 'The Yen/Dollar Agreement: liberalizing Japanese Capital Markets', *Policy Analyses in International Economics*, no. 9, December 1984, Washington, DC, Institute for International Economics, 1984, p. 54.
3 Suzuki Yoshio, *Japan's Economic Performance and International Role*, Tokyo, University of Tokyo Press, 1989, p. 42.

4 Ibid., pp. 42–3.
5 Peter F. Drucker, *The New Realities: in Government and Politics, in Economics and Business, in Society and World View*, New York, Harper and Row, 1989, p. 120.
6 For more detail, see 'Super-industrialism and the New Japan', *Tokyo Business Today* (March 1989). The article was written by David Williams, based on research by Sato Takashi and Fukuma Masaki, published in the *Shūkan Tōyō Keizai*, 19 January 1989, pp. 4–16.
7 *Nikkan Kōgyō Shinbun Shuzai-han-hen* (The Special Reporting Section of the Nikkan Kōgyō newspaper) (ed), *Shin 'Maekawa Ripōto' ga Shimesu Michi: Nihon wo Kōkawaeru* (The Way Shown by the 'New' Maekawa Report: This is How Japan Can Change), Tokyo, Nikkan Shobō, 1987.
8 Ibid., pp. 1–5.
9 Leon Hollerman, *Japan, Disincorporated: The Economic Liberalization Process*, Stanford, Calif., Hoover Institution Press, 1988, p. xvi.

6 THE MINISTRY OF FINANCE AND THE JAPANESE MIRACLE

1 Kuribayashi Yoshimitsu, *Ōkura-shō: Ginkō-kyoku* (The Ministry of Finance: The Banking Bureau), Tokyo, Kōdan-sha, 1988; *Ōkura-sho: Shukei-kyoku* (The Ministry of Finance: The Budget Bureau), Tokyo, Kōdan-sha, 1990; *Ōkura-shō: Shuzei-kyoku* (The Ministry of Finance: The Tax Administration Bureau), Tokyo, Kōdan-sha, 1991; *Ōkura-shō: Shōken-kyoku* (The Ministry of Finance: The Securities Bureau), Tokyo, Kōdan-sha, 1991.
2 Kuribayashi Yoshimitsu, *Ōkura-shō: Ginkō-kyoku* (The Ministry of Finance: the Banking Bureau), Tokyo, Kōdan-sha, 1988, p. 3.
3 Kishimoto Kōichi, *Politics in Modern Japan: Development and Organization*, Tokyo, Japan Echo Inc., 1988, third edition, p. 3.
4 Ibid.
5 Itō Daiichi, *Genzai Nihon Kanryō-sei no Bunseki* (The Japanese Bureaucracy Today: an Analysis), Tokyo, Tokyo Daigaku Shuppan-kai, 1980, p. v.

7 JAPANESE INDUSTRIAL POLICY: THE GREAT DEBATE

1 E. Sydney Crawcour, 'Industrialization and Technological Change, 1885–1920', in Peter Duus (ed.), *The Cambridge History of Japan, Volume 6, The Twentieth Century*, Cambridge, England, Cambridge University Press, 1988, p. 387.
2 Ibid., pp. 389–90.
3 Ibid., p. 446.
4 Ibid., p. 450.
5 Iwata Masakazu, *Ōkubo Toshimichi: The Bismarck of Japan*, Berkeley and Los Angeles, University of California Press, 1964, p. 50.
6 Marius B. Jansen, *Sakamoto Ryōma and the Meiji Restoration*, Stanford, Calif., Stanford University Press, 1971, p. 3.
7 T. J. Pempel, *Policy and Politics in Japan: Creative Conservativism*, Philadelphia, Temple University Press, 1982. It is important to note that

Pempel's notion of Japanese conservatism bears only small resemblance to neo-conservativism in America. The closer Western policy practice approaches the model of the public choice school, the more it departs from the Japanese model.

8 In this description of the birth of the Japanese shipping industry, I am indebted to the account of William D. Wray, *Mitsubishi and the NYK, 1870–1914: Business Strategy in the Japanese Shipping Industry*, Cambridge, Mass. and London, Harvard University Press, 1984.

9 Ibid., p. 84.

10 Ibid., p. 88.

11 Ibid., pp. 92–3.

12 Hosomi Takashi and Okumura Ariyoshi, 'Japanese Industrial Policy', in John Pinder (ed.), *National Industrial Strategies and the World Economy*, London, Allanheld, Osmun/Croom Helm, 1982, p. 123.

13 Tsuruda Toshimasa, *Sengo Nihon no Sangyō Seisaku* (Industrial Policy in Postwar Japan), Tokyo, Nihon Keizai Shinbun-sha, 1982, p. 9.

14 Komiya Ryutarō, Okuna Masahiro and Suzumura Kotarō (eds), *Nihon no Sangyō Seisaku* (Japanese Industrial Policy), Tokyo, Tokyo Daigaku Shuppan-kai, 1984, published in English translation as *Industrial Policy of Japan*, Tokyo, Academic Press, 1988.

15 This is a brief statement of what is a complex problem. My intention is to address this complexity in a future book on the relationship between the European political tradition and the Japanese experience of government.

16 Peter Halfpenny, 'Positivism' in David Miller *et al.* (eds), *The Blackwell Encyclopedia of Political Thought*, Oxford, Basil Blackwell, 1991, pp. 395–7.

17 David Friedman, *The Misunderstood Miracle: Industrial Development and Political Change in Japan*, Ithaca, NY, Cornell University Press, 1988.

18 Hugh Patrick and Larry Meissner (eds), *Japan's High Technology Industries: Lessons and Limitations of Industrial Policy*, Seattle, Wash., University of Washington Press/Tokyo, University of Tokyo Press, 1986, and Komiya Ryutarō, Okuna Masahiro and Suzumura Kotarō (eds), op. cit.

19 P.A. Samuelson, *Economics*, New York, McGraw-Hill, 1948; Richard G. Lipsey, *An Introduction to Positive Economics*, London, Weidenfeld and Nicolson, 1963.

20 Some examples of this view are cited in Martin Staniland, *What is Political Economy?: A Study of Social Theory and Underdevelopment*, New Haven, Conn., Yale University Press, 1985, pp. 27–8.

21 Frank K. Upham, 'Legal Informality and Industrial Policy', *Law and Social Change in Postwar Japan*, Cambridge, Mass., Harvard University Press, 1987, p. 170.

22 Ibid., p. 171.

8 POLITICS AND POLICIES SINCE THE BUBBLE

1 Chalmers Johnson, *MITI and the Japanese Miracle: The Growth of Industrial Policy, 1925–1975*, Stanford, Calif., Stanford University Press, 1982; Suzuki Yoshio (ed.), *The Japanese Financial System*, Oxford, Clarendon Press, 1987.

2 For a detailed and liberal view of the issue, see Mikami Naoyuki, '*Saigo no Kabe wa Katakuna Jichi-shō*' (The Final Line of Resistance: the Stubborn Ministry of Home Affairs), *Shūkan Tōyō Keizai* (16 May 1992), pp. 108–11.

3 The criticism of the main players of Japan's financial system has been extensive in the quality and tabloid press, but the journalist Ubukata Yukio, in his unflinchingly negative *Ginkō vs. Shōken: Fuhai no Kōzō to Shin Tenkai* (Banks vs. Securities Companies: Structural Corruption and its New Face), Tokyo, Kōdan-sha, 1992, makes the pained point that the Japanese public has been all too forgiving and passive in the face of elite machinations, as demonstrated in the speculative bubble of the late 1980s.

4 The continued importance of the economic bureaucracy must be stressed not only because of anti-bureaucratic bias that continues to colour most journalism in English about Japanese politics and public policy (this odd business where the bureaucracy is blamed for private sector corruption), but also because of the pronounced tendency to dismiss the bureaucracy in recent political-scientific analysis of the Japanese political scene.

In the case of the Ministry of Finance, liberalization inevitably means a changing, some would claim diminished, role. But what has been striking during the transition from a nationalist framework to a liberal order has been the way that the bureaucratic agencies have reasserted their importance in the struggle to reform the post-war system in a liberal direction. This has certainly proved true in the case of MITI and the problem of Japan's trade surplus, of MOF in Japanese financial liberalization, and the Ministry of Posts and Telecommunications in the break up of NTT. For the last, see Ian Gow, 'Re-regulation, Competition and New Industries in Japanese Telecommunications' in *The Promotion and Regulation of Industry in Japan*, edited by Stephen Wilks and Maurice Wright, London, Macmillan, 1992, pp. 256–85.

5 The ferocity of this attack on Japan's financial authorities and the elite consensus about the likelihood of an economic recovery late in 1992 is suggested by the title of a longish article in the tabloid news weekly *Shūkan Posuto* titled '*Mieno Nichigin Sosai no "Keiki Kaifuku" no Dai Uso*' (The Big Lies in Bank of Japan Governor Mieno's Prediction of an Economic Recovery), 5 June 1992 issue, pp. 32–7. The number of such articles appearing in the popular press during the spring and early summer of 1992 was phenomenal, reflecting the pain and influence of those hit hardest by the bursting of Japan's 1980s speculative bubble.

6 See, for example, Yamazaki Taketoshi, '*"Nomura Shintaku Ginkō": San-do-me Shōjiku*' (Nomura Trust Bank: Lucky on the Third Try) and '*"Kōgin Shōken" no Takawarai ga Kikoeru*' (IBJ Securities: The Sound of Confident Laughter), in *Kinyū Bejinesu* (The Financial Business), June 1992, pp. 26–9, 30–2.

7 This of course means the end of the escort system, which in turn will require a sustained period of restructuring in the banking and securities industry. Change there will be, but whether the apocalyptic vision of total revolution, endorsed by Ubutaka Yukio (op. cit., pp. 9–11), among others, will stand remains to be proven by events.

8 Morita Akio, '*"Nihon-gata Keiei" ga Abunai*' (Japanese-style Management is in Crisis), *Bungei-Shunjū*, February 1992, pp. 94–103.

9 *Tsūshō-sangyō-sho Tsūsan Seisaku-kyoku* (MITI International Trade Policy Bureau), *Heisei Yonen Tsūsan-shō Hakusho* (1992 MITI White Paper), Tokyo, Tsūshō-sangyō Chōsa-kai, May 1992. For a liberal analysis of some of the key data deployed by the MITI analysts, see '*Isogareru "Sentaku no Jiyū" no Kakudai*' (The Drive to Enhance the 'Freedom to

Choose' Must Be Accelerated) in *Shūkan Tōyō Keizai* (The Weekly Toyo Keizai), 16 May 1992, pp. 36–9.

9   A JAPANESE LESSON: LANGUAGE AND NATIONALISM

1 William T. McLeod (ed.), *The New Collins Concise English Dictionary*, London and Glasgow, Williams Collins & Son, 1982, p. 749.
2 Shinmura Izuru (ed.), *Kōjien*, Tokyo, Iwanami-shoten, 1988, third edition, p. 876.
3 Ibid., p. 657.
4 William Little *et al.*, *Shorter Oxford English Dictionary*, third edition, London, Oxford University Press, 1973, Volume I, p. 1386.
5 Frances FitzGerald, *Fire in the Lake: The Vietnamese and the Americans in Vietnam*, Boston, Little, Brown and Company, 1972, p. 7.
6 Isaiah Berlin, 'Nationalism: Past Neglect and Present Power', *Against the Current: Essays in the History of Ideas*, Oxford, Clarendon Press, 1989, pp. 333–55.
7 Confucius, *The Analects*, translated by D.C. Lau, Middlesex, England, Penguin, 1979, p. 115.

10   JAPAN, GERMANY AND THE ALTERNATIVE TRADITION IN MODERN PUBLIC POLICY

1 Peter Hennessy, *Whitehall*, London, Secker and Warburg, 1989, p. 88.
2 Ibid., p. 95.
3 Ibid., p. 120.
4 George Steiner, *In Bluebeard's Castle: Some Notes Towards the Redefinition of Culture*, New Haven, Conn., Yale University Press, 1971, p. 18.
5 Friedrich List, *The National System of Political Economy*, translated by S.S. Lloyd, London, Longman, Green & Co., 1922, p. 98.
6 Ibid., p. 89.
7 Ibid., pp. 99–100.
8 Ibid., pp. 97–8.
9 Herman Finer, *The Theory and Practice of Modern Government*, London, Methuen, 1932, p. 1183.
10 S.E. Finer, 'State- and Nation-Building in Europe: The Role of the Military' in Charles Tilly (ed.), *The Formation of National States in Western Europe*, Princeton, NJ, Princeton University Press, 1975, p. 97.
11 Herman Finer, op. cit., p. 1191.
12 Ibid., p. 1193. Effective centralization was, of course, limited.
13 Ibid., p. 1195.
14 Ibid. Cf. W. Hubatsch, *Frederick the Great*, London, Thames & Hudson, 1973.
15 Roger Hausheer, 'Fichte', in David Miller *et al.* (eds), *The Blackwell Encyclopedia of Political Thought*, Oxford, Basil Blackwell, 1991, pp. 154–5.
16 Tsuruta Toshimasa, *Sengo Nihon no Sangyō Seisaku* (Industrial Policy in Post-war Japan), Tokyo, Nihon Keizai Shinbun-sha, 1982, pp. 2–3.
17 Ibid., p. 4.

18 Kent E. Calder, *Crisis and Compensation: Public Policy and Political Stability in Japan, 1949–1986*, Princeton, NJ, Princeton University Press, 1988, p. 135.

11 MAKING HISTORY: JAPAN'S GRAND NARRATIVE AND THE POLICYMAKER

1 Frederic Jameson, 'Foreword', in Jean-François Lyotard, *The Postmodern Condition: A Report on Knowledge*, translated by Geoff Bennington and Brian Massumi, Manchester, Manchester University Press, 1984, p. ix.
2 Ibid.
3 Thomas R. Zengage and C. Tait Ratcliffe, *The Japanese Century: Challenge and Response*, Hong Kong, Longman Group, 1988.
4 Edward J. Lincoln, *Japan's Unequal Trade*, Washington, The Brookings Institution, 1990.
5 Quoted in E. Sydney Crawcour, 'Industrialization and Technological Change, 1885–1920, in Peter Duus (ed.), *The Cambridge History of Japan, Volume 6, The Twentieth Century*, Cambridge, England, Cambridge University Press, 1988, p. 389.

12 THE REVOLUTIONARY 1980s AND THE RISE OF JAPANESE PUBLIC POLICY STUDIES

1 Thomas S. Kuhn, *The Structure of Scientific Revolutions*, Chicago, University of Chicago Press, 1970, second edition, but see also Imre Lakatos and Alan Musgrave, *Criticism and the Growth of Knowledge*, London, Cambridge University Press, 1970.
2 Roy J. Hofheinz, Jr. and Kent E. Calder, *The Eastasia Edge*, New York, Basic Books, 1982; Kent E. Calder, *Crisis and Compensation: Public Policy and Political Stability in Japan, 1949–1986*, Princeton, NJ, Princeton University Press, 1988.
3 Ezra F. Vogel, *Japan as Number One: Lessons for America*, Tokyo, Charles E. Tuttle Co., 1980 [1979].
4 Chalmers Johnson, *MITI and the Japanese Miracle: The Growth of Industrial Policy, 1925–1975*, Stanford, Calif., Stanford University Press, 1982.
5 J.A.A. Stockwin, *Japan: Divided Politics in a Growth Economy*, New York and London, W.W. Norton, second edition, 1982.
6 J.A.A. Stockwin, *et al.*, *Dynamic and Immobilist Politics in Japan*, London, Macmillan Press, 1988.
7 Kuhn, op. cit.
8 T.J. Pempel, *Policy and Politics in Japan: Creative Conservativism*, Philadelphia, Temple University Press, 1982.
9 Ezra F. Vogel, *Comeback*, Tokyo, Charles E. Tuttle Co., 1985.
10 Ronald Dore, *Flexible Rigidities: Industrial Policy and Structural Adjustment in the Japanese Economy, 1970–1980*, London, The Athlone Press, 1986.
11 Ronald Dore, *Taking Japan Seriously: A Confucian Perspective on Leading Economic Issues*, London, The Athlone Press, 1987.
12 Karl Boger, *Postwar Industrial Policy in Japan: An Annotated Bibliography*, Metuchen, NJ and London, The Scarecrow Press, 1988.

13 Daniel I. Okimoto, *Between MITI and the Market: Japanese Industrial Policy for High Technology*, Stanford, Calif., Stanford University Press, 1989; Richard J. Samuels, *The Business of the Japanese State: Energy Markets in Comparative and Historical Perspective*, Ithaca and London, Cornell University Press, 1987; Frances McCall Rosenbluth, *Financial Politics in Contemporary Japan*, Ithaca, Cornell University Press, 1989; Chalmers Johnson, Laura D'Andrea Tyson and John Zysman (eds), *Politics and Productivity: How Japan's Development Strategy Works*, New York, Harper Business, 1989.

14 Aurelia George, 'Japanese Interest Group Behaviour: an Institutional Approach', in J.A.A. Stockwin, *Dynamic and Immobilist Politics in Japan*, op. cit.

15 Kozo Yamamura and Yasukichi Yasuba (eds), *The Political Economy of Japan, Volume 1: The Domestic Transformation*, Stanford, Calif., Stanford University Press, 1987; Inoguchi Takashi and Daniel I. Okimoto (eds), *The Political Economy of Japan, Volume 2: The Changing International Context*, Stanford, Calif., Stanford University Press, 1988.

16 Daniel I. Okimoto and Thomas P. Rohlen (eds), *Inside the Japanese System: Readings on Contemporary Society and Political Economy*, Stanford, Calif., Stanford University Press, 1988.

17 Hugh Patrick and Henry Rosovosky (eds), *Asia's New Giant: How the Japanese Economy Works*, Washington, DC, The Brookings Institution, 1976.

18 Philip H. Trezise and Yukio Suzuki, 'Politics, Government, and Economic Growth in Japan' in Hugh Patrick and Henry Rosovosky, op. cit., p. 757.

19 Richard B. McKenzie and Gordon Tullock, *Modern Political Economy: An Introduction to Economics*, Tokyo, McGraw-Hill/Kōdan-sha, 1978.

20 Okimoto, op. cit.

13 YELLOW ATHENA: THE JAPANESE MODEL AND 'THE END OF HISTORY'

1 Francis Fukuyama, 'The End of History?', *The National Interest*, Summer 1989 issue, pp. 3–18.

2 *Hegel's Philosophy of Right*, translated by T. M. Knox, Oxford, Clarendon Press, 1952.

3 Alexandre Kojève, *Introduction to the Reading of Hegel: Lectures on the Phenomenology of Spirit*, assembled by Raymond Queneau, edited by Allan Bloom, translated by James H. Nichols, Jr., Ithaca and London, Cornell University Press, 1969, footnote on pp. 161–2.

4 Fukuyama, op. cit., p. 3.

5 Ibid., pp. 3–4.

6 Ibid., pp. 4–5 and p. 8.

7 Georg Lukács, *The Young Hegel: Studies in the Relations between Dialectics and Economics*, translated by Rodney Livingstone, London, Merlin Press, 1975.

8 The notion of 'ontology/Ontology' will be developed in a forthcoming study by David Williams.

9 This essay is found in Isaiah Berlin, *The Crooked Timber of Humanity: Chapters in the History of Ideas*, London, John Murray, 1990, pp. 1–19.

10 Ibid., pp. 5–6.
11 Ibid., p. 11.
12 Martin Bernal, *Black Athena: The Afroasiatic Roots of Classical Civilization, Vol. I: The Fabrication of Ancient Greece 1785–1985*, London, Free Association Books, 1987.
13 Friedrich List, *The National System of Political Economy*, translated by Sampson S. Lloyd, London, Longman, Green and Co., 1922, p. 98.
14 Ibid., p. 99.
15 John Plamenatz, *Man and Society: A Critical Examination of Some Important Social and Political Theories from Machiavelli to Marx*, London, Longman, 1963.
16 Ibid., Vol. II, pp. 232–3.
17 Ibid., Vol. II, p. 245.
18 Ibid., Vol. II, pp. 245–6.
19 Hegel, op. cit., Addition 158 to par. 265, p. 281.
20 Plamenatz, op. cit., p. 242.

14 JAPANESE PUBLIC POLICY AS FOREIGN POLICY: A POST-WAR REVOLUTION?

1 For an incisive critique of the traditional position, see Alan S. Milward, *War, Economy and Society, 1939–1945*, Harmondsworth, Middlesex, Penguin Books, 1987.
2 This rejects the arguments to the contrary put forward in Lester Thurow's *Head to Head: The Coming Economic Battle between Japan, Europe and America*, New York, William Morrow and Co., 1992, p. 20. Citing the total GNP figures for the United States as a measure of its ability to finance the war is unpersuasive. The days when Washington alone decided, organized and paid for military initiatives such as NATO are gone. This reflects new financial limits. Japan did not ask for Washington's intervention in the conflict. Indeed it is not obvious that Desert Storm was in Japan's interest, *in any sense.*
3 Edward J. Lincoln, *Japan's Unequal Trade*, Washington, DC, The Brookings Institution, 1990, p. 1.
4 John Maynard Keynes, *The General Theory of Employment, Interest and Money*, London, Macmillan, 1936, pp. 333–71.
5 Alvin H. Hansen, *A Guide to Keynes*, New York, McGraw-Hill, 1953, p. 216.
6 Kozo Yamamura (ed.), *Japan's Economic Structure: Should It Change?*, Seattle, Wash., Society of Japanese Studies, 1990.
7 Jacob Viner, *The Long View and the Short: Studies in Economic Theory and Policy*, New York, Free Press, 1958, p. 286.
8 Yamamura, op. cit., p. 11 (Yamamura summarizing Ronald Dore's critique).

15 UNBLINKING POLITICS: McCARTHYISM, GRAND THEORY AND WILD EMPIRICISM

1 Robert Wade has done much to correct this misperception in the English-language literature in his excellent *Governing the Market: Economic Theory*

and the Role of Government in East Asian Industrialization, Princeton, NJ,
Princeton University Press, 1991. Yet, even here, the problem is not just one
of ideological and cultural interference with the true facts of a particular
Asian polity. It is also a problem of methodology. The implicit anti-
empiricism is also at work in a collection of studies titled *Sekai no Naka no
Sangyō Seisaku: Bōdaresu Keizai e no Taiō* (Industrial Policy in World
Perspective: Responding to a Borderless Economy), the 38th Annual Report
of the Japan Economic Policy Association of Waseda University, published
in 1990. If even native Japanese, reared in the nationalist climate of the post-
war economic miracle, can fall foul of this problem, then the resistant
features of the system demand inspired scrutiny.

2 This is both a question of the quality of analysis and the degree of breadth
aimed for in thinking about Japan. This issue is examined in the discussion of
micro empiricism later in this chapter, but what must be emphasized here is
the need to understand Japan as a whole. Whatever differences of approach
and emphasis divide the authors, a comparable breadth of understanding is
sought by Robert E. Ward in *Japan's Political System* (Englewood Hills, NJ,
Prentice-Hall, 1967), by J.A.A. Stockwin in *Japan: Divided Politics in a
Growth Economy*, London, Weidenfeld & Nicolson, 1982; by Bradley M.
Richardson and Scott C. Flanagan in *Politics in Japan*, Boston, Little Brown
and Co., 1984; and, more recently, in the 1990 American Political Science
Association Annual Meeting seminar led by Kent Calder. This last effort
included papers by T.J. Pempel, Shigeko N. Fukai and Haruhiro Fukui,
Stephen J. Anderson, Ellis S. Krauss, and Roger Bowen, and they have been
published under the title 'Introducing Japan into the Comparative Politics
Curriculum' in *Political Science*, March 1992, pp. 5–73.

Politics, as an object of serious journalistic commentary or undergraduate
teaching, is inconceivable without a commitment to this level of
generalization and penetration. But the thrust of anti-Johnsonian
revisionism, in the micro-empirical mode, as reflected in the writings of
David Friedman, Richard Samuels and some of the papers gathered in
Stephen Wilks and Maurice Wright (eds), *The Promotion and Regulation of
Industry in Japan*, London, Macmillan, 1992, does not easily translate into a
more complete picture of the Japanese political system. These revisionists are
aware of the problem. Thus in the essay 'The Comparative Context of
Japanese Political Economy', Wilks and Wright rightly conclude that: 'Case
studies are not automatically cumulative. They are easily compartmental-
ized, isolated and forgotten. They have to be informed by a wider framework
and operate in interaction with it' (ibid., p. 18). But not just any 'wider
framework' will do. The question one is forced to ask is: How well does a
particular piece of micro empiricism, its design, execution and findings,
integrate into the larger macro framework? In this context, unguided
empiricism, micro or otherwise, may be scientifically respectable, but what
claims does it make on those of us who must teach and inform the wider
community about the nature of Japanese politics?

3 Yet here the distinction between the presenters of arguments in public
forums and the researchers who compiled the information must be stressed.
See, for example, Ellis S. Krauss and Isobel Coles 'Built-in Impediments' in
Kozo Yamamura (ed.), *Japan's Economic Structure: Should It Change?*,
Seattle, Wash., Society for Japanese Studies, 1990, pp. 333–58.

4 Theodore Cohen, *Remaking Japan: The American Occupation as New Deal*, edited by Herbert Passin, New York, The Free Press, 1987, p. 20.
5 Ibid.
6 Ibid., p. 21.
7 Ibid.
8 Ibid., p. 23.
9 Ibid.
10 Ibid., p. 24. The argument over the larger character of Occupation policymaking must be fought on the broadest level of generalization. A closer look at any of the areas of policymaking will reveal a more detailed and confused picture. The special expertise of the old Japan hand was especially germane to the reform of so-called 'State Shinto' (*Kokka* or *Kokkateki Shintō*). William Woodward, one of the prime movers in this sphere of Occupation reforms, acknowledges that the Religions Division of SCAP tried, 'to secure the services of Dr. Daniel C. Holtom, the well-known Shinto scholar, but his health would not permit him to travel. A request was also made for a specialist in Buddhism and Shinto and if there had been qualified American Buddhists or Shintoists available, they certainly would have been employed. Since none was found the position went to Walter Nichols, who was born in Japan and knew the language but was not a specialist in religion.' William P. Woodward, *The Allied Occupation of Japan and Japanese Religions*, Leiden, E.J. Brill, 1972, p. 26.
   The problem of reforming Japanese religious institutions challenges the notion that Japan experts had no obvious contribution to make to Occupation policy and that such expertise was irrelevant to 'the broader realities' of SCAP need. It is was the sort of problem which undermines the blithe assumption that Japan was 'just like any other country'. Woodward challenges some of the simplicities of the SCAP approach to the issue as it was influenced by the business of defining Shinto and the precise nature of its contribution to the pre-war Japanese nationalist ideology. On this problem, see also Wilhelmus H.M. Creemers, *Shrine Shinto after World War II*, Leiden, E.J. Brill, 1968, and more recently, Helen Hardacre, *Shinto and the State, 1868–1988*, Princeton, NJ, Princeton University Press, 1989.
11 Francis Fukuyama, *The End of History and the Last Man*, London, Hamish Hamilton, 1992.
12 Francis Fukuyama, 'The End of History?', *The National Interest*, Summer 1989.
13 Ibid. The place of 'America' in Fukuyama's overall schema has evolved since the publication of his essay in *The National Interest*. There the triumphalist celebration in the US of the victory of the American way of life is exploited by Fukuyama both to make a point and also to invite interest in the writings of those Europeans, such as Kojève, who recognized the nature of America's success during the twentieth century. But in *The End of History and the Last Man*, this 'America' is submerged in the larger notion of the Western (read 'European') discourse on the nature of communal politics since Plato's Athens. It is the Western world as a whole that Fukuyama appears to hope to 'recentre' in his book. This reflects a growing doubt about the recent evolution of 'the American way of life'.
   Since writing the book, these doubts have deepened. In what was one of the best of all the discussions of his work in Japan, where Fukuyama's book was a bestseller, Komori Yoshihisa, chief Washington correspondent for the

Sankei Shinbun, the conservative Japanese daily, questioned Fukuyama on this very point. In particular he sought Fukuyama's reaction to criticism from Japanese nationalist intellectuals, such as Umehara Takashi, on the question of whether the faltering of the American dream since the 1980s marks the approaching defeat of the modern Western model.

The Komori interview was published in *Chūō Kōron* under the title '*Nihon no Chōsen ga "Rekishi" o Hiraku*' (The Japanese Challenge Will Restart History) in May 1992. In it, Fukuyama concedes the failings of contemporary America. He appears to be pessimistic about the capacity of the US political system to right itself, and flatly denies that the 'end of history' represents a triumph for American capitalism. In particular, he observes that it is the West European continental model of politics and economics that is taking hold in post-communist Eastern Europe, not the American model. But on Japan, Fukuyama is consistently negative. He acknowledges Japan's importance, but Japan is, in his philosophical perspective, distinctly marginal. Japan has not made the modern world, nor does she have the capacity to change it. The title given to the Komori interview reflects a position that Fukuyama does not share.

14 John Dunn, 'In the Glare of Recognition', *Times Literary Supplement*, 24 April, 1992, p. 6. and Alan Ryan, 'Professor Hegel Goes to Washington', *New York Review of Books*, 26 March 1992, pp. 7–13.

15 Takeuchi Yoshimi, '*Kindai to wa Nani ka*' (What is Modernity?) in *Takeuchi Yoshimi Zenshū* (The Complete Works of Takeuchi Yoshimi), Tokyo, 1980, vol. 4, p. 130. Here and below, I have used the translation of the essay from Sakai Naoki, 'Modernity and Its Critique: The Problem of Universalism and Particularism'. The translation quoted appears on p. 115 of Sakai Naoki, 'Modernity and Its Critique: The Problem of Universalism' in Masao Miyoshi and H.D. Harootunian (eds), *Postmodernism and Japan*, Durham and London, Duke University Press, 1989, pp. 93–122.

16 Sakai Naoki, 'Modernity and Its Critique: The Problem of Universalism' in *Postmodernism and Japan*, edited by Masao Miyoshi and H.D. Harootunian, Durham and London, Duke University Press, 1989, p. 95.

17 This term, so prominent in Edward W. Said's writings, is the object of sustained assault in his *Orientalism*, Harmondsworth, Middlesex, Penguin Books, 1985 (1978).

18 Sakai, op. cit., p. 95.

19 Ibid., p. 117.

20 Roland Barthes, 'Chateaubriand: Life of Rancé', *New Critical Essays*, translated by Richard Howard, Berkeley and Los Angeles, University of California Press, 1990, p. 43.

21 J.A.A. Stockwin *et al.*, *Dynamic and Immobilist Politics in Japan*, London, Macmillan Press, 1988.

22 I have chosen to concentrate on the Wilks–Wright study because of its commitment to overturning the Johnson thesis (see Chalmers Johnson, *MITI and the Japanese Miracle*, Stanford, Calif., Stanford University Press, 1982), and because it tackles some of the methodological problems often ignored in political scientific analysis of the Japanese scene. The Wilks–Wright study was useful also because it included an article by Muramatsu Michio, author of the controversial study *Sengo Nihon no Kanryōsei* (The Bureaucratic System in Postwar Japan), Tokyo, Tōyō Keizai Shinpō-sha, 1982, which forcefully challenged the orthodox view that bureaucrats

dominate ministers in the Japanese system. Muramatsu's argument was further developed in Yung H. Park's *Bureaucrats and Ministers in Contemporary Japanese Government*, Berkeley, Institute of East Asian Studies of the University of California-Berkeley, 1986. This book merits close attention, especially from scholars who hold contrary views. B.C. Koh's study, *Japan's Administrative Elite*, Berkeley, University of California Press, 1989, is a fine example of thorough fair-mindedness.

23 Chalmers Johnson, op. cit. This is not to say that there are no other books on Japanese politics that may be labelled 'highly original, influential and important' (*Collins English Dictionary*), that is, 'seminal' in a usefully vague sense, but to assert that no other post-war study by a Western author comes close to rivalling the generative powers of Johnson's text. 'Seminal' here is taken in its derivation from the Latin *semen* or seed. Johnson's Japan-as-developmental-state thesis has provoked a wider and deeper critical response among Western political scientists than any other recent study. *MITI and the Japanese Miracle*, whatever its defects, must be regarded as seminal.

24 Wilks and Wright, op cit.: Itō Daiichi, 'Government–Industry Relations in a Dual Regulatory Scheme: Engineering Research Associations as Policy Instruments', pp. 51–80; Jeremy Howells and Ian Neary, 'Science and Technology Policy in Japan: The Pharmaceutical Industry and New Technology', pp. 81–109; Tanaka Masami, 'Government Policy and Biotechnology in Japan: The Pattern and Impact of Rivalry Between Ministries', pp. 110–31; Michael K. Young, 'Structural Adjustment of Mature Industries in Japan: Legal Institutions, Industry Association and Bargaining', pp. 135–66; Richard Boyd and Nagamori Seiichi, 'Industry Policy-making in Practice: Electoral, Diplomatic and Other Adjustments to Crisis in the Japanese Shipbuilding Industry', pp. 167–204.

Other studies in the Wilks–Wright volume are: Martin Edmonds, 'Defence Interests and United States Policy for Telecommunications', pp. 207–32; Kevin Morgan and Douglas Pitt, 'Communities, Communications and Change: The Dialetic of Development in US Telecommunications', pp. 233–55; Ian Gow, 'Re-regulation, Competition and New Industries in Japanese Telecommunications', pp. 256–85; Muramatsu Michio, 'The "Enhancement" of the Ministry of Posts and Telecommunications to Meet the Challenge of Telecommunications Innovation', pp. 286–308.

25 'Japanese Business Methods: Couldn't We All Do a Little Bit Worse?', *The Economist*, 4–10 April 1992, pp. 19–22.

26 David Friedman, *The Misunderstood Miracle: Industrial Development and Political Change in Japan*, Ithaca, NY, Cornell University Press, 1988.

27 Ibid., p. 4.

28 Immanuel Kant, *The Critique of Pure Reason*, translated by Norman Kemp Smith, London, Macmillan, 1929 (1787), p. 540.

29 The danger of 'unpacking' is, I believe, what Kant had in mind when he warned that:

> This twofold interest manifests itself also among students of nature in the diversity of their ways of thinking. Those who are more especially speculative are, we may almost say, hostile to heterogeneity, and are always on the watch for the unity of the genus; *those, on the other hand, who are more especially empirical, are constantly endeavouring to differentiate nature in such manifold fashion as almost to extinguish the*

> *hope of ever being able to determine its appearances in accordance with universal principles.*　　　　　　　　　　　　　　　(ibid., italics added)

30　Kozo Yamamura and Yasukichi Yasuba (eds), *The Political Economy of Japan, Volume I: The Domestic Transformation*, Stanford, Calif., Stanford University Press, 1987.

31　Reviewing the work of Western political scientists on Japan during the past three decades, Samuels has observed that:

> Overall, Japanese political studies was marked by a failure to cumulate knowledge and to build upon previous research while advancing conceptual frameworks. As William Steslicke aptly put it, as a result, 'we have many pearls, but few necklaces'.

> Quoted in Richard J. Samuels, 'Japanese Political Studies and the Myth of the Independent Intellectual', in Richard J. Samuels and Myron Weiner (eds), *The Political Culture of Foreign Area Studies: Essay in Honor of Lucian W. Pye*, Washington, DC, Pergammon-Brassey's, 1992, pp. 17–59. The quote is on p. 30.

16　THE RECEDING ROAR: LAST THOUGHTS ON THE JAPANESE MIRACLE

1　The depth of nationalist concern was nicely reflected in the title of Keio University Professor Shimada Haruo's article ' "Japan Moderu" wa Shinazu' (The Japan Model Will Not Die) in the February issue of *Bungei Shunjū*, pp. 138–49. See also Tachi Ryūichirō, '*Keiki Chōsei to Kasanatta Shisutemu no Tenkan: "Nihon-kei" kara "Eibei-kei" e*' (Not Just a Business Downturn but a System in Revolution: Why it is Time to Move from the Japanese Model to the Anglo-American Model), *Ekonomisuto*, 27 April 1992, pp. 22–8. It is the timing of Tachi's remarks that gave them their force. His arguments are not substantially different from those he offered in his book *Kin-yū Sai-hensei no Shiten* (The Reform of the Japanese Financial System in Perspective), Tokyo, Tōyō Keizai Shinpō-sha, 1985.

2　Shindō Muneyuki, *Gyōsei Shidō: Kanchō to Gyōkai no Aida* (Administrative Guidance: Between the Bureaucracy and the Private Sector), Tokyo, Iwanami Shinsho, 1992.

3　Daniel I. Okimoto, *Between MITI and the Market: Japanese Industrial Policy for High Technology*, Stanford, Calif., Stanford University Press, 1989, p. 3–4.

List of works cited

Barthes, Roland, 'Chateaubriand: Life of Rancé', *New Critical Essays*, translated by Richard Howard, Berkeley and Los Angeles, University of California Press, 1990.

Bergsten, C. Fred, 'What to do about the US–Japan Economic Conflict', *Foreign Affairs*, vol. 60, no. 5, Summer 1982, pp. 1054–75.

—— 'The United States Trade Deficit and the Dollar', Statement before the Senate Committee on Banking, Housing and Urban Affairs, Subcommittee on International Finance and Monetary Policy, Washington, 6 June 1984, p. 4, cited in Jeffrey A. Frankel, 'The Yen/Dollar Agreement: Liberalizing Japanese Capital Markets', *Policy Analyses in International Economics*, no. 9, December 1984, Washington, DC, Institute for International Economics, 1984.

Berlin, Sir Isaiah, 'Nationalism: Past Neglect and Present Power', *Against the Current: Essays in the History of Ideas*, Oxford, Clarendon Press, 1989.

—— 'The Pursuit of the Ideal', *The Crooked Timber of Humanity: Chapters in the History of Ideas*, London, John Murray, 1990.

Bernal, Martin, *Black Athena: The Afroasiatic Roots of Classical Civilization, Vol. I: The Fabrication of Ancient Greece 1785–1985*, London, Free Association Books, 1987.

Boger, Karl, *Postwar Industrial Policy in Japan: An Annotated Bibliography*, Metuchen, NJ and London, The Scarecrow Press, 1988.

Boyd, Richard and Nagamori Seiichi, 'Industry Policy-making in Practice: Electoral, Diplomatic and Other Adjustments to Crisis in the Japanese Shipbuilding Industry', in Stephen Wilks and Maurice Wright (eds), *The Promotion and Regulation of Industry in Japan*, London, Macmillan, 1992.

Calder, Kent. E., *Crisis and Compensation: Public Policy and Political Stability in Japan, 1949–1986*, Princeton, NJ, Princeton University Press, 1988.

Calder, Kent E. (ed.) 'Introducing Japan into the Comparative Politics Curriculum' in *Political Science*, March 1992, pp. 5–73.

Campbell, John Creighton, *Contemporary Japanese Budget Politics*, Berkeley, Calif., University of California Press, 1977.

Cohen, Theodore, *Remaking Japan: The American Occupation as New Deal*, edited by Herbert Passin, New York, The Free Press, 1987.

Confucius, *The Analects*, translated by D.C. Lau, Middlesex, England, Penguin, 1979.

Crawcour, E. Sydney, 'Industrialization and Technological Change, 1885–1920', in Peter Duus (ed.), *The Cambridge History of Japan, Volume 6, The Twentieth Century*, Cambridge, England, Cambridge University Press, 1988.

Creemers, Wilhelmus H.M., *Shrine Shinto after World War II*, Leiden, E.J. Brill, 1968.

Dore, Ronald, *Flexible Rigidities: Industrial Policy and Structural Adjustment in the Japanese Economy, 1970–1980*, London, The Athlone Press, 1986.

—— *Taking Japan Seriously: A Confucian Perspective on Leading Economic Issues*, London, The Athlone Press, 1987.

Drucker, Peter F., *The New Realities: In Government and Politics, in Economics and Business, in Society and World View*, New York, Harper and Row, 1989.

Dunn, John, 'In the Glare of Recognition', *Times Literary Supplement*, 24 April 1992, p. 6.

Duus, Peter (ed.), *The Cambridge History of Japan, Volume 6, The Twentieth Century*, Cambridge, England, Cambridge University Press, 1988, p. 385–450.

—— *Feudalism in Japan*, New York, Alfred A. Knopf, 1976, second edition.

The Economist, 'Central Banks: America v Japan – The Rewards of Independence', 25–31 January 1992, p. 19.

—— 'Japanese Business Methods: Couldn't We All Do a Little Bit Worse?', 4–10 April 1992, pp. 19–22.

Edmonds, Martin, 'Defence Interests and United States Policy in Telecommunications', in Stephen Wilks and Maurice Wright (eds), *The Promotion and Regulation of Industry in Japan*, London, Macmillan, 1992, pp. 207–32.

Farnsworth, Lee W., 'Japan's Changing Policy-making Structure', *The World Economy*, vol. 12, no. 2, June 1989, pp. 163–74.

Finer, Herman, *The Theory and Practice of Modern Government*, London, Methuen, 1932.

Finer, S.E., 'State- and Nation-Building in Europe: The Role of the Military' in Charles Tilly (ed.), *The Formation of National States in Western Europe*, Princeton, NJ, Princeton University Press, 1975.

FitzGerald, Frances, *Fire in the Lake: The Vietnamese and the Americans in Vietnam*, Boston, Little, Brown and Company, 1972.

Frankel, Jeffrey A., 'The Yen/Dollar Agreement: Liberalizing Japanese Capital Markets', *Policy Analysis in International Economics*, no. 9, December 1984, Washington, DC, Institute for International Economics, 1984.

Friedman, David, *The Misunderstood Miracle: Industrial Development and Political Change in Japan*, Ithaca, NY, Cornell University Press, 1988.

Fukuyama, Francis, 'The End of History?', *The National Interest*, Summer 1989 issue, pp. 3–18.

—— *The End of History and the Last Man*, London, Hamish Hamilton, 1992.

Garon, Sheldon, *The State and Labor in Modern Japan*, Berkeley and Los Angeles, University of California Press, 1987.

George, Aurelia, 'Japanese Interest Group Behaviour: An Institutional Approach', in J.A.A. Stockwin *et al.*, *Dynamic and Immobilist Politics in Japan*, London, Macmillan Press, 1988.

Gluck, Carol, *Japan's Modern Myths: Ideology in the Late Meiji Period*, Princeton, NJ, Princeton University Press, 1985.

Gow, Ian, 'Re-regulation, Competition and New Industries in Japanese Telecommunications' in Stephen Wilks and Maurice Wright (eds), *The Promotion and Regulation of Industry in Japan*, London, Macmillan, 1992.

Halfpenny, Peter, 'Positivism' in David Miller *et al.* (eds), *The Blackwell Encyclopedia of Political Thought*, Oxford, Basil Blackwell, 1991, p. 395.

Hansen, Alvin H., *A Guide to Keynes*, New York, McGraw-Hill, 1953.

Hardacre, Helen, *Shinto and the State, 1868–1988,* Princeton, NJ, Princeton University Press, 1989.

Hausheer, Roger, 'Fichte' in David Miller *et al.* (ed.), *The Blackwell Encyclopedia of Political Thought*, Oxford, Basil Blackwell, 1991.

Hegel, Georg Wilhelm Friedrich, *Hegel's Philosophy of Right*, translated by T.M. Knox, Oxford, Clarendon Press, 1952.

Hennessy, Peter, *Whitehall*, London, Secker and Warburg, 1989.

Hofheinz, Roy, Jr. and Calder, Kent E., *The Eastasia Edge*, New York, Basic Books, 1982.

Hollerman, Leon, *Japan, Disincorporated: The Economic Liberalization Process*, Stanford, Calif., Hoover Institution Press, 1988.

Honneth, Axel *et al.* (eds), *Philosophical Interventions in the Unfinished Project of Enlightenment*, Cambridge, Mass., The MIT Press, 1992.

Hosomi Takashi and Okumura Ariyoshi, 'Japanese Industrial Policy', in John Pinder (ed.), *National Industrial Strategies and the World Economy*, London, Allanheld, Osmun/Croom Helm, 1982.

Howells, Jeremy and Neary, Ian, 'Science and Technology Policy in Japan: The Pharmaceutical Industry and New Technology', in Stephen Wilks and Maurice Wright (eds), *The Promotion and Regulation of Industry in Japan*, London, Macmillan, 1992.

Inoguchi Takashi and Okimoto, Daniel I. (eds), *The Political Economy of Japan, Volume 2: The Changing International Context*, Stanford, Calif., Stanford University Press, 1988.

Itō Daiichi, *Genzai Nihon Kanryō-sei no Bunseki* (The Japanese Bureaucracy Today: an Analysis), Tokyo, Tokyo Daigaku Shuppan-kai, 1980.

—— 'Government-Industry Relations in a Dual Regulatory Scheme: Engineering Research Associations as Policy Instruments', in Stephen Wilks and Maurice Wright (eds) *The Promotion and Regulation of Industry in Japan*, London, Macmillan, 1992.

Iwata, Masakazu, *Ōkubo Toshimichi: The Bismarck of Japan*, Berkeley and Los Angeles, University of California Press, 1964.

Jameson, Frederic, 'Foreword', in Jean-François Lyotard, *The Postmodern Condition: A Report on Knowledge*, translated by Geoff Bennington and Brian Massumi, Manchester, Manchester University Press, 1984.

Jansen, Marius B., *Sakamoto Ryōma and the Meiji Restoration*, Stanford, Calif., Stanford University Press, 1971.

Japan Economic Policy Association of Waseda University, *Sekai no Naka no Sangyō Seisaku: Bōdaresu Keizai e no Taiō* (Industrial Policy in World Perspective: Responding to a Borderless Economy), 38th Annual Report, 1990.

Johnson, Chalmers, *MITI and the Japanese Miracle: The Growth of Industrial Policy, 1925–1975*, Stanford, Calif., Stanford University Press, 1982.

Johnson, Chalmers; Tyson, Laura D'Andrea; Zysman, John (eds), *Politics and Productivity: How Japan's Development Strategy Works*, New York, HarperBusiness, 1989.

Kant, Immanuel, *The Critique of Pure Reason*, trans. by Norman Kemp Smith, London, Macmillan, 1929.

Keynes, John Maynard, *The General Theory of Employment, Interest and Money*, London, Macmillan, 1936.

Kishimoto Kōichi, *Politics in Modern Japan: Development and Organization*, Tokyo, Japan Echo Inc., 1988, third edition.

Koh, B.C., *Japan's Administrative Elite*, Berkeley, University of California Press, 1989.

Kojève, Alexandre, *Introduction to the Reading of Hegel: Lectures on the Phenomenology of Spirit*, assembled by Raymond Queneau, edited by Allan Bloom, translated by James H. Nichols, Jr., Ithaca and London, Cornell University Press, 1969.

Komiya Ryutarō, Okuna Masahiro and Suzumura Kotaro (eds), *Nihon no Sangyō Seisaku* (Japanese Industrial Policy), Tokyo, Tokyo Daigaku Shuppan-kai, 1984, published in English translation as *Industrial Policy of Japan*, Tokyo, Academic Press, 1988.

Komori Yoshihisa, '*Nihon no Chōsen ga "Rekishi" o Hiraku*' (The Japanese Challenge Will Restart History) in *Chūō Kōron*, May 1992, pp. 90–9.

Krauss, Ellis S. and Coles, Isobel, 'Built-in Impediments' in Yamamura Kozo, (ed.), *Japan's Economic Structure: Should it Change?*, Washington, DC, Society for Japanese Studies, 1990.

Kuhn, Thomas S., *The Structure of Scientific Revolutions*, Chicago, University of Chicago Press, 1970, second edition.

Kuribayashi Yoshimitsu, *Ōkura-shō: Ginkō-kyoku* (The Ministry of Finance: The Banking Bureau), Tokyo, Kōdan-sha, 1988.

—— *Ōkura-shō: Shukei-kyoku* (The Ministry of Finance: The Budget Bureau), Tokyo, Kōdan-sha, 1990.

—— *Ōkura-shō: Shuzei-kyoku* (The Ministry of Finance: The Tax Administration Bureau), Tokyo, Kōdan-sha, 1991.

—— *Ōkura-shō: Shōken-kyoku* (The Ministry of Finance: The Securities Bureau), Tokyo, Kōdan-sha, 1991.

Lakatos, Imre and Musgrave, Alan (eds), *Criticism and the Growth of Knowledge*, London, Cambridge University Press, 1970.

Large, Stephen S., *Emperor Hirohito & Showa Japan: A Political Biography*, London, Routledge, 1992.

Lincoln, Edward J., *Japan's Unequal Trade*, Washington, DC, The Brookings Institution, 1990.

Lipsey, Richard G., *An Introduction to Positive Economics*, Weidenfeld and Nicolson, 1963.

List, Friedrich, *The National System of Political Economy*, translated by S.S. Lloyd, London, Longman, Green and Co., 1922.

Little, William *et al.*, *Shorter Oxford English Dictionary*, third edition, London, Oxford University Press, 1973.

Longley, Clifford, 'Religious Schools Must Uphold Common Values', *The Times*, 11 January 1992, p. 10.

Lukács, Georg, *The Young Hegel: Studies in the Relations between Dialectics and Economics*, translated by Rodney Livingstone, London, Merlin Press, 1975.

Lyotard, Jean-François, *The Postmodern Condition: A Report on Knowledge*, translated by Geoff Bennington and Brian Massumi, Manchester, Manchester University Press, 1984.

McKenzie, Richard B. and Tullock, Gordon, *Modern Political Economy: An Introduction to Economics*, Tokyo, McGraw-Hill/Kōdan-sha, 1978.

McLeod, William T. (ed.), *The New Collins Concise English Dictionary*, London and Glasgow, William Collins and Son, 1982.

Madison, James, *Federalist Paper No. 10*, New York, 1787.

Mikami Naoyuki, 'Saigo no Kabe wa Katakuna Jichi-shō' (The Final Line of Resistance: The Stubborn Ministry of Home Affairs), *Shūkan Tōyō Keizai*, 16 May 1992, pp. 108–11.

Miller, David *et al.* (eds), *The Blackwell Encyclopedia of Political Thought*, Oxford, Basil Blackwell, 1991.

Milward, Alan S., *War, Economy and Society, 1939–1945*, Harmondsworth, Middlesex, Penguin Books, 1987.

Miyoshi, Masao and Harootunian, H.D. (eds), *Postmodernism and Japan*, Durham and London, Duke University Press, 1989.

Morgan, Kevin and Pitt, Douglas, 'Communities, Communications and Change: The Dialectic of Development in US Telecommunications', in Stephen Wilks and Maurice Wright (eds), *The Promotion and Regulation of Industry in Japan*, London, Macmillan, 1992.

Morita Akio, '"Nihon-gata Keiei" ga Abunai' (Japanese-style Management is in Crisis), *Bungei-Shunjū*, February 1992, pp. 94–103.

Muramatsu Michio, *Sengo Nihon no Kanryōsei* (The Bureaucratic System in Postwar Japan), Tokyo, Tōyō Keizai Shinpō-sha, 1982.

—— 'The "Enhancement" of the Ministry of Posts and Telecommunications to Meet the Challenge of Telecommunications Innovation', in Stephen Wilks and Maurice Wright (eds), *The Promotion and Regulation of Industry in Japan*, London, Macmillan, 1992.

Najita, Tetsuo, *Japan: The Intellectual Foundations of Modern Japanese Politics*, Chicago, University of Chicago Press, 1980.

Namiki Nobuyoshi, *Tsūsanshō no Shūen: Shakai Kōzo no Henkaku wa Kanō ka* (The End of MITI: Is the Structural Change of Society still Possible?), Tokyo, Daiyamondo-sha, 1989.

Neary, Ian (ed.), *War, Revolution and Japan*, Folkstone, Kent, Japan Library, 1993.

Nikkan Kōgyō Shinbun Shuzai-han-hen (The Special Reporting Section of the *Nikkan Kōgyō* newspaper), (ed.) *Shin 'Maekawa Ripōto' ga Shimesu Michi: Nihon wo Kōkawaeru* (The Way Shown by the 'New' Maekawa Report: This Is How Japan can Change), Tokyo, Nikkan Shobō, 1987.

Okimoto, Daniel I., *Between MITI and the Market: Japanese Industrial Policy for High Technology*, Stanford, Calif., Stanford University Press, 1989.

Okimoto, Daniel I. and Rohlen, Thomas P. (eds), *Inside the Japanese System: Readings on Contemporary Society and Political Economy*, Stanford, Calif., Stanford University Press, 1988.

Ōtsuka Hisao, *Dai-roku-kan: Kokumin Keizai, Ōtsuka Hisao Chosaku-shū* (Volume Six: National Economics, The Collected Work of Otsuka Hisao), Tokyo, Iwanami-shoten, 1969.

Park, Yung H., *Bureaucrats and Ministers in Contemporary Japanese Government*, Berkeley, Institute of East Asian Studies of the University of California-Berkeley, 1986.

Patrick, Hugh and Meissner, Larry (eds), *Japan's High Technology Industries: Lessons and Limitations of Industrial Policy*, Seattle, Wash., University of Washington Press/Tokyo, University of Tokyo Press, 1986.

226   *List of works cited*

Patrick, Hugh and Rosovsky, Henry (eds), *Asia's New Giant: How the Japanese Economy Works*, Washington, DC, The Brookings Institution, 1976.

Pempel, T.J., *Policy and Politics in Japan: Creative Conservatism*, Philadelphia, Temple University Press, 1982.

Plamenatz, John, *Man and Society: A Critical Examination of Some Important Social and Political Theories from Machiavelli to Marx*, London, Longman, 1963.

Richardson, Bradley M. and Flanagan, Scott C., *Politics in Japan*, Boston, Little Brown and Company, 1984.

Rorty, R. (ed.), *The Linguistic Turn*, Chicago, Univesity of Chicago Press, 1967.

Rorty, R., *Philosophy and the Mirror of Nature*, Princeton, NJ, Princeton University Press, 1979.

Rosenbluth, Frances McCall, *Financial Politics in Contemporary Japan*, Ithaca, Cornell University Press, 1989.

Ryan, Alan, 'Professor Hegel Goes to Washington', *New York Review of Books*, 26 March 1992, pp. 7–13.

Said, Edward W., *Orientalism*, Harmondsworth, Middlesex, Penguin Books, 1985.

Sakai Naoki, 'Modernity and Its Critique: The Problem of Universalism and Particularism', in Masao Miyoshi and H.D. Harootunian (eds), *Postmodernism and Japan*, Durham and London, Duke University Press, 1989.

Samuels, Richard J., *The Politics of Regional Policy: Localities Incorporated?*, Princeton, NJ, Princeton University Press, 1983.

—— *The Business of the Japanese State: Energy Markets in Comparative and Historical Perspective*, Ithaca and London, Cornell University Press, 1987.

—— 'Japanese Political Studies and the Myth of Independent Intellectual', in Richard J. Samuels and Myron Weiner (eds), *The Political Culture of Foreign Area Studies: Essay in Honor of Lucian W. Pye*, Washington, DC, Pergammon-Brassey's, 1992, pp. 17–59.

Samuelson, P.A., *Economics*, New York, McGraw-Hill, 1948.

Sataka Makoto, *Nihon Kanryō Hakusho* (White Paper on the Japanese Bureaucracy), Tokyo, Kōdan-sha, 1989.

Shimada, Haruo, '"Japan Moderu" wa Shinazu' (The Japan Model will not Die), *Bungei Shunjū*, February 1992 issue, pp. 138–49.

Shinmura Izuru (ed.), *Kōjien*, Tokyo, Iwanami-shoten, 1988, third edition.

Shindō Muneyuki, *Gyōsei Shidō: Kanchō to Gyōkai no Aida* (Administrative Guidance: Between the Bureaucracy and the Private Sector), Tokyo, Iwanami Shincho, 1992.

Shūkan Posuto (The Weekly Post) '*Mieno Nichigin Sosai no "Keiki Kaifuku" no Dai Uso* (The Big Lies in Bank of Japan Governor Mieno's Prediction of an Economic Recovery), 5 June 1992, pp. 32–7.

Shūkan Tōyō Keizai (The Weekly Toyo Keizai), '*Isogareru "Sentaku no Jiyu" no Kakudai*' (The Drive to Enhance the 'Freedom to Choose' Must Be Accelerated), 16 May 1992, pp. 36–9.

Staniland, Martin, *What is Political Economy?: A Study of Social Theory and Underdevelopment*, New Haven, Conn., Yale University Press, 1985.

Steiner, George, *In Bluebeard's Castle: Some Notes Towards the Redefinition of Culture*, New Haven, Conn., Yale University Press, 1971.

Stockwin, J.A.A., *Japan: Divided Politics in a Growth Economy*, New York and London, W.W. Norton, 1982, second edition.

Stockwin, J.A.A. *et al.*, *Dynamic and Immobilist Politics in Japan*, London, Macmillan Press, 1988.

Suzuki Yoshio (ed.), *The Japanese Financial System*, Oxford, Clarendon Press, 1987.

—— *Japan's Economic Performance and International Role*, Tokyo, University of Tokyo Press, 1989.

Tachi Ryūichiro, *Kin-yū Sai-hensei no Shiten* (The Reform of the Japanese Financial System in Perspective), Tokyo, Tōyō Keizai Shinpo-sha, 1985.

—— '*Keiki Chōsei to Kasanatta Shisutemu no Tenkan: "Nihon-gata" kara "Eibei-gata" e*' (Not Just as Business Downturn but a System in Revolution: Why it is Time to Move from the Japanese Model to the Anglo-American Model), *Ekonomisuto*, 27 April 1992, pp. 22–8.

Takeuchi Yoshimi, '*Kindai to wa Nani ka*' (What is Modernity?) in *Takeuchi Yoshimi Zenshū* (The Complete Works of Takeuchi Yoshimi), vol. 4, Tokyo, 1980.

Tanaka Masami, 'Government Policy and Biotechnology in Japan: The Pattern and Impact of Rivalry Between Ministries', in Stephen Wilks and Maurice Wright (eds), *The Promotion and Regulation of Industry in Japan*, London, Macmillan, 1992.

Taylor, Charles, 'Inwardness and the Culture of Modernity', in Axel Honneth *et al.* (eds), *Philosophical Interventions in the Unfinished Project of Enlightenment*, Cambridge, Mass., The MIT Press, 1992.

Thurow, Lester, *Head to Head: The Coming Economic Battle between Japan, Europe and America*, New York, William Morrow and Co., 1992.

Tilly, Charles (ed.), *The Formation of National States in Western Europe*, Princeton, NJ, Princeton University Press, 1975.

Tokyo Business Today, A Bad Case of Japanese Disease (Special Issue), Tokyo, Tōyō Keizai Shinpō-sha, January/February 1993, vol. 61, no. 1.

Trezise, Philip H. and Suzuki Yukio, 'Politics, Government, and Economic Growth in Japan', in Hugh Patrick and Henry Rosovsky (eds), *Asia's New Giant: How the Japanese Economy Works*, Washington, DC, The Brookings Institution, 1976.

Tsuruda Toshimasa, *Sengo Nihon no Sangyō Seisaku* (Industrial Policy in Postwar Japan) Tokyo, Nihon Keizai Shinbun-sha, 1982.

Tsushō-sangyō-shō Tsūsan Seisaku-kyoku (MITI International Trade Policy Bureau), *Heisei Yon-nen Tsūsan-shō Hakusho* (1992 MITI White Paper), Tokyo, Tsūsho-sangyō Chōsa-kai, May 1992. (Both complete and summary volumes are published under the same title.)

Ubukata Yukio, *Ginkō vs. Shōken: Fuhai no Kōzō to Shin Tenkai* (Banks vs. Securities Companies: Structural Corruption and its New Face), Tokyo, Kōdan-sha, 1992.

Uchibashi, Katsuhito, '*Kaisetsu*', in Sataka Makoto, *Nihon Kanryō Hakusho* (White Paper on the Japanese Bureaucracy), Tokyo, Kōdan-sha, 1989, pp. 330–6.

Upham, Frank K., 'Legal Informality and Industrial Policy', *Law and Social Change in Postwar Japan*, Cambridge, Mass., Harvard University Press, 1987.

Viner, Jacob, *The Long View and the Short: Studies in Economic Theory and Policy*, New York, Free Press, 1958.

Vogel, Ezra F., *Japan as Number One: Lessons for America*, Tokyo, Charles E. Tuttle Co., 1980.

—— *Comeback*, Tokyo, Charles E. Tuttle Co., 1985.

Wade, Robert, *Governing the Market: Economic Theory and the Role of Government in East Asian Industrialization*, Princeton, NJ, Princeton University Press, 1991.

Ward, Robert E., *Japan's Political System*, Englewood Hills, NJ, Prentice-Hall, 1967.

Wilks, Stephen and Wright, Maurice (eds), *The Promotion and Regulation of Industry in Japan*, London, Macmillan, 1992.

Williams, David, 'Super-industrialism and the New Japan', *Tokyo Business Today*, Tokyo, March 1989, pp. 14–19.

—— 'Reporting the Death of the Emperor Showa', Oxford, Nissan Occasional Paper Series, no. 14, 1990.

—— The Revolutionary 1980s: 'Towards a New Era in the Euro-American Science of Japanese Government', Marburg, Germany, Philipps-Universität Marburg, Center for Japanese Studies, Occasional Paper, January 1991.

—— 'Yellow Athena: The Japanese Model and the East European Revolution', in Ian Neary (ed.), *War, Revolution and Japan*, Folkestone, Kent, Japan Library, 1993.

Woodward, William P., *The Allied Occupation of Japan and Japanese Religions*, Leiden, E.J. Brill, 1972.

Wray, William D., *Mitsubishi and the NYK, 1870–1914: Business Strategy in the Japanese Shipping Industry*, Cambridge, Mass. and London, Harvard University Press, 1984.

Yamaguchi Jirō, *Ōkura Kanryō no Shihai no Shūen* (The End of MOF Domination), Tokyo, Iwanami-Shoten, 1987.

Yamamura, Kozo (ed.), *Japan's Economic Structure: Should it Change?*, Seattle, Wash., Society of Japanese Studies, 1990.

Yamamura, Kozo and Yasuba, Yasukichi (eds), *The Political Economy of Japan, Volume 1: The Domestic Transformation*, Stanford, Calif., Stanford University Press, 1987.

Yamazaki Taketoshi, '"Nomura Shintaku Ginkō": San-do-me Shōjiku' (Nomura Trust Bank: Lucky on the Third Try) and '"Kōgin Shōken" no Takawarai ga Kikoeru' (IBJ Securities: The Sound of Confident Laughter), in *Kinyū Bijinesu* (The Financial Business), June 1992, pp. 26–9, 30–2.

Young, Michael K., 'Structural Adjustment of Mature Industries in Japan: Legal Institutions, Industry Association and Bargaining', in Stephen Wilks and Maurice Wright (eds), *The Promotion and Regulation of Industry in Japan*, London, Macmillan, 1992.

Zengage, Thomas R. and Ratcliffe, C. Tait, *The Japanese Century: Challenge and Response*, Hong Kong, Longman Group, 1988.

Index

absolute knowledge 162–3
academics' understanding of Asia
    181–6, 192, 193–6
acultural modernity xv–xvi
agriculture in Japan, 37, 43, 70,
    134–5
aircraft: FSX fighter affair 53, 62
Americanization/American way of
    life 157, 158–9, 160, 162, 187, 191,
    196
Anglo-American: economic
    expectations 98; economic model
    23, 107, 116, 124; ontology 168;
    political tradition 159, 168; school
    of modern economics 69, 84–5,
    121, 141, 152, 162, 192, 194, 203;
    see also Western
anti-liberalism in Japan 21, 27
anti-statism 168, 196
Archilochus 147
Aristotle 190
armaments industries 5, 9, 123
armed forces 9, 27, 28, 80
arms trade 171–2
Asia see East Asia
Asian studies 181–6
Athena 166; Yellow 165, 166, 170
Athens (classical) 106, 166, 190
Australia 4, 106, 118; Oxford–
    Australia school 149, 195
authority and deference 69–70
automobile industry in US 130–1

Bachelard, G. 158, 168
Bacon, F. 85, 88
Bagehot, W. 203, 205

bakafu 23, 26, 32, 80, 115
Bank of Japan (BOJ) 95; policy
    making by 20
Banking Bureau (MOF) 65–6, 72–3,
    94, 96
banks/banking: European
    Community (EC) 72; Japan 65–6,
    71–4, 94, 96–7
Barthes, R. 21, 193, 199
Bentham, J. 164, 168–9
Bergsten, C.F. 52, 53
Berlin, I. 6–8, 114, 165, 167
Bernal, M. 166
Bismarck, O. von 23, 123, 131–2
Boger, K. 149
BOJ see Bank of Japan
bourgeois business class 27
Boyd, R. 197
Brandenburg see Prussia
Britain/British 5, 7, 22, 42, 140;
    academics' understanding of Asia
    195, 197; education 90; empiricism
    10, 11; Labour Party 88–91;
    nationalism 113; productivity 90;
    protectionism 83, 83–4, 114–15;
    public policy 10; stock market 67;
    see also England, Western
bureaucracy: Confucian 30, 38, 111,
    115, 116; East Asian attitudes to
    38–9, 70; Germany/Prussia 122–3,
    124–6; and interest groups 25, 29;
    Japan 19–23, 28, 40–2, 48, 95–6,
    116; judicial scrutiny of 91; Meiji
    26; and party politics 42, 47–8,
    95–6, 155; policy-making 40–2,

47–8, 91, 124, 148, 155; pre–Meiji era 23, 115; as service 29, 30, 38–9; UK 171–8; Western attitudes to 38–9, 70
bureaucratism 29–30, 38
bureaucrats 37; as heroes 38
Bush, G./Bush administration 11–12, 52–3, 56–8, 61–4, 84, 99, 142, 164, 183, 185
business interests 25, 27, 29, 30, 37, 155, 177
business in Japan: exclusionary practices 63

Calder, K.E. 39, 42–6, 132, 147, 149, 150, 151
California 23
Cameralism 126
Canada 4, 140; provinces of 22
capital inflows to US 53
capital markets: Plaza Accord 51, 52, 53–5, 56–7
cartels 36–7, 63
catching up with West 140–2
centralization in Japan 22–6, 78–9
chauvinism 114
Cheney, D. 64
China/Chinese: mentality 160; political philosophy 39; relations with Japan 27, 80, 123; relations with US 181, 182–3; student power 31, *see also* Confucius/Confucianism
Churchill, W.S. 118
city banks 97
civil service *see* bureaucracy
civil society 157, 163–4, 168–70
Clinton, Bill/Clinton administration 52, 84, 88–9
coal industry 66
Cohen, T. 184, 185, 186
Cold War, end of 8–9
collective identity 119–20, 127–8, 167–8
communism, failure of 157–9, 172, 187
company meetings, disruption of 32
competitiveness of US industry 54, 84
computer systems, fifth generation 7
Comte, A. 85

Confucius/Confucianism 30, 31, 38, 69, 70, 111, 115, 116
conservatism, creative 79, 210
constitution: of 1947 151; MacArthur 20; Meiji 19–20, 27, 34
convergence theory 196, *see also* Americanization
convoy–protection by MOF 66, 73, 98
Cooper, T. 120, 167
Corbett, J. 87
corporatism 28
corruption 28, 29, 30–1, 45, 46–7, 62, 96, *see also* scandals
costs of production 55–6
counter–elite 29
Crawcour, E.S. 76–8
creative conservatism 79, 210
credit banks 71–2, 97
crime *see* yakuza
cultural modernity xv–xvi

Dai-ichi Kangyō (bank) 72
Daiwa (securities house) 67
de Gaulle, C. 7
deconstruction/post-structuralists 21, 190
defence industries 5, 9, 123
defence policy of US 62, 64
deference 69–70
demand expansion and trade imbalance 57–8
democracy 106–7; Japan 148
Democratic Party, US 62, 88–9, 138
Deposit Insurance Corporation 97
deregulation 69, 71; financial markets 69–71
devaluation 54; of US dollar 54, 55, 57; *see also* exchange rates
Diet (Parliament) 19, 20–1, 27, 30, 151
direction of trade, and investment 54
Dodge, J./Dodge line 136
Dore, R. xiii
Drucker, P.F. 6, 9, 54, 55, 149
Dunn, J. 188

East Asia 8; bureaucracy 38–9, 70; economic growth 175, 176; and Hong Kong 122; philosophy 69
Eastern Europe: collapse of

communism 172; post–communist reconstruction 157–9, 163–4
Eatwell, J. 89
economic change in Japan 134–9
economic forces, supremacy of 157–8
economic growth *see* growth
economic man 158
economic nationalism 58, 81, 82, 178
economics: empiricism 85–8, 179; and foreign policy 9, 51; and political science 149, 154; positivism 75, 77, 85–8, 154–5, 179, 199
Edo administration 19, 23–4, 26, 79–80, 115–16
education: Germany/Prussia 129; Japan, and national identity 8, 24; Britain 90
electronics industry: Japan 7; market-share pact 52; USA 7
elite, ruling 29
emperor 23, 27, 32–5
empiricism 199; British 10, 11; in economics 85–8, 179; wild 198, 200
end of history 187–8, 189, 193
energy costs 44
England 4, 83
English thought 162 (Manchester School); limitations of 168–9
English language thought/thinking 6, 37, 39, 65, 71, 106, 113, 168–9; writing in about Japan 12, 37, 88, 180
Enlightment beliefs 85, 107–8, 122, 129, 133, 157, 191
equality 189
ethnic minorities in Japan 93, 109
ethnicity and national identity 111, 113–14, 189–90
Eto Jun 192
Europe/Europeans 4, Continental thought/thinking 10–11; Continental institutions 139, 218; Continental tradition xiv, 112, 115, 159, 162, 168; Eurocentrism 190; European thought 217; free trade 114–15; Post-Renaissance 166, 193; protectionism 130, 131; Revolution (1989–91) xvi
European Community (EC): banking 72; and British empiricism 10, 11; Japan Policy 142; protectionism 91
exchange rates: Japan 57; and trade imbalance 57; US 53–4
expansionism 8; Japanese 135

Fair Trade Commission 36
fairness 71
family 168
Farnsworth, L.W. 208
federalism 23, 24
Ferguson, A. 164
Fichte, J.G. 127, 128–9, 131
fifth generation computer systems 7
Finance Ministry *see* Ministry of Finance
financial markets: Japan 47, 65–74
Finer, H. 123, 126
Finer, S.E. xiii
fiscal policy: Japan 45; US 53–4
FitzGerald, F. 111–12, 181
Flanagan, S.C. 216
Fontenelle, B. 165
foreign policy 171–9
Formosa 123
France 5, 22, 93, 140; compared with Japan 116; *départements* of 22; French Revolution 34, 116, 161–2; as model 23; philosophy 133, 162, 167
free enterprise 69, 194
free trade 52, 69, 189, 194; Europe 114–15; Germany 129–30; US 130–1
Friedman, D. 87, 196–7
Friedman, M. 108, 122, 160
FSX fighter affair 53, 62
Fuji Bank 96
Fujiwara family 19
Fukuyama, F. xiii, xiv, xvi, 157–8, 161–3, 169, 180, 187, 188–93, 194, 217–18

gangsters *see* yakuza
Garon, S. 41
General Agreement on Tariffs and Trade (GATT): Uruguay round 52
geo-politics 8–9
German historical school 83, 206
German philosophy 159–64
Germany 4, 22, 140; bureaucracy 122–3, 124–6; compared with

Japan 107, 108, 113, 116; democracy 107; economic policy 58; economic theories 120–1; education 129; formation of 123–32; free trade 129–30; GNP 58; as model 89; for Japan 23, 27, 113, 116, 122–32; nationalism 113, 115, 127–9; protectionism 84, 130, 131; stock market 67; Weimar 23
Glass–Steagall Act 72
global financial integration 72
Gluck, C. 8
goals 128; of Japanese 11, 26, 79, 142; national 105
government *see* state
grand theory 186–91, 194
Greeks (ancient) 6, 66, 72, 166
Grew, J. 181, 184, 186
gross national product (GNP) 6, 66, 72, 140, 142
Group of Seven (G–7) 57–8, 59, 106–7; Paris Summit (1989) 62
growth 43–4; from above/below 76–7; East Asia 175, 176; Japan 134–42, 179, 192
Gulf War (1990–1) 53, 64, 111, 171–4, 215

Habermas, J. 133, 192, 193
Hamilton, A. 66, 183
heavy industry 66, 172
Hegel, G.W.F./Hegelianism xvi, 133, 157, 159–60, 161–4, 166, 168, 169–70, 187, 188, 190
Heiwa-dō group 94
Hennessy, P. 39, 118
Herder, J.G. 127–8, 131, 165
Herodatus 106
heroes, bureaucrats as 38
hierarchies in Japan 70
high-speed growth 136–7
high-tech industries: Japanese supremacy 7
high yen (*endaka*) recession 55, 92
Hilldring, J.H. 184–5
Hirohito (Shōwa) 32, 33–5
historical awareness 139–40
history: direction of 189; end of 187–8, 189; as myth 133–4
Hitachi Ltd 56
Hitler, A. 118

Hobbes, T. 118, 119, 189, 190
Hofheinz, R. 39
Holland 4, 83
Hollerman, L. 61
Home Ministry 28, 139
Hong Kong 67, 122
Hosokawa Morihiro xiv
Hosomi Takashi 82
housing costs 63
Hull, C. 84
humaneness of rulers 70
Hume, D. 85, 169
Hungary 172

IBJ (Industrial Bank of Japan) 71–2, 74, 96, 198
IBM and Japanese electronics industry 7
idealism (cultural) 29, 31, 35
ideology and nationalism 7–8
Ikeda Hayato 7, 137
imperial power 23, 27, 32–5
imperialism, Western 23, 78–9, 80, 140
imports to Japan 58, 62
imports to US: voluntary restraints 58
income levels 137
individual: and markets 120, 152; and nation 109, 167–8; subordination of 70
Industrial Bank of Japan (IBJ) 71–2, 73–4, 96, 198
industrial policy xii, 113; England 83, 86–7; Japan 43–4, 57, 75–91, 196–7
industrialism 34, 51, 76–8, 135
industries: steel 55–6; strategic 66; sunrise 76; sunset 55, 57
Industry Ministry *see* Ministry of International Trade and Industry
infant industries 66, 83
Inoguchi Takashi 152
institutions: Japanese banking 71; of market 67
interest rates: Japan 94; US 53–4
interests 37, 148, 155; business 25, 29, 30, 37, 155; private 25; public 25
international relations 9, 171–9
International Trade Ministry *see* Ministry of International Trade and Industry

internationalization: financial markets 71, 72
investment 63, 73, 135, 137; and direction of trade 54; foreign 53, 54, 68, 138–9; and growth 55, 56, 57; private 68; state direction of 66; steel industry 55–6
Iraq: Gulf War (1990–1) 53, 64, 111, 171–4
iron and steel industry: Japan 55–6
Italy (bureaucrats) 91
Itō Daiichi 70
Itō Hirobumi 35, 132
Itoman affair 94
Iwakura Mission 123
Iwasaki Yatarō 77
Iwata Masakazu 78

James, H. 183
Jameson, F. 133
Jansen, M.B. 79
Japan: as developmental state 164, 195; as evil empire 51; as model 89, 165
Jevons, W.S. 86
Johnson, C. xiii, 41–2, 78, 86, 88, 92, 124, 148, 150, 195, 196–7, 204
journalism *see* media
Joyce, J. 198
judicial scrutiny of bureaucracy 91

kagemusha 20
Kaifu Toshiki 62
kamikaze 32
Kanemaru Shin 48
Kant, I. 166, 190, 197, 199, 219
Keidranen 99
Keynes, J.M./Keynesianism 27, 122, 135, 142, 178, 199–200
Kishomoto Kōichi 70
knowledge, absolute 162–3
Kojève, A. 160, 161, 162, 165, 170, 187
Kokusai Kōgyō 94
Komiya Ryutarō 84, 86
Komori, Yoshihisa 217–18
Korea 31, 39, 42, 123, 164, 175, 182
Korean minority in Japan 93
Kuhn, T.S. 145, 148
Kuribayashi Yoshimitsu 65–6, 94
Kurosawa Akira 20

Kyōwa affair 94

Labour Party, Britain 88–91, 155
laissez–faire 78, 120, 204
land: prices 63, 94; reform 46
language: and culture 127–8; Japanese 108–13; and political reality 112–13; and untranslatability xv; war idioms 119
Lattimore, O. 181
laws, positivistic 87
left wing in Japan 28, 29, 30–1, 116
Lenin, V. 172
Liberal Democratic Party (LDP) 28, 29, 30, 36–7, 42, 43–8, 62, 96, 137, 138
liberalism 3, 35, 46, 159–63, 187, 188; Japan 24, 27, 93, 94, 98, 99, 106–7, 108, 205
liberalization 69, 71, 79, 141–2, 164; financial markets 65, 69–74, 95, 98, 138–9
Lincoln, E.J. 141, 176
List, F. xii, 64, 66, 79, 81, 83, 114, 120–2, 159, 167
Livy, T.V. 172
local government 129
Locke, J. 115, 162, 164, 190
Longley, C. 10–11
Louvre Accord (1987) 57–8
loyalty 30
Lukács, G. 133
Lyotard, J.F. 133

MacArthur, D./MacArthur shogunate 20, 34, 46, 64, *see also* occupation by US
McCarthy, J./McCarthyism 180–3
Machiavelli, N. 129, 165, 167, 190; Florence of 190
McKenzie, R.B. 154
macro theory 194–5, 196, 197
Madison, J. 24, 147, 191
Maekawa Haruo/Maekawa Reports xiv, 25, 39, 51, 52, 57–61, 64
Mafia *see* yakuza
Malaysia 155
marginalization of Japan 191–3
market forces 106–7, 152, 160, 163, 178, 194, 196; financial system

73–4, 98; and growth 77–8;
'liberalizing' Japan 12–13, 52, 136,
  196, 204–5; and the state 167–8;
  US policy tools and goals 53, 56,
  89; and war and peace 120–2
market share 43–4
markets: foreign penetration 65; and
  individuals 120; institutions 67;
  state intervention 63
Marshall, A. 84, 86, 153
Maruyama Masao 205
Marx, K. 122, 190, 196
master and slave 188
Matsuno Toshihiko 96
Matsushita Electric 56
media 199–200; Japan 44, 95
  megalothymia 189, 190
Meiji Restoration 26, 32, 142
Meiji state 19–20, 21, 24, 25–7, 34–5,
  80–1, 115–16, 134–5, 141, 164
Meissner, L. 86
mercantilism 177–9
meso theory 194, 196, 197
Mexico 106
micro research and analysis 194, 196,
  197–9, 216, 219
Mieno Yasushi 95–6, 211
militarism 172–7, 188–9
Mill, J.S. 84, 108, 115, 153
mining industry 66
Ministry of Commerce and Industry
  (MCI) 78, 80
Ministry of Finance (MOF) 28, 40,
  43, 47, 65–74, 211; and Bank of
  Japan 20; and banking 96–7;
  Banking Bureau 65–6, 72–3, 94,
  96; convoy-protection 66, 73, 98;
  and financial markets 47, 65–74,
  94–8; and investment 66;
  Kuribayashi on 65, 94; and
  liberalization 72–3; and MITI 66;
  Securities Bureau 67–8; values of
  71; Yamaguchi on 40
Ministry of International Trade and
  Industry (MITI) 7, 28, 40, 43, 91;
  and investment 57; Johnson on 41–
  2, 78, 124; and MCI 178; and
  MOF 66; Namiki on 40; and
  philosophy 169; policy goals 99,
  124; studies of 149–50; values of 71
Ministry of Transport (MOT) 48

Mishima, Y. 35
MITI *see* Ministry of International
  Trade and Industry
Mitsubishi shipping 80–2
Miyazawa Kiichi 96, 208
modernity xv–xvi, 164, 187, 191,
  192–3
modernization xv, 113; of Japan
  24–6, 34–5, 79, 105, 134–5, 141,
  165
Modernization School xvi, 155, 191,
  192
MOF *see* Ministry of Finance
Mondale, W. 89
monetarism/monetarists 158, 163,
  169, 178, 199–200
monetary policy 21; US 53–4
money politics 47
monism 165
monopolies 63
Montesquieu, C. 20
Morishima Tōzō xii
Morita Akio 99
Muramatsu Michio 218–19
myth and history 133–4

Nagamori Seiichi 197
Najita, T. 29, 30, 33, 41
Nakasone Yasuhiro 58, 59, 164
Namiki Nobuyoshi 40
Napoleon Bonaparte 114, 127
narrative, history as 39, 133–4
nation 10, 108–12, 113, 167; Japanese
  8, 69, 79, 110–12; and markets 120;
  and state 122; *see also* state
nation–state 108–9
national economy 66–7
national greatness 203
national identity 114
national purpose 142
nationalism 3, 8, 9, 113–16; Britain
  113; economic 178; and European
  Community (EC) 10; Germany
  113, 115, 127–9; Japan 23–6, 34–5,
  65, 92–3, 98, 108, 115–16, 134, 151,
  177–9, 189, 205; Slav 128
nationality 167; Japan 93
neo-classical/neo-liberal theories 78,
  84–5, 88, 158–9, 160, 162–3, 179
neo-mercantilism 177–9
New Zealand 4

Nietzsche, F. 128, 190, 191
Niigata 46–7
Nikkan Kōgyō Shinbun 59–61
Nikkei index 67–8
Nikkō (securities house) 67
Nippon Steel 55–6
Nippon Telegraph and Telephone (NTT) 95
Nissan 90
Nixon, R.M./Nixon administration 44, 52, 137
Nomura Securities 32, 47, 67, 72, 97
'normalizing' Japan 134, 141–2
Norman, E.H. 181
nuclear weapons 9
NYK (firm) 82

objectives *see* goals
occupation by United States 20, 28, 34, 46, 64, 115–16, 136, 180, 184–6
Ogyū Sorai 128
oil imports from Iraq 173–4
oil shocks 44, 92, 137–8, 146
Okimoto, D.I. 88, 151, 152, 154, 204
Ōkubo Toshimichi 24, 78, 80
Okumura Ariyoshi 82
Okuna Masahiro 84
Onoue Nui 96
ontology 168
Orientalism 192
Ōtsuka Hisao xii, 206
overtaking the West 140–2, 190

P & O 80, 81–2
Pacific Mail Company 80–1
Palm Springs summit (1990) 64
Paris 22
Parliament *see* Diet
party politics/politicians 21, 27, 28, 37, 42–8, 95–6, 155, *see also* Liberal Democratic Party; political parties
paternalism 70, 111
Patrick, H. 86, 153
patriotism 114
peace 120–2; as aftermath to war 118–19
peasants, Japanese 115–16, 151
Pempel, T.J. 41, 79, 209–10
Peoples Action Party (Singapore) 96
Plamenatz, J. 168–9

Plato 165, 166, 189, 190
Plaza Accord 51, 52, 53–5, 56–7
pluralism 108, 148, 155, 164, 165–6, 167
Poland 158, 164, 172, 173
police 24, 28
policymaking 19–26, 78–9; Bank of Japan (BOJ) 20; by bureaucracy 40–2, 47–8, 91, 124, 148, 155
policy tools 80–1
policy tribes (*zoku*) 19, 48, 208
political economy 152–5, 167
political parties 44, 46, *see also* Liberal Democratic Party; party politics
political philosophy, Japanese 19–1
political science 42; and economics 149, 154; of Japan 42, 43, 145–56, 216
politics, comparative 106
polycentrism of Japan 19–26, 78–9
Popper, K. 15, 120, 135
pork–barrel patronage 28, 43, 45, 47, 148
positivism in economics 75, 77, 85–8, 154–5, 179, 199
post–war expansion 135–6, 165
Potsdam agreement 34
power: division of 19–26, 111; international 5, 156; passion for 188–9; polycentrism of Japan 19–26
power industry 66
press *see* media
price-fixing 36–7
prices of steel 55–6
private gain 69, 77
private interests 25, 69, 77, 98
private investment 68
private sector and the state 77
productivity: UK 90, 91; and war 118
property prices 63, 94
protectionism: Europe 130, 131; European Community 91; Germany 84, 130, 131; UK 83–4, 114–15; US 58, 84, 130–1
Proust, M. 140, 165
Prussia 124–31, *see also* Germany
public choice theory 77
public interests 25, 98
public policy 110–11, 131, 203; G–7

countries 107; Britain 10;
Germany/Prussia 127; Japan 3–9,
43–4, 51, 59, 68, 70–1, 78, 79, 80–1,
94, 107, 116, 145–56; Western
models 203–4; *see also* industrial
policy; state
public policy studies 145–56
public procurement 63
public service *see* bureaucracy
public works spending 62
purity of spirit 29–30, 31, 32

racial *see* ethnic
rationalization of industry 55–6, 57
Rawls, J. 108, 166
Reagan, R./Reagan administration
52–4, 56–8, 62, 84
reality and research 197
reality and surface 21
rebates to retailers 63
recognition of Japan 191–3
Recruit scandal 28, 30, 62, 96
regulation 69–70
Reich, R.B. 88–9
Reischauer, E.O. 181
relativism 165
research, levels of 194–9
retail stores 62
revisionism, anti-Japanese 39, 51,
155–6, 195
Ricardo, D. 84
Richardson, B.M. 216
Rohlen, T.P. 152
Roosevelt, F.D 185
Rorty, R. xvi
Rosenbluth, F.M. 150
Rosovsky, H. 153
ruling elite 29
Russia/Russians: imperialism 6;
mentality 160; reconstruction 158,
172, 187, *see also* USSR
Russian Revolution (1917): effect on
global society 6–7
Russo-Japanese War (1904–5) 26, 27,
117, 123, 134
Ryan, A. 188
Ryūkyū Islands 80

Saddam Hussein 173
Sagawa Kyūbin 32, 48, 94, 96
Sahashi Shigeru 40

Said, E.W. 192 (*Orientalism*)
Saigō Takamori 123
Sakai Naoki 191–2, 193
Sakata Makoto 41
Samuels, R.J. 199, 220
samurai 27, 115
Sanwa Bank 96
Satsuma 24, 78, 80
savings in Japan 57, 63, 97
Say, J.B. 120, 167
scandals 32, 45, 47–8; financial 94;
Nomura 32, 47; Recruit 28, 30, 62,
96; securities houses 67–8
science, relationship with technology
9
science and technology: effect on
global society 6–7
sectoral analysis 194, 196
Securities Bureau 67–8
securities houses 67–8, 72, 95, 97–8
self-esteem 188
semiconductor industry 25
service ethos *see* bureaucracy
shadow power in Japan 20
share prices 67–8, 95
shareholders' meetings: disruption by
sōkaiya–yakuza 32
Shimane 45–7
Shinkin Bank Association 97
Shinkin credit associations 96
Shintoism 32, 116, 217
Shindō Muneyuki 204
shipping 80–2
Shōwa (Hirohito) 32, 33–5
Showa Restoration 32, 34
SII *see* Structural Impediments
Initiative
Singapore 96, 155, 175
Slav nationalism 128
slave and master 188
Smith, Adam 121
Snow, E. 181
social democracy: and industrial
policy 88–9
social welfare: Prussia 132
society: civil 157, 163–4, 168–70
Socrates 166
sōkaiya–yakuza 32
Sparta 106
spirit, purity of 29–30, 31
the state 25, 105, 108–12, 128–9, 167–

8; and civil society 168–70;
Japanese 22–6, 65, 189; and market
forces 167–8; and nation 122; and
private sector 77; service to *see*
bureaucracy; *see also* nation
State Department, US 184–5
state intervention 89; and growth
76–8; in investment 66, 76; in
markets 63
state-led banking 72
state philosophy: contrast between
West and Japan 71
steel industry in Japan 55–6
Steiner, G. 119
Stein, H., Baron von 126–9
stock market 67–9, 95
Stockwin, J.A.A. 20, 148, 195, 216
Strauss, L. 188
structural change: Japan 11–12, 25,
39, 42, 58–64, 79, 183–4; US 12
Structural Impediments Initiative
(SII) 11–12, 51, 53, 61–4, 183
student radicalism 31
subordination of individual 70
sunrise industries 76
sunset industries 55, 57
super-industrialism 51, 55–7, 63
surface and reality 21
Suzuki Yoshio 92
Suzuki Yukio 153
Suzumura Kotaŕ 84

Tachi Ryūichiro 203–4, 220
Taishō 41
Taiwan 39, 42, 175, 182–3
Takahashi Korekiyo 142
Takeshita Noboru 45, 48, 62
Takeuchi Yoshimi 186, 187, 191
Tanaka Kakuei 19, 20, 46, 48
taxation in Prussia 125–6
Taylor, C. xvi, xvii
technology: and democracy 107;
effect on global society 6–7, 133;
relationship with science 9
technology transfer to Japan 62
Thatcher, M. 10, 22, 160, 167
theory, levels of 186–91, 194–9
'thinking nationalism' 8, 190
Third World 4, 5, 34
tobashi 98
Tocqueville, A. 190

Tokugawa Ieyasu 26
Tokugawa shogunate 19, 26, 164
Tokyo 22, 52
Tokyo District Public Prosecutors 48
'Tokyo Primary' (1992) 25
Tokyo Sagawa Kyūbin 32, 48, 94
Tokyo summit (1986) 59
Tokyo University 177
Tōshiba affair 40; sanctions 52
Tōyo Shinkin 94, 96, 97, 198
Toyota 90
trade imbalance: and demand
expansion 57–8; and exchange
rates 57; with US 12, 39, 52–5, 56,
57–64
Trade Ministry *see* Ministry of
International Trade and Industry
trade sanctions 62
trade surplus, Japanese 58
translation of Japanese 112–13
Tresize, P.H. 153
tripartite alliance in Japan 28, 29, 44
Truman, H./Truman administration
184
trust banks 97
truth–telling 180–6
Tsuruda Toshimasa 83, 129–31
Tullock, G. 154

Uchibashi Katsuhito 40–1
Umehara Takashi 192
unification: of Germany 123–32; of
Japan 123
United States 4, 5; academics'
understanding of Asia 181–6, 195;
Americanization/American way of
life 157, 158–9, 160, 162;
automobile industry 130–1; capital
inflows 53; and China 181, 182–3;
Civil War 116; competitiveness 54;
defence policy 62; deficit 58;
Democratic Party 88–9; economic
philosophy 69; electronics industry
7; exchange rates 53–4; financial
system 72; fiscal policy 53–4;
foreign investment by 54; foreign
investment in 54; foreign policy
175–6; free trade 130–1; interest
rates 53–4; militarism 174–6;
monetary policy 53–4;
protectionism 58, 62, 84; as

regulatory state 42; State Department 184–5; states 22; structural change 12; Vietnam War 111–12, 176; *see also* Western
United States–Japan Security Pact 31, 44
United States relations with Japan 51–3; academic influences 181–6; interdependence 51–2; market remedies 54–5; occupation 28, 115–16, 136, 180, 184–6; (*see also* MacArthur) Plaza Accord 51, 52, 53–5, 56–7; Structural Impediments Initiative (SII) 11–12, 39, 53; trade imbalance 12, 39, 52–5, 56, 57–64
Uno Sōsuke 62
Upham, F.K. 91
Uruguay round (GATT) 52
USSR 140; collapse of 5, 64; Western attitudes xiii–xiv; *see also* Russia

Venice 4
Venice summit 59
Verdi, G. 13, 92
Vico, G. 165
Vietnam War 111–12, 175–6
Viner, J. 178–9
Vogel, E.F. 148, 194
voluntary restraints on imports to United States 58

Wade, R. xiii
wages 55
Wales 4
war 119–22; First World War 117, 119, 175; twentieth century 131;

Second World War 32, 117–18, 135, 140, 178; (*see also* occupation); and bureaucracy 117–18; and politics 120; and productivity 118
Ward, R.E. 216
Weber, M. 70, 124, 190, 192, 193
West, catching up with/overtaking 140–2
Western academics' understanding of Asia 181–6, 192, 193–6
Western attitudes: to bureaucracy 38–9, 70; to USSR xiii–xiv
Western culture 187, 191–2, *see also* Americanization
Western imperialism 23, 78–9, 80, 140
Western market models 203–5
Western philosophy 159
Western pressures to 'normalize' 134, 141–2, 194
Wilks, S. 195–9, 216
Wilson, W. 175
Wray, W.D. 81–2
Wright, M. 195–9, 216

yakuza 31–2; economic gangsters 47–8
Yamaichi Securities 68, 98
Yamamura Kozo 152, 178, 198
Yamazaki Ansai 128
Yasuba Yasukichi 152, 198
yen *see* exchange rates

zaibatsu 27, 28
zoku (policy tribes) 19, 48, 208